SOCIAL MEDIA
HOMICIDE CONFESSIONS

Stories of killers and their victims

Elizabeth Yardley

First published in Great Britain in 2017 by

Policy Press
University of Bristol
1-9 Old Park Hill
Bristol
BS2 8BB
UK
t: +44 (0)117 954 5940
pp-info@bristol.ac.uk
www.policypress.co.uk

North America office:
Policy Press
c/o The University of Chicago Press
1427 East 60th Street
Chicago, IL 60637, USA
t: +1 773 702 7700
f: +1 773-702-9756
sales@press.uchicago.edu
www.press.uchicago.edu

British Library Cataloguing in Publication Data
A catalogue record for this book is available from the British Library

Library of Congress Cataloging-in-Publication Data
A catalog record for this book has been requested

ISBN 978-1-4473-2801-8 paperback
ISBN 978-1-4473-2800-1 hardcover
ISBN 978-1-4473-2804-9 ePub
ISBN 978-1-4473-2805-6 Mobi
ISBN 978-1-4473-2803-2 epdf

Cover design by Hayes Design
Front cover image: istock
Printed and bound in Great Britain by Clays Ltd, St Ives plc
Policy Press uses environmentally responsible print partners

This book is dedicated to the memories of

Jennifer Alfonso, Emily Janzen,

Laurel Janzen, Shelley Janzen,

Charles Taylor and other victims, who are

all too often absent from the stories of

their own homicides.

Contents

Acknowledgements

I would like to thank the following people and organisations, as this book would not have been possible without their support and assistance: Mum and Dad and Michael and Cheryl Hughes for their unwavering belief in me and their ability to convince me to occasionally step away from the laptop; Professor David Wilson for showing me what real, applied criminology means and being the best mentor and role model any academic could wish for; Victoria Pittman and Rebecca Tomlinson at Policy Press, who saw the seeds of an idea and provided the encouragement and advice that I needed to develop it into something real; Barb McClintock of British Columbia Coroner's Service and Cindi McCoy of the Court of Appeals of Virginia for their helpfulness and efficiency in providing me with access to information in the Janzen and Taylor cases respectively; and staff and students in the Department of Criminology and Faculty of Business, Law and Social Sciences at Birmingham City University for creating such a dynamic and inspirational place to be a criminologist – I am privileged to be among you.

Thank you also to the anonymous reviewers who took the time to offer thoughtful and constructive comments on the proposal and drafts of this book.

ONE

From 'happy slapping' to 'Facebook murder': networked media in violent crime

This book examines three cases in which perpetrators confessed on social media to committing homicides. The confessions included text-based content justifying the killings and, in two cases, images of the victims' dead bodies. Such cases might be interpreted as anomalies, extreme examples of individuals desperate for attention and notoriety in a time in which to be is to be seen. However, within this book, the author argues that these cases evade such a simplistic explanation. While narcissism is indeed a piece of the puzzle, it is simply one factor among a messy combination of others. Making sense of such acts requires criminologists to acknowledge the complex contexts in which they occur. It demands that we draw on our existing understandings of homicide, but it also requires that we venture into new territory. One of the most important stops on this journey is the media and communications literature, within which scholars have developed innovative and fruitful approaches to better understand the contemporary social world, its digital culture (Miller, 2011) and the mediatised construction of our realities (Couldry and Hepp, 2017). Within this introductory chapter, the author explains how the topic of *media in homicide* first came to her attention, identifies the foundations on which the research in this book was built and provides an overview of the content and cases explored therein.

In recent years, the role of networked media in violent crime has emerged as a prominent popular cultural concern. Over a decade ago, a *Guardian* journalist expressed significant concern about a phenomenon termed 'happy slapping' (Honigsbaum, 2005). Happy slapping is an orchestrated attack, in which perpetrators physically set upon a victim – often an unfortunate stranger in the wrong place at the wrong time – film the assault on their mobile phones and then share it with peers via networked media (Mann, 2009; Chan et al, 2012; Palasinski, 2013). This is essentially a crime enacted for the camera – a concept that Surette (2015a) has recently termed 'performance crime'. In the years that followed, the author came across further references to networked media in violent crime. The mainstream media were increasingly drawing attention to particular online spaces in cases of homicide. Of note was the social networking site Facebook. One article, entitled 'Teenager jailed for Facebook murder', reported on the 2009 killing of 18-year-old Londoner Salum Kombo by a 14-year-old with whom he had exchanged insults on Facebook (Hughes, 2010). Another told the story of Hayley Williams' killing at the hands of her former partner Brian Lewis after she changed her relationship status on a social networking site to single (Hughes, 2009). A further piece described how sex offender Peter Chapman posed as a teenage boy on Facebook to lure, rape and murder 17-year-old Ashleigh Hall in 2009 (Carter, 2010).

As a result of the author's interest in these cases, she embarked on a study with a colleague to explore homicides involving Facebook (Yardley and Wilson, 2015). The 48 homicides examined within the study were in many ways typical of homicide in general – most perpetrators were male and there was a close social relationship between the victim and the perpetrator. However, female victims and homicide-suicides were overrepresented and there appeared to be associations between particular types of homicide and the ways in which Facebook had been used. For example, perpetrators of domestic homicide were often 'reactors', angered by Facebook content posted by their intimate partner. In newer relationships, 'fantasist' perpetrators used Facebook to support a self that was unrepresentative of reality. There were multiple cases of 'informers', who had used Facebook to announce that they were going to commit a homicide, that they had just committed a homicide, or both. The informer-type incidents included domestic cases where an intimate partner or child had been killed, confrontational 'honour contests' among male strangers or acquaintances (Polk, 1994) and instances of intense jealousy or revenge encompassing several victim–perpetrator relationships. These findings suggested that networked technology *meant* different things to different perpetrators of different types of homicide. Facebook played a role in their presentation of self (Goffman, 1959) and the establishment and maintenance of their relationships with others – particularly their victims. These self-presentations were socially and culturally rooted, symptomatic of broader currents of meaning. Informers were particularly interesting to the author, given the way in which their acts served as attempts to assert power and take control of the narrative around a homicide, while simultaneously silencing the victim.

The study into 'Facebook murder' highlighted the necessity of further enquiry around networked media in homicide. Such research would have to better understand the meaning and significance of networked media in these cases by exploring the wider context. Individuals use a unique blend of networked media in their everyday lives – often termed 'polymedia' (Madianou and Miller, 2013). The more intimate people's social relationships, the more complex the media blend becomes (Baym, 2010). Given that homicide most often occurs between individuals with close social relationships, the need to understand these repertoires becomes even more important. How were the individuals affected by homicide using networked media in their everyday lives? To what extent were their actions around the homicide consistent or inconsistent with this? What role did networked media play in their performances of self, connections to others and sense of *being* in the world? How should criminologists take account of networked media in their research around homicide?

In order to address these questions, criminologists must draw on broader conceptual frameworks. Making sense of 'media' is a key part of this. In particular, it is necessary to appreciate that while criminologists have only been analysing networked media for a decade or so, media has been intricately threaded into the fabric of everyday life for centuries. As such, it is important to briefly explore contributions of media and communications scholars in making sense of media in social life in general.

> From clocks to telegraphs to radio and television, new media have always woven themselves into everyday life, interfering with existing patterns of spatiotemporal life, generating new rhythms and spaces. The migration of computer technology from industry and research laboratory to the home over the past thirty years or so has intensified these processes ... over time, some new digital media have become unremarkable due to their familiarity and ubiquity, and others have been refashioned or displaced, we see not a Narnia or Matrix-like division of virtual and actual worlds, but rather a complicated interweaving of mediated, lived, time and space ... (Lister et al, 2009, p 237)

The past three decades have seen significant shifts in media. Advances in networked technology have built the foundations for further developments such as social networking sites like Facebook and Twitter, content-sharing platforms like YouTube and Reddit and video-calling facilities like Skype. Innovations in computer hardware enable us to engage with media on a range of devices including the traditional desktop machine, the portable laptop or tablet and the ever-present smartphone. While all technologies were at some point new (Marvin, 1997), it cannot be denied that since the last quarter of the 20th century we have seen a significant shift in the nature and extent of media in everyday life.

The mid- to late 1990s saw a proliferation of academic output from scholars who considered the implications of newer media for social life. Crucial concerns focused on the interplay of developing technologies with more established media. The work of Bolter and Grusin (1999) is particularly prominent in this regard; their concept of *remediation* is based on the premise that newer media have not replaced older media – rather, they coexist, each shaping and refashioning the other. The ideas of continuity and change are long-running themes for media and communications scholars. Over 30 years prior to Bolter and Grusin, Marshall McLuhan famously stated that 'the "content" of any medium is always another medium' (1968, pp 15-16). The often quoted phrase 'the medium is the message' (McLuhan, 1964, p 7) suggests that it is not what *flows through* media that should be the focus of our studies but *media itself* in terms of how its scale has an impact on our relationship with others and the social world. Writing in the mid-1990s about the development of the internet, Mark Poster claimed that potential for impact lay in the sudden increase in capacity for information transmission that came with this new technology. He went on to consider implications for identity, subjectivity and performance, identifying an 'explosion of narrativity' and noting that email and bulletin boards were 'inundated by stories.... The appeal is strong to tell one's tale to others, to many, many others' (Poster, 1995, p 91). This work formed part of a considerable body of academic literature trying to make sense of the implications of shifts in media at the turn of the millennium, which posed questions encompassing embodiment, identity, performance, anonymity, community and belonging (see, for example, Stone, 1995; Turkle, 1995; Castells, 1996; Baym, 1998; Hayles, 1999; Manovich, 2001).

More recently, Thompson (2005) has drawn attention to the concept of 'mediated visibility', in which to be is to be seen and individuals use new forms of visibility as weapons to tackle everyday struggles and challenges. Miller (2011) has argued that making sense of changes to social life involves looking at more than just the internet, emphasising not only the *technical characteristics* of media (digital, interactive, networked, hypertextual, automated and databased) but also *cultural forms* in relation to how media are created, encountered and used, and *immersive experiences* centring on the relationships between media and user. While the degree to which technology shapes the social and vice versa remains a point of contention – stemming from a longstanding debate between supporters of media theorists Raymond Williams and Marshall McLuhan (for a comprehensive overview, see Lister et al, 2009) – arguments that media fundamentally affect our sense of being in the world continue to proliferate, evident across a wide body of literature. Scholars exploring the mobile telephone, for example, and its more recent incarnation the smartphone, emphasise the way in which these technologies support shifting connections between social and physical proximity in enabling us to be both absent and present (Fortunati, 2002, 2005; Gergen, 2002; Licoppe, 2004; Rettie, 2009; Hjorth et al, 2012; Miller, 2014). So too the considerable body of work exploring social media debates a range of impacts on the maintenance of existing social connections and the establishment of new ones (Fuchs, 2008; Baym, 2010; Papacharissi, 2011; Chambers, 2013).

Researchers emphasise fluidity and continuity, an overlap between the online and the offline in their claims these worlds are far from separate (Baym, 1998; Kennedy, 2006; Lister et al, 2009; Miller, 2011). This is well summarised by Lister et al: 'cyberspace ... is not more separate from the material world than any other kind of mediated experience and indeed precisely because of its ubiquity may in fact be more seamlessly and intimately stitched into everyday life' (2009, p 217). Some go further in claiming that media are essentially *environmental* and create the setting for social life while staunchly emphasising that such scenery is in a constant state of flux – as social realities are fashioned and refashioned in the presence of and through their interaction with media (Schulz, 2004; Silverstone, 2007).

There is sometimes a tendency, particularly among criminologists, to distinguish 'old' from 'new' media. The former have been described as 'few-to-many' and 'one-way' (Yar, 2012, p 249), with television, radio and film texts produced by a small number of individuals for consumption by a larger viewer society or synopticon (Mathieson, 1997). New media arguably disrupt this model. Innovation in computer hardware and software has increasingly enabled those without professional skills in media production to develop their own texts (or user-generated content), while the development of the internet and World Wide Web has created new opportunities for the dissemination of such texts, with fewer restrictions in relation to time and space (Harvey, 1989). It is argued that this leads to a blurring of the lines between producers and consumers, writers and readers, actors and audiences, spawning terminology that captures this hybridity: 'prosumer' (Ritzer and Jurgenson, 2010); 'produsage' (Bruns, 2008); and peer producer (Bauwens, 2006). Jenkins (2006) highlights the democratic effect of such convergence and the opportunities this creates at grassroots or participatory levels. Miller (2011) points to the extension of fan culture, in which people with a common interest often create fan websites, search for information, and connect with like-minded others, challenging the exclusive control of the producer. Caution is, however, required when contrasting old with new media, as too heavy a focus on change has obscured continuity (Silverstone, 1999). It is difficult, if not impossible, to argue that consumers of old media were passive, uncritical recipients of the representations they encountered. Audiences have always had – and will always have – a diverse range of opinion, expressed through the channels available to them. The networked and digital affordances associated with newer media forms have, however, broadened and accelerated this process. They have widened opportunities for people to create, share and respond to content through a greater range of channels at faster speeds. This has led to some shifts in not just the extent but also the nature of consumption. Senft (2008, 2013) points to the differing way in which people consume content on social media platforms compared with print, film or television – rather than gazing or glancing, they are 'grabbing' in a segmented and tangible way, which has implications for our understandings of participation, agency, power and control in our encounters with media. In essence, the social practices of creating and engaging continue, albeit at a different pace, on a wider scale, and in new virtual spaces, where the norms guiding behaviour are characterised by complexity (Poster, 1999; Rice, 1999; Suler, 2004; Baym, 2010).

In the same way that prosocial activities like keeping in touch with friends and family are embedded within the networked context, so too are criminal and antisocial activities. Criminologists were quick to begin exploring such phenomena – perhaps too quick. Characteristic of the criminological tendency to dichotomise, Wall (2007) distinguished between computer-oriented and computer-assisted crimes. The former encompasses new crimes that have emerged through the affordances of networked technologies – for example, computer hacking and the distribution of malicious software. The latter relates to old crimes in new times – crimes that take on a new lease of life through networked technology, which has enabled them to increase in scope or scale. This includes crimes like fraud, theft and distribution of illegal materials. Wall (2007) also proposes a 'transformation test', in which scholars are urged to consider whether the crime would still exist if the internet was taken away. The transformation test, like the dichotomy of 'old' and 'new' media or online and offline, is indicative of the positivist nature of some areas of criminology – mimicking the natural sciences in creating distinct categories, dependent and independent variables (Young, 2011). To date, this has created problems in making sense of networked media and violent crime. A better understanding of face-to-face, embodied violence via these conceptual frameworks is challenging. Networked society is messy, and characterised by continuities, blurred lines and multiple layers. Violence in a networked society is also messy. It develops in a range of places and spaces to which different people attach different meanings. It manifests itself in different ways – from a disparaging comment on Twitter to a fatal physical confrontation. Stories like the ones mentioned previously are continuing to make the news. Criminal justice systems are incorporating behaviour around media into policy and practice – for example, the Sentencing Council for England and Wales has proposed tougher punishments on young people who film their crimes and post them on social media (Sentencing Council, 2016). Governments and voluntary sector organisations continue to issue guidance around how to stay safe online. But while networked media in violent crime is a key topic for general discussion and concern, it remains under-researched by criminologists.

Now is an important time to take networked media in homicide seriously and this book is the author's attempt to do so from a criminological perspective. The book aims to develop further insights into how networked media are being used in relation to homicide, and introduce better conceptual and theoretical frameworks within which to situate such research. It does so through critiquing current criminological sense making around homicide and media, drawing on concepts from media and communications studies literature, developing an analytical framework within which to explore a range of case studies and considering how the lessons learned can be applied. The journey begins in Chapter Two, where the author outlines existing criminological insights into homicide and identifies the key themes and perspectives that emerge at the intersection of homicide and media. Chapter Three broadens the conceptual and theoretical scope to encompass concepts from media and communications studies, considering the extent to which criminologists have embraced these ideas and highlighting promising areas on which to build. Chapter Four outlines the ontological, epistemological and methodological considerations of the empirical research reported in this book and proposes a new approach towards analysing media in crime – Ethnographic Media Practice Analysis for Criminology. Thereafter, Chapters Five to Seven focus on networked media in specific cases.

Chapter Five examines the murder of Jennifer Alfonso by her husband Derek Medina in Florida, US. Chapter Six examines the Janzen familicide in British Columbia, Canada. The murder of Charles Taylor by his daughter in law Amanda Taylor in Virginia, US is the focus of Chapter Seven. Finally, Chapter Eight considers the cases collectively in the context of the relevant conceptual frameworks and concludes by proposing ways forward for future criminological enquiry into media in homicide.

TWO

Homicide and media: 'realities' and 'representations'

This chapter explores criminological insights into homicide and its representation in mainstream media. It is important to explore these realities and representations as they help form the contextual landscape of the cases that are considered in this book. It is tempting to think of perpetrators like Derek Medina, Randy Janzen and Amanda Taylor as aberrations who are fundamentally different from the rest of us. It is also tempting to make sense of their social media posts in relation to the crimes they committed as simply another manifestation of their transgression, one more thing that marks them out as deviant, criminal and 'other'. However, these individuals have lived out their lives in the same world as us. Prior to committing homicide, they have obtained information about this type of crime and *consumed* it in the same way that the rest of us do – through mediated representations. Prior to committing homicide, their knowledge of this type of crime is highly likely to have been shaped by listening to the same news stories, watching the same dramas, documentaries and films, reading the same novels and true crime books and engaging with the same social media platforms as the rest of us. They did not live in a vacuum. Before they were killers – and indeed afterwards – they were 'prosumers' (Ritzer and Jurgenson, 2010) of mediated representations of homicide, as we all are. Therefore an appreciation of the nature of this context is essential if we are to develop a deeper insights into what they *did* with media around the homicides they committed. This chapter will begin by exploring criminological insights into homicide, addressing questions of definition, scale and nature. Thereafter, the author will identify the key themes and perspectives that emerge around the intersection of homicide and media to explore how criminologists have made sense of homicide in media in terms of what emerges as important as well as what is missing from such analyses.

Homicide

In its very broadest sense, homicide refers to the unlawful taking of a life, to which a range of penalties applies based on the extent of culpability and intention. Legal penalties vary from one jurisdiction to the next. For example, many states within the US differentiate between first- and second-degree murder based on a lack of premeditation in relation to the latter. Within England and Wales, murder and manslaughter both include an intention to harm the victim, but manslaughter applies where there are circumstances that reduce the gravity of the crime – for instance, the killer was provoked or not in control of their behaviour. Other legal penalties apply in different situations. For example, infanticide applies in England and Wales to a mother who kills her biological child in the first year of its life and who has 'not fully recovered from the effects of having given birth' (1938 Infanticide Act). In addition, there are often provisions in law that account for the use of a vehicle in taking the life of another person – in England and Wales this is known as causing death by dangerous driving (1988 Road Traffic Act), while in the US the term 'vehicular homicide' – or a variation of this – is applied in states where such laws exist. Finally, an offence known as corporate manslaughter came into force in 2008 in England and Wales, in which *organisations* can be found guilty of the offence and fined if their activities cause someone's death (2007 Corporate Manslaughter and Corporate Homicide Act).

It is common to assume that any of the aforementioned types of homicide are highly unlikely to go unrecorded in official crime figures. While many property or drug offences may never become part of official crime statistics, it could be argued that this is much less likely to happen in relation to homicide. We assume that friends and relatives of homicide victims will discover their bodies or note their absence, prompting law enforcement to investigate. However, Brookman explored the 'dark figure' of unrecorded homicides (2005, p 20). She noted that there may be many homicide victims whose bodies have never been found. While it is indeed possible to gain a conviction where a body is not present – for example, the conviction of Bradley Murdoch for the 2001 murder of British tourist Peter Falconio in Australia – it is challenging to gather and present evidence that a court will accept within an appropriate burden of proof – most often 'beyond reasonable doubt'. Brookman also argued that a proportion of missing people may be the victims of homicide. Even in cases where a body has been discovered, issues around establishing a cause of death may further obscure homicides – some perpetrators are more able to conceal homicides than others and some medical terms, such as Sudden Infant Death Syndrome or 'cot death', may act to obscure suspicious deaths. Lastly, Brookman notes that the range of inquest verdicts available to coroners may also distort homicide figures. Therefore, when dealing with official statistics, the numbers presented may not be a true or accurate reflection of all homicides that have taken place. What we often take to be the 'reality' – official statistics or 'hard facts' – are themselves merely representations.

Turning to explore official statistics, several patterns do, however, emerge in relation to the scale of homicide relative to other types of crime and the social dynamics of those affected by it. First, homicide is relatively rare compared with other types of crime (D'Cruze et al, 2006). Considering figures for England and Wales, there were 518 recorded homicides in the year ending March 2015 (ONS, 2016a). Compared with other crimes in the same period – for example, over 1.7 million theft offences, over 50,000 robbery offences and nearly 170,000 drug offences – numbers of recorded homicides are indeed relatively small (ONS, 2016b). Second, there has been a general decline in the number of homicides recorded in recent years – from over 800 per year in the early 2000s in England and Wales to the aforementioned 518 for the year ending March 2015 (ONS, 2016a). Similar downward trends have also been reported in the US, where the homicide rate declined by nearly 50% between 1992 and 2011, reaching its lowest level since 1963 (Smith and Cooper, 2013).

Examining the socio-demographics of homicide, scholars point to three overall themes. Homicide is a largely male-perpetrated crime, men are overrepresented as victims, and victim and perpetrator often have a close social connection (Polk, 1994; Rock, 1998; D'Cruze et al, 2006). In relation to male perpetration, 90% of homicide suspects in England and Wales in the year ending March 2015 were men (ONS, 2016a). In terms of victimhood, men are overrepresented as victims – with male victimisation in the US between 1992 and 2011 being 3.6 times that for women (Smith and Cooper, 2013). Homicides commonly feature a close social relationship between victim and perpetrator – stranger homicides are relatively rare. It is, however, difficult to ascertain accurate figures for stranger homicides, given that the 'stranger' category in official data often includes cases where the suspect is not known. However, reasons for misconceptions around stranger homicides are addressed by criminologists Hough and McCorkle, who argue as follows:

> When hearing *stranger homicide,* a number of people immediately conjure thoughts of lurking serial killers. In fact, most of the stranger killings are cases resulting from confrontational violence or are gang-related ... where participants do not *know* one another but believe they have

opposing gang affiliations. (Hough and McCorkle, 2017, p 21, emphasis added)

The close social relationships that characterise homicides go some way towards a high clearance rate for this type of crime – investigators are able to quickly identify suspects given their social and geographical proximity to the victim. For example, figures for England and Wales in the year 2012/13 show a homicide detection rate of 90%, compared with 28.5% for sexual offences and 18% for theft (Smith et al, 2013). Exploring the links between victim and perpetrator further, Brookman (2005) identifies 'domestic' homicide as the most common type of homicide, where connections are based on family relationships or intimate partnerships. Male and female infants aged under 12 months have the highest victimisation rate regarding family relationship homicides, with the majority killed by a parent (Brookman and Maguire, 2003). In terms of sexual intimacy or 'intimate partner' homicides, these cases predominantly feature a male perpetrator and a female victim. Female victims are more likely than men to be killed by a partner or an ex-partner – 41% and 6%, respectively, in England and Wales (ONS, 2016a). While female and infant victims feature heavily in domestic cases, male victims are overrepresented in cases based on other types of social connection. Polk (1994) and Brookman (2005) highlight the maleness of confrontational homicide. In these cases, fights or assaults have escalated and the homicide is the outcome of attempts to maintain honour and reputation particularly among men from working-class backgrounds, where violence may be entwined with ideas of masculinity (Toch, 1969; Polk, 1994, 1999). Brookman (2005) identifies men aged 16–35 years as most at risk of involvement in a homicide as a victim or suspect, with black and Asian men particularly vulnerable. This is certainly the case in the US, where individuals who are young (particularly aged 25–34 years), black and male have the highest victimisation rate (Smith and Cooper, 2013).

Therefore, while even the official statistics may not tell the full story, homicide is a crime with a set of clear characteristics. It is rare and declining. It is a male-dominated act in which men are disproportionately represented as perpetrators and victims. Those involved are known to one another more often than not and homicides are more likely than other types of crime to be cleared up by law enforcement. However, when we venture beyond the official statistics and criminological analysis to explore media representations of homicide, the picture becomes somewhat distorted.

Representing homicide

This section critically considers media representations of homicide, outlining and exploring the nature and extent of their deviation from official and criminological understandings and the implications for the subject of this book. Homicide is a subject of popular fascination (Biressi and Bloom, 2001) – one that has been drawing audiences since at least the times of the Greek and Roman dramatists (Turnbull, 2014). The 'Lombrosian overtones' evident in considerations of those who kill indicate the need for explanations that position killers as different from the rest of us, as aberrations of nature, obscuring the broader range of biological, psychological and sociological explanations offered by social science (Dowler et al, 2006, p 840). The invention of the printing press in the 15th century gave sense making around homicide a new lease of life. In exploring the history of crime fiction, Knight (2010) identifies homicide as a prominent theme in Elizabethan and Jacobean crime stories:

> They can be very grisly: the axe-murderer was hired by the children's father ... Mr Page is murdered by the wife and her hired assistants ... Mr Trat, a curate, is killed on the highway and then, in his own house, cut up, boiled and salted. (Knight, 2010, p 3)

Later literary publications both entertained and informed audiences. One notable example was the Newgate Calendar, a collection of true crime accounts that emerged in the early 17th century (Turnbull, 2010, 2014). The 19th century saw the proliferation of 'penny bloods', renamed penny 'dreadfuls' in the 1860s. These books were fictional tales of highwaymen, deviant aristocrats and determined policemen hunting down criminals (Flanders, 2013). Penny dreadfuls caused uproar among polite society and there was particular concern around the impact of such publications – particularly on young minds. Following the conviction of 12- and 13-year-old brothers Robert and Nathaniel Coombes for the murder of their mother in 1895, campaigners called for a ban on penny dreadfuls, arguing that they inflamed the imaginations of children to such a degree that they could lead to murder (Summerscale, 2016). Despite this, the crime genre thrived. The factual and the fictional came to borrow from one another – William Roughhead's accounts of the Deacon Brodie murder trial in Edinburgh were remodelled by Robert Louis Stevenson into the well-known fictional work, the *Strange Case of Dr Jekyll and Mr Hyde*

(Seltzer, 2008). With the emergence of the large and small screen, homicide was often the plot around which films, television programmes and documentaries emerged and it continues to be a staple topic for entertainment media. Therefore, despite its relative rarity, homicide is a prominent crime when we examine its presence in media (Ferrell, 2005). Within fiction, news, drama, film and true crime, coverage of homicide vastly eclipses that of the property crimes that constitute the majority of police-recorded crime (Maguire, 2002). As such, it is a longstanding and lucrative cultural product.

Criminologists examining the rendezvous of homicide and media assert that not only is homicide *overrepresented*, but it is also subject to varying degrees of *misrepresentation*. As stated previously, the individuals at the centre of the cases this book examines are not only the producers of content around the crimes they commit, they are also *consumers* of media representations of homicide. The criminological concepts and theories explored within this section are useful in mapping the contemporary mediascape within which perpetrator-produced media exists. This mediascape is a hall of mirrors in which the street scripts the screen and the screen scripts the street (Hayward and Young, 2004). Crime literature is often adapted for television and film, the characters it portrays developing significant fan followings and emerging as key figures in the contemporary zeitgeist. The homicides covered on the evening news are reproduced on the websites of news organisations, which are linked to elsewhere online and pored over by people wanting to comment and discuss further. The homicide behind the headline of a newspaper may one day be explored in a documentary, written up as a true crime account, serialised as a podcast or inspire a television drama. Contemporary audiences go back and forth on a daily basis between various types of media, obscuring the distinction between news and entertainment (Carrabine, 2008). This section will not therefore attempt to forcibly separate the media genres in which homicide is represented but will identify the key criminological ideas around its representation and consider the implications for the cases that this book focuses on.

Perhaps the most powerful points made about homicide in media have developed around the concept of 'news values' (Galtung and Ruge, 1965; Chibnall, 1977; Jewkes, 2015). News values could be described as the unwritten rules of journalism, a list of criteria that contribute to the creation of news stories with widespread appeal or 'newsworthiness'. Not all homicides will make the news. It is important therefore to examine news values as they help explain why particular homicides are accorded significance while others go unreported. The

12 news values identified by criminologist Yvonne Jewkes (2015) are particularly valuable in this regard, given that they were developed specifically in relation to crime news. It could be argued that most known homicides are conducive to the news values of 'predictability' and 'simplification'. In terms of predictability, events in the aftermath of homicide allow news organisations to plan their coverage ahead of time and follow the key milestones of the case – a suspect is charged, the defendant appears in court, there may be a trial, and, if found guilty, the convicted person will be sentenced. In relation to simplification, stories of homicide can be reduced to a small number of explanatory categories – the perpetrator was mad or bad, righteous or evil, the product of nature or nurture (D'Cruze et al, 2006). However, this is where similarities end and other news values come to the fore, all stemming from the homicide reaching a particular 'threshold' that makes it worthy of a place in the news. The degree of violence and extent of visual spectacle or graphic imagery involved plays a role, as does the presence of sex, celebrity and the ability to individualise those involved. Hence the newsworthiness of the murder of South African law graduate and model Reeva Steenkamp was significantly enhanced by the combination of the multiple gunshot wounds she suffered, images of the bloody crime scene and her intimate relationship with her killer Oscar Pistorius – a world-famous sports personality. In addition, homicides with a sense of proximity, involving children, embodying risk and reinforcing conservative ideology are also likely to meet thresholds for newsworthiness. The murder of Liverpool toddler James Bulger is illustrative of this: James could have been anyone's child, taken while on a trip to the local shops with his mother, an activity that thousands of parents with young children engage in every day. The fact that he was taken and killed by two 10-year-olds stimulated debate around the making of a murderer and the role of the family – a cornerstone institution of British neoliberal society – in creating children who kill.

In addition to news values, criminologists also draw on the concept of the 'ideal victim' in exploring news media representations of homicide. Ideal victims are people who 'when hit by crime – are most readily given the complete and legitimate status of being a victim' (Christie, 1986, p 18). They include society's most vulnerable – for instance, the frail pensioner and the dependent child. As one criminologist notes, "'if it bleeds it leads" is not entirely truthful, as "it really depends on who is bleeding"' (Dowler, cited in Dowler et al, 2006, p 841). One study found disproportionate emphasis on rare types of homicide, which included vulnerable or ideal victims (Peelo et al, 2004). Several other studies have highlighted ethnic disparities, with disproportionate emphasis on white over black and Hispanic victims (Johnstone et al, 1994; Sorenson et al, 1998; Weiss and Chermak, 1998; Paulsen, 2003). Female victims are also overrepresented (Sorensen et al, 1998), an observation that has been applied to crime drama as well as crime news, distorting the male-dominated nature of this crime in reality (Rader et al, 2016). Other research takes a different stance, arguing that the key determinant of coverage is the extent to which homicides deviate from or reinforce culturally rooted norms and expectations (Pritchard and Hughes, 1997; Lundman, 2003; Gruenewald et al, 2009, 2013). For example, in relation to the US city of Baltimore, where the majority of homicide victims are black, Schildkraut and Donley (2012) noted that killings involving white, female, or older victims – and those in which victims are stabbed or asphyxiated – are particularly overrepresented in news.

Criminologists have also analysed the narratives created around homicide in news media. Dowler et al (2006) claim that news media frequently devalue domestic homicides in which women are killed by current or former intimate partners, holding victims partially responsible for their victimisation – a perspective rooted in patriarchal ideas of femininity and gender. In her analysis of newspaper coverage of such homicides, Cathy Ferrand Bullock (2007) identified a tendency to 'other' those involved, presenting such cases as different, one-off incidents and diluting women's victimhood by emphasising the impact of the homicide on those other than the victim:

> Together these journalistic choices created coverage that tended to omit or obscure the ideas of domestic violence as a longer-term experience that leads to the victim's death, as stemming from patterns of domination and control, as part of the larger problem of gender inequality that allows men to brutalise women. (Bullock, 2007, p 47)

These findings were echoed and further developed in another study. Having analysed news reporting of 72 cases of femicide, Monckton-Smith (2012) argued that news media reinforce the dominant discourse of heterosexual romantic love, which rationalises such homicides. In addition, media are not the sole advocates of these narratives – they stood alongside those of the police and courts in mutually reinforcing these discourses. Monckton Smith's study supports the findings of Dowler et al (2006) and Bullock (2007) in discovering significant 'victim blaming' and framing of the homicides as *exceptional* events rather than the culmination of entrenched patterns of abuse. In addition, Monckton-Smith identifies other narratives evident in news reports. These were an emphasis on the perpetrator being drunk or under the influence of substances (and therefore less culpable), assumptions that victims of abuse are lying, pity for the perpetrator and the framing of male violence as an expression of love and intensity of feelings. Similar conclusions are drawn by Walklate and Petrie in their consideration of newspaper reporting of filicide-suicides, where responsibility for such tragedies is placed 'solely on individuals while sidestepping any consideration of collective social responsibility as an element of causality' (2013, p 276). It is important to examine this framing because representation will affect reality to varying degrees. News media have a role in shaping public opinion and policy responses to violent crimes like homicide. In marginalising the victim's perspective, there is a risk of minimising the significance of particular types of homicide through rationalising them within hegemonic discourses of 'love'.

As most of us are not personally affected by homicide, we get our information about it from media (Surette, 2015b). We tend to accord greater legitimacy to media representations involving law enforcement personnel and other 'experts'; when reality television emerged in the 1980s, therefore, its representation of homicide came under close watch by criminologists. Reality crime television claimed to offer realistic representations of crime, perpetrators and victims (Fishman and Cavender, 1998). The conservative political context lent further legitimacy to the criminal justice professionals on our screens – tempering our insecurities by presenting law and order as the guardian of neoliberal ideological values and institutions. This type of programming therefore not only filled an increasing number of television channels but also tapped into popular cultural concerns and insecurities. Jermyn (2007) traces its roots to the launch of BBC's Crimewatch in 1984, which, she argues, was a trailblazer, clearing a path for a number of other shows such as America's Most Wanted and Police, Camera, Action!. A homicide was often the leading case in this landmark programme and for several years the presenter Nick Ross ended the show with the comment 'Don't have nightmares' (Soothill, 1998, p 156). Crimewatch did not challenge the status quo, emphasising instead the pathology of the criminal at a micro level – supporting the political rhetoric of individual responsibility and agency over structure (Jermyn, 2007). It did not tackle issues of domestic violence – a much more considerable risk to women than stranger attacks – and Crimewatch's aesthetics often had more in common with the sensationalism characteristic of news media, particularly in terms of its reconstructions (Jermyn, 2007). As such, it can be argued that portrayals of homicide in early true crime television fall victim to the same criticisms aimed at crime news and crime drama – homicide is overrepresented, misrepresented and decontextualised.

The concerns of overrepresentation and misrepresentation voiced by criminologists studying news media and early reality television representations of homicide are echoed to various degrees by those exploring homicide in other types of media. Durham et al (1995) conducted a critical review of homicide in true crime books – a longstanding literary genre with its roots in the early modern period (Wiltenburg, 2004; Seltzer, 2007), its contemporary manifestation arguably set in motion by Truman Capote's *In Cold Blood* (1965). Arguing that true crime books represent not only a distorted image of the crime itself, but also of the criminal justice outcomes, Durham and colleagues stated:

> ... true crime presents cases involving higher status White victims who are often killed by related middle- or upper-class White offenders, including females, using guns and a variety of other methods. Unlike many Uniform Crime Reports homicides, the crime did not occur subsequent to arguments and were often the result of a plot to inherit money or gain revenge on a family member. Offenders are generally caught and convicted and, when compared to the overall distribution of homicide case outcomes, significant numbers are sentenced to death. (Durham et al, 1995, p 150)

In relation to film, Young (2010a) argues that the portrayal of widespread opportunistic victimisation in serial killer films echoes the risk concept seen in crime news and presents ideal rather than actual victim groups: 'The serial killer film locates criminality in any suburb, any neighbourhood, dispersing the threat of victimisation ... victims may be selected for reasons as arbitrary as checking into the "wrong" motel or happening to be a size 14 in clothes' (2010a, p 75). Young also identifies a clear interweaving of the seriality in mass popular culture and the repetition-compulsion in serial homicide within these films – they are essentially tapping into the zeitgeist. However, it could also be argued that this genre *offsets* the anxiety it creates through heavy focus on detectives who pursue and ultimately catch the serial killer. In effect, such portrayals attempt to restore faith in criminal justice as the guardian of neoliberal values, and, in so doing, they imitate news media's handling of homicide.

In relation to television crime drama, Fabianic notes the overrepresentation of white victims and offenders and individualistic explanations for the homicides, concluding 'little, if any effort is made to connect them to basic social institutions.... Fiction markets better than reality' (1997, pp 201-2). Soulliere (2003) refutes this, claiming that crime dramas are relatively *accurate* in that most killers are known to their victims, women are killed by their current or former intimate partners and killings take place in homes. Soulliere also argued that producers are increasingly serving viewer demands for more *authentic* portrayals – partly attributable to the increasing popularity of reality television. Remaining inaccuracies and omissions – for example, intricately planned homicides and a neglect of structural factors – were attributed to the audience demand for dramatic effect. As well as inaccuracies, criminologists have noted victim blaming in crime drama, although some claim that male characters are subject to a greater degree of victim blaming than female characters (Rader et al, 2016). Crime drama has, however, evolved from the high-speed cop series of the 1950s and 1960s, through 'forensic realism' with its emphasis on wounds, bodies and corpses, to 'post-forensics', in which the complex narratives and differing perspectives of the characters are explored (Jermyn, 2013). Therefore it can be argued that as the genre has developed, it has become more sophisticated, turning the questions of 'Howdunit?' and 'Whodunit?' to 'Whydunit?'.

In his consideration of the contemporary true crime genre in television, Mark Seltzer (2008) makes similar observations. He recognises the somewhat voyeuristic motivations that drive our fascination with true crime, particularly violent crime, which he describes as symptomatic of our contemporary 'wound culture' (Seltzer, 1998, 2007, 2008). He describes trauma, violence and terror as key gathering points between the individual and the collective in a pathological public sphere, a 'theatre for the living' (2008, p 14) in the 'strange attraction of the murder leisure industry' (2008, p 35). Seltzer argues that there exists a compulsion in modern society towards observation, particularly of torn and open bodies and torn and open people or 'psyches' (Seltzer, 1998). This plays out in various ways in true crime, where viewers see what those affected by the crime did *not* see and access multiple viewpoints as 'spokesvictims' (2008, p 20) of crime recount their experiences. In addition, Seltzer offers insight into the presence of the simplification and individualisation news values in true crime – arguing that true crime sheds light on these news values, even if it does not tackle them. True crime, he argues, highlights the difficulties in singling out motives and explanations and ascribing them to individuals. The device through which it highlights this difficulty is tackled is the retrospective, 'by which causes and motives are reattached to the effects of the acts (the torn body)' (2008, p 26).

Therefore in relation to crime drama and true crime, it appears that while some criticise such media in terms of overrepresentation and misrepresentation, these genres mark a significant departure from crime news and early reality crime television in one important way. We can argue that there is room to at least *identify* the complex context of homicide in crime drama and true crime, even if the degree to which it is explored and interrogated falls short of the depth seen in academic analysis of this type of crime. By its very nature, crime news has to deliver a compact, efficient, and effective product – there is little room for ambiguity when time and column inches are limited. Simplicity is less of a requirement for crime drama and true crime television, as audiences are increasingly seeking out insights into the grey areas, asking questions that are more demanding and defy simple answers. Jermyn (2013) sums up this cultural turn in her consideration of the popular HBO series The Wire:

> The series notably eschewed any interest in lab forensics or spectacular corpses to instead develop intricate narratives built around multiple, intertwined characters and story arcs, tracking both the complex execution of crime (particularly the drug trade) and the quotidian nature of police work. Its devoted fans, and the burgeoning scholarly interest in it, surely speak of an active audience base desirous of crime drama that returns to and concentrates on characters and social context, on motive and human interaction, above the explication of the minutiae of scientific evidence. (2013, p 109)

Delving into complex narratives and the psychology of their protagonists requires a lengthier true crime format – more likely to be a series than a self-contained episode or freestanding documentary. The serialised single story is beginning to emerge as a popular new format for true crime. A recent example is HBO's The Jinx (2015), a six-part series directed by Andrew Jarecki that explored the Manhattan real estate heir Robert Durst's alleged involvement in several homicides. Durst's status as a member of a wealthy, well-known New York family also highlights the convergence of true crime television and celebrity – our contemporary preoccupation with and valuing of commodified public figures (Cashmore, 2014). Murderers perceived to have transgressed not only legal but also moral codes are accorded considerable notoriety and become 'iniquitous criminal celebrities' (Penfold-Mounce, 2009). Notable among such criminal celebrities are female murderers such as Myra Hindley, convicted for the murders of several children alongside her partner Ian Brady, and Aileen Wuornos, executed in 2002 following her convictions for killing men while working as a prostitute in Florida. They have not only broken the law, but have also disrupted social norms and expectations in which violence is the very antithesis of femininity. The act of homicide in itself is therefore insufficient to attain celebrity status.

> The iniquitous criminal refers to a criminal individual who achieves celebrity due to their well-knownness for committing unforgivable horror crimes, which are actions inspiring a universal public fear, loathing and disgust on a national or international basis. Unforgivable crimes by the iniquitous criminal are horror crimes that target the vulnerable such as the old or the very young and involve sexual assault, abuse or large-scale murder, often using torture, sadism and cannibalism. The association with such crimes leads the iniquitous criminal to possess the strongest longevity and celebrity status of all the criminal-celebrity categories. (Penfold-Mounce, 2009, p 90)

News and entertainment media play a significant role in the maintenance of this celebrity status. Murderers continue to make the news during their prison sentences and their transgression is reanalysed in true crime books and documentaries. As media organisations revisit these cases and use them as ongoing reference points, they become 'mega cases' (Soothill et al, 2002, Peelo et al, 2004), further cementing the iniquitous murderer as a cultural anti-hero.

Many of these points have been magnified in recent years, given the proliferation of networked media and the increased participatory opportunities that have come along with these shifts. The opportunities for increasing numbers of people to create and share content and the acceleration at which these processes occur is 'the biggest change that media-criminologists have witnessed' (Jewkes, 2015, p 4). The visual has become an increasingly important component of social life in networked society via the ubiquitous smartphone camera. Referring to this 'photographic culture', Carney notes:

> Our photographic culture involves us all in the social practices of spectacular production ... we are both actors and audience ... the photographic spectacle is no mere image, backdrop, illustration or portrait *of* our lives. It flows through us as part of our social being. It is not an image of our lives; it is part of our lives. (2010, p 18, original emphasis)

The nature of media texts and the way in which we receive, consume and interact with them has changed. In the past when we wanted to engage with a particular representation of homicide, we could discuss it with friends and family and perhaps write a letter to the editor of a newspaper if we took issue with that representation. Now we have considerably more participatory opportunities – we can post a comment on an online news article, we can tweet about a television programme using a hashtag or we can join one of the multiple online websleuth communities to discuss and debate particular cases (Yardley et al, 2015, 2016). We are able to produce our own critical or counter-representations even if we have little in the way of formal media production training. The surge in true crime podcasting is evidence of the ease with which people are now able to participate in the mediated representation of homicide. In an article exploring the appeal true crime podcasts, David Whelan shares his thoughts and those of Aaron, a host of the Generation Why podcast:

> The allure of these podcasts is that they function as brilliant unfinished stories that leave you, the listener, to fill in the blank spaces – we are hardwired to love a good gruesome death as well as mystery. True crime is a combination of both, and there is no way to stop it – because death, tragedy, and mystery belong to no one. "Once a crime hits the news it no longer belongs to private individuals," says Aaron. "The public wants and needs to know more about it. It started with newspapers and television and continues on with podcasts." (Whelan, 2016)

In producing and consuming – or 'prosuming' (Ritzer and Jurgenson, 2010) – mediated representations of homicide, we are engaging in a form of 'witnessing'. This goes beyond passive watching or observing; it is active, performed and embodied (Young, 2005, 2010a, 2010b; Carney, 2010; Howie, 2012). The landscape of mediated representations of homicide has changed. Opportunities to participate – to be seen and heard – are now more accessible to more people, the criminal and the law-abiding alike.

From the literature explored in this chapter, it is clear that homicide continues to be a contemporary fascination. The comments made in this regard by Lesser over 20 years ago still hold true: 'We all seem to be interested in murderers these days. They are our truth and our fiction; they are our truth *as* fiction, and vice versa' (Lesser, 1993,cited in Biressi and Bloom, 2001, p 1). People buy the newspapers, watch the television dramas, read the novels and listen to the podcasts that accord a rare crime a considerable presence. Through networked technologies we also participate in the production and consumption of media representations of homicide to an unprecedented extent. Killers are embedded in a context in which homicide is a highly visible, accessible and lucrative cultural product. Their mediascape is our mediascape. When perpetrators create their own media in relation to the homicides they commit, we should therefore be examining these actions as constitutive of the homicide–fixated wound culture (Seltzer, 1998, 2007, 2008) within which they occur. We should continue asking the question 'What does media do with homicide?'. However, we now need to supplement this with the more pressing questions of 'What do those involved in homicide do with media?' and 'How can this be understood within the bigger picture of mediated representations of homicide?'. In our preoccupation with homicide in media, we have neglected media in homicide. The next chapter considers these points in more detail and charts a path towards filling this void.

THREE

Media in homicide: from consumption to participation

The previous chapter outlined the nature and extent of homicide and considered how criminology has engaged with questions of media around this crime. It was established that to date, criminologists have largely analysed media *representations* of homicide as opposed to what those involved in homicide *do* with media. Within this chapter, the author identifies the work of a small group of criminologists who have started to grapple with these issues alongside promising approaches from media and communications studies. The chapter begins by further exploring the shifts in media noted in Chapter One and the extent to which criminologists have accommodated these changes in their work. Thereafter, the criminological literature around school shootings will be considered because of the unique way in which scholars working in this field explore perpetrators' use of media. The chapter concludes by proposing stronger links between these strands of literature – which to date have run parallel, but have rarely intersected.

Mediatisation

In Chapter One, the author explored the questions of media with which she had grappled when researching 'Facebook murder' (Yardley and Wilson, 2015). This involved mining the media and communications studies literature to understand the wider context of such crimes. This literature is a rich repository of conceptual and theoretical frameworks for making better sense of media in homicide. The past five years have seen a rapid expansion of scholarly activity further exploring media in everyday life (Couldry, 2012; Deuze, 2012, 2014; Couldry and Hepp, 2013, 2017; Hepp and Krotz, 2014; Hepp et al, 2015). One of the concepts these scholars draw attention to is invisibility – as newer media become more intricately interwoven into the fabric of everyday life, they become older media, blending into the background and taken for granted (Deuze, 2012, 2014). Researchers deploy a range of terms to emphasise the importance of media in the social, for example 'mediapolis' (Silverstone, 2007), 'media life' (Deuze, 2012), 'mediatized worlds' (Couldry, 2012) and 'mediascapes' (Appadurai, 1990). A key distinction is drawn between the terms 'mediated' and 'mediatised':

> While 'mediation' refers to the process of communication in general – that is how communication has to be understood as involving the ongoing mediation of meaning construction, 'mediatization' is a category designed to describe change.... Mediatization reflects how the overall consequences of multiple processes of mediation have changed with the emergence of different kinds of media. (Couldry and Hepp, 2013, p 197)

Rather than conceptualising media in positivist terms as an independent variable, something that *comes in* from *out there* and has an impact on us – as criminologists have tended to do – media and communications scholars take a different approach. As opposed to describing a life lived *with* media, they take as their focus a life lived *in* media:

> You live *in* media. Who you are, what you do, and what all of this means to you does not exist outside of media. Media are to us as water is to fish. This does not mean life is determined by media – it just suggests that whether we like it or not, every aspect of our lives takes place in media ... the uses and appropriations of media can be seen as fused with *everything* people do, *everywhere* people are, *everyone* people aspire to be. There is no external to media life – whatever we perceive as escape hatch, passage out, or potential Delete key is just an illusion. In fact we can only *imagine* a life outside of media. (Deuze, 2012, p x)

One strand of the mediatisation literature focuses on the concept of 'media logic' – exploring the modus operandi of the media in distributing resources of a material and symbolic nature, and in so doing, using formal and informal rules (Hjarvard, 2008). However, the author shares the view of Lundby (2009) that an emphasis on media logic diverts attention from the microsociological interactions in which media are used, shaped and given meaning. As such, those who place these interactions at the centre of their analysis hold greater potential to inform the study of media in homicide. Couldry (2004, 2012) has contributed considerably to conceptual development around mediatisation in this respect. He emphasises the need to, 'decentre media research from the study of media texts or production structures (important though these are) and redirect it onto the study of the open-ended range of practices focused directly or indirectly on media' (2004, p 117). Labelling his approach 'media as practice', Couldry stresses the importance of exploring what media imply for the social lives of those who use them. In this respect, inquiry focuses on the needs-led, routinised use of media in everyday life, and, in so doing, contextualises these practices within the social. This is of particular relevance for this book, which explores homicide confessions on social media. Whether media is an aim, object, both or neither, its constituent role in the social realities of the individuals involved is the key starting point. Couldry defines media in broad terms, including not only institutionally produced media like television, radio, press and film, but also the individually produced media interwoven with this more traditional content across a variety of platforms. Couldry summarises the underlying premises of his approach as follows:

> ... a practice approach to media frames its questions by reference, not to media considered as objects, texts, apparatuses of perception of production processes, but to what people are doing in relation to media in the contexts in which they act. Such a media sociology is interested in actions that *involve* media without necessarily having media as their aim or object; and actions whose possibility is *conditioned by* the prior existence, presencing or functioning of media. We can combine those interests into a single, apparently naïve question ... *what are people doing that is related to media?* (Couldry, 2012, p 35, original emphasis)

Couldry's contribution to the mediatisation debates may be valuable for criminologists asking this question in relation to crime and deviance. The self is increasingly performed on and through networked media, an array of 'resources' that enable us to narrate, represent and maintain ourselves as social actors (Couldry and Hepp, 2017). How these resources are deployed around crime and deviance is an important direction for criminological research. Couldry identifies four key media practices – or things we *do* with media – that offer an important conceptual framework: searching and search enabling; showing and being shown; presencing; and archiving.

Couldry argues that 'searching' is now culturally embedded and goes beyond the tools associated with online search engines like Google. Searching has led to the development of other practices, which includes sharing links and stylised content with others, and setting up alerts and

RSS feeds. These are the tools through which people seek to refine their access to an array of information of potential relevance to them. Couldry argues that this new type of 'dispersed agency' (2012, p 46) is a significant contrast with the past. The idea of witnessing is central to 'showing' and 'being shown'. Acts are now available for us to *see*, rather than simply read or hear about from others. In relation to the cases considered in this book, what we are witnessing has moved on to encompass not only professionally produced media products around homicide, but also content produced by those *involved in* and *affected by* these crimes. Couldry cites the video-sharing site YouTube as a key tool for this type of media practice, a 'vast new space of showing' (2012, p 47). Couldry makes some salient points for criminologists in identifying antisocial motivations for showing, citing the examples of humiliating others or the desire to

> ... triumph oneself through the act of showing, as in the exultant videos by school shooters. In past eras (and sometimes still today) heads of war victims were placed on stakes for all to see. Now perhaps there is no need: a video of an attack within minutes can be posted online or circulated by mobile phone amongst friends. (2012, p 49)

Couldry argues that these media practices are associated with the dissolving boundaries around private life, stating that being shown is an ever-present possibility in contemporary social life. 'Presencing' is described as 'acts of managing through media a continuous presence-to-others across space' (2012, p 49). This is concerned with the dissemination of information about oneself in order to sustain a sense of public presence. Couldry emphasises the importance of a permanent site in public space for the display of the self – a Twitter or Facebook profile, a personal webpage or blog, for example. Presencing is a response to 'an emerging requirement in everyday life to have a public presence beyond one's bodily presence, to construct an objectification of oneself' (Couldry, 2012, p 50). 'Archiving', is described as

> ... presencing's equivalent in time.... While the effort of presencing is directed at the difficulties of maintaining a presence in public space ... archiving ... is the individual's practice of managing in time the whole mass of informational and image traces s/he continually produces, so that over time, they add up to something acceptable and perhaps even graspable as a history. (2012, pp 51-52)

Archiving supports people's general desire to pass on some type of legacy, leaving a story of their lives behind – this is as relevant for homicide perpetrators as it is for everyone else. Archiving is nothing new, but in contemporary mediatised worlds this practice occurs amid new conceptualisations of time and space (Harvey, 1989), in which the past is more readily accessible in the present than has ever been the case.

In addition to the four key practices, Couldry acknowledges that some of what people do in relation to media is inherently complex, involving combinations of the activities described here alongside non-media-related practices. He argues that these may feature particular sequences of separate actions or messy composites in which actions bleed into and affect each other. He cites several examples, including how people keep up with the news – not only through watching a prime-time TV news bulletin, but also through glancing at news headline on an internet homepage, receiving an alert on a smartphone, or picking up a free newspaper on the way home. Couldry argues that keeping up with the news is a highly variable articulation of smaller practices that will continue to change and evolve in relation to the organisation of everyday life. In addition, Couldry emphasises the apparent contradiction between the complex practices of keeping all channels open and screening out, noting

> By choosing from a vast range of 'apps', people screen out much of the infinite media environment to create a 'chosen' interface – a customized media manifold if you like – that is both manageable and seemingly personal. (2012, p 56)

This has clear implications for Seltzer's notion of wound culture discussed earlier (2007, 2008). Those drawn to trauma and suffering are able to tailor their own wound culture polymedia (Madianou and Miller, 2013). As such, they each have unique portals into the murder leisure industry – choosing and subscribing to a personalised range of true crime podcasts, networked websleuthing spaces, Twitter feeds and Facebook pages, on-demand films and television shows.

While there has been considerable conceptual and theoretical development around mediatisation, empirical studies are few and far between. However, mediatisation holds considerable potential for the topic under consideration in this book. If life is lived in and through media, so too is homicide and our prosumption of it (Ritzer and Jurgenson, 2010). The next section explores cultural criminology – a field of criminology that has much in common with the mediatisation literature. As such, it holds considerable potential to shape approaches to studying media in homicide.

Cultural criminology: nurturing the mediatisation seed

Cultural criminology represents a significant departure from its orthodox counterpart. As scholars of culture, its followers are committed to a continued emphasis on the learned and shared values, attitudes and behaviours of social groups. As *criminologists*, they focus on those considered deviant in breaching social expectations, both formal and informal. Challenging the concept of the 'mainstream' from which these groups deviate, cultural criminologists explore how crime and criminals come to be labelled as such and how these processes play out at a range of social sites – from the individual micro-sociological lived experience to the institutional macro-sociological structures that frame, enable and constrain the everyday. This is neither a top-down determinism nor a bottom-up constructionism but a messy combination of both:

> ... cultural criminology seeks to highlight the interaction between these two elements: the relationship and the interaction between constructions upwards and constructions downwards. Its focus is always upon the continuous generation of meaning around interaction; rules created, rules broken, a constant interplay of moral entrepreneurship, moral innovation and transgression. (Hayward and Young, 2004, p 259)

Questions of identity are central ones for cultural criminologists, with reference in particular to the notion of the 'transgressive subject':

> ... what we are witnessing today is a crisis of being in a society where self-fulfilment, expression, and immediacy are paramount values, yet the possibilities of realizing such dreams are strictly curtailed by the increasing bureaucratization of work (its so-called McDonaldization) and the commodification of leisure. Crime and transgression in this new context can be seen as the breaking through of restraints, a realization of immediacy and a reassertion of identity and ontology. In this sense, identity becomes woven into rule-breaking. (Hayward and Young, 2004, p 267)

The question of media is a central one for cultural criminologists. They are concerned with exploring not only the way in which media organisations report on criminal and deviant acts, but also the ways in which those involved in such activities actively use media in constructing, maintaining and shaping their identities and realities. Cultural criminologists use the concept of 'loops' to describe this phenomena (Ferrell et al, 2008, 2015). Loops depict the process by which 'everyday life recreates itself in its own image' (Ferrell et al, 2008, p 130). As lives are made visible and infused with meaning through media, this then feeds back into those lives themselves. So, for example, with reference to gangs, it could be argued that mainstream media representations of gangs and the media produced by gang members (for instance YouTube videos and posts on social networking sites) feed into and give meaning to the experiences of gang members and others' perceptions of them, which in turn are then further represented and fed back in a continuous circle. Ferrell and colleagues argue that while these loops can remain self-contained, constantly playing back on themselves, they more commonly connect up to other loops in larger 'spirals' of culture and crime (Ferrell et al, 2008, 2015).

One of the early studies in cultural criminology explored the lives of BASE jumpers in the late 1990s (Ferrell et al, 2001). BASE is an acronym representing the four fixed places from which participants might parachute themselves – bridges, antennas, spans and Earth. BASE jumping is an example of 'edgework' – the invention, adoption and performance of risky activities. While the fieldwork and publication of Ferrell and colleagues' 2001 article occurred within a media landscape somewhat different from the one we inhabit today, the findings have clear relevance for the contemporary context. Ferrell et al (2001) critically considered media in relation the Bridge Day events in 1997 and 1998. Bridge Day is described as an opportunity giving 'some 300 BASE jumpers from around the world a once-a-year opportunity to jump legally from the bridge' (Ferrell et al, 2001, p 181). The bridge is the 876-foot high New River Gorge Bridge in Fayette County, West Virginia, US. The paper highlights the multidirectional and multilevel nature of media around Bridge Day. Professional photographers and videographers were present at Bridge Day to film the events. This had an impact on the BASE jumpers in the sense that there was an expectation for them to fulfil the demands of these individuals to create the desired images that might end up in television commercials or popular channels like MTV. The jumpers were to a degree dependent on these individuals to ensure that coverage of the event reached mainstream channels, enhancing the legitimacy of their sport.

However, the BASE jumpers also created their own media through the use of helmet cameras and internet bulletin boards within which they challenged the narratives created about them by media organisations. This event also took place at a time when sharing video content online was a more complex process requiring more technical skill that it does today; however, members of the community distributed VHS tapes and other merchandise post-event. This elongated Bridge Day and embodied the idea of the screen scripting the street and the street scripting the screen:

> ... a subculture that is less the passive object of mass media attention than it is the active producer of its own image ... they operate collectively to construct a world awash with their own recurring images and elongated, mediated meanings.... BASE jumpers have in many ways made the media their own as well.... In attaching media machines to their bodies and their activities, they produce as well as consume; they inaugurate their own complex flows of information and thus shape a mediated world as much as they are shaped by it. (Ferrell et al, 2001, p 191)

In a similar vein, Encheva and colleagues (2013) explored how media are embedded into the practices of graffiti artists and skaters. This study suggests that the media practices of these groups are contributing towards the mainstreaming and social acceptability of a previously underground, deviant way of life:

> ... media-saturated societies have challenged the capacity of apparently secretive criminal and deviant subcultures to maintain these conditions. By embedding media in their then underground practices, skaters and graffiti writers have come to the surface of society and mainstream culture ... deviant subcultures were handed a tool for legitimating their activities and influencing the general public's view of the subcultures as not just rebellious and resistant by instead emphasizing their artistic and performative skills. (2013,.p 21)

These examples, alongside the studies of violent crime discussed earlier, demonstrate that the question of crime and media is far from a simple one of cause and effect and very much one of mirrors, reflections, loops and spirals (Hayward and Young, 2004; Ferrell et al, 2008, 2015).

Despite this, the conceptual frameworks that typify such studies are still the exception rather than the rule in criminology. Cultural criminologists share the author's concern with the superficial nature of wider criminological sense making around media, arguing that criminologists have not dug deep enough into networked media and its implications for social life (Hayward, 2012; Ferrell et al, 2015). It is worth briefly exploring some of the problems with orthodox criminological theorising around crime and networked media, most notably in relation to violent crime. Despite a plethora of output around 'cybercrime' in recent years (see, for example, Wall, 2007; Jewkes and Yar, 2010; Yar, 2013), criminologists continue to dichotomise, separating the online from the offline, the virtual from the real, and assuming that crime associated with networked technology occupies a conceptual category of its own, distinct from the 'terrestrial' crimes with which criminologists are more familiar. As such, criminologists have difficulty in making sense of violent crime in relation to networked media. An example of such a study is one in which the researcher searched for reports of homicides involving the internet and found 'Very few killings were identifiable that had any cyber element described' (Wykes, 2010, p 378). In positioning the internet as an independent variable, the context in which it had meaning for those involved was not considered and the question of what victims and perpetrators were *doing* with media more broadly was not posed. Such approaches have not escaped scrutiny from within the discipline. Most notable among the critical voices is Brown (2006, 2011), who argues that the cybercrime literature has tended to select from – rather than build on – existing theory, stating: 'There is simply no such thing as a "technological" crime ... as distinct from an "embodied" crime' (2006, p 236). In terms of violent crime in general and homicide in particular, the cybercrime literature has considerable difficulty in reconciling a body-to-body crime with the disembodied and virtual characteristics that criminologists have attributed to media like the internet. These critical observations are echoed by the cultural criminologists:

> Conceptually, ongoing criminological and legal work on cybercrime is primarily concerned with *diffusion,* whether in terms of the increased criminal opportunities afforded by decentralized networks or the potential diffusion of victimhood associated with digital crimes such as phishing scams or identity theft.... As cultural criminologists, we're not interested in setting up rigid and ultimately false distinctions between virtual and real-world experience ...

our line of analysis attempts to move beyond old formulae and established dualisms ... rather than focusing solely upon models of diffusion or thinking about the Internet simply as a digital tool, we should instead focus upon the *experience of the Internet* – how it functions in particular ways for particular purposes. This in turns allows us to think about digital/online (criminal) activities as a *process*, that is, as a phenomena in constant dialogue and transformation with other phenomena/technologies. (Ferrell et al, 2015, pp 170-1, original emphasis)

Ferrell et al (2015) then go on to highlight a particular homicide case with reference to these concepts. They discuss the case of Elliot Rodger, who killed six people in Santa Barbara in 2014. They draw attention to Rodger's video blogging and widely circulated, lengthy manifesto, noting that his desire to be seen is clear, as is his 'knowing awareness of his non-degradable digital "presence", his *eternal mediated being* ... both before and after his own physical death' (Ferrell et al, 2015, p 175, original emphasis). Unlike the BASE jumpers, skateboarders and graffiti artists, for whom media practices are inherently subcultural, Ferrell et al (2015) discuss Rodger's use of media in terms of Majid Yar's 'will to representation' concept (2012), in which it is argued that Rodger is one of many criminals who play out their crimes for an intended audience. The affordances of social media facilitates 'performance crime', in which law breaking is enacted and performed for the camera in response to an increasing preoccupation with the idea that to be is to be seen, which necessitates the practice of sharing (Surette, 2015a). They are able to draw on advances in media and communication technologies to get their messages out to a wide audience. These technologies have altered their sense of being in the world (Miller, 2011) by providing a platform from which they are able to share their narratives within wound culture (Seltzer, 2007, 2008), whereby others are drawn to, seek out and share trauma and suffering.

Given the proliferation of homicide images posted by the perpetrators in the cases examined in this book, it is also important to note the increasing emphasis placed on the visual within cultural criminology. While visual criminologists appear not to have moved very far from questions of mass media representation discussed in the preceding chapter, their conceptual contributions are of potential value, particularly the idea of the spectacle, which resonates strongly with showing and being shown (Couldry, 2012).

> The photographic spectacle is part of that aspect of the mass media which is *practical* or *performative* rather than *communicative* … events might not have occurred without the presence of cameras…. In short, it matters less what the photographic spectacle 'means', what it 'represents', what it symbolizes, and more what it *does* in the real … the photograph was itself *part* of the event. (Carney, 2010, p 30, original emphasis)

Advances in computer hardware and software enable individuals to create their own photographic spectacles, a point that Carney touches on in a more recent piece, noting the considerable extent and intensity of photographic force in the 21st century (Carney, 2015). This is echoed by Ferrell and Van der Voorde in their consideration of amateur photographers, who 'post and share images in such numbers that collectively, they create a sweeping, polymorphous archive of everyday life' (2010, p 47). One particular type of photograph that has become ubiquitous amid widespread adoption of camera phones and smartphones is the 'selfie'. These self-portraits, which are both objects and practices, are infused with meanings about contemporary cultures, social divisions and values as to 'how people ought to represent, document and share their behaviours' (Senft and Baym, 2015, p 1589). The idea of the spectacle is a central one for life and crime in media and is especially relevant for homicide, particularly given the prominence of the visual in the homicide confessions explored in this book. The existence of such behaviour suggests that homicide perpetrators are now better able to produce and control spectacle around their crimes, as opposed to this power being concentrated in the hands of media organisations. Among society's amateur image makers will be those creating images around homicide. A greater number of hands control the images of crime and criminals that percolate through 21st-century society, and include those of media organisations as well as those of perpetrators, victims and other stakeholders in crime. Revisiting Carney's points on the spectacle further emphasises this:

> If we are spectators, we are active. We bring to the power of spectacle our own desires, our own social practices and our own practical spectatorship … the lines of force running in and through an image are unruly. They do not follow straight lines. (Carney, 2010, p 19)

As such, exploring images must be about much more than simply seeing them as objects awaiting our interpretation. Young (2014) proposes an approach she terms 'criminological aesthetics', in which criminologists analyse *both* the image *and* the relationship between the spectator and the image. A further important concept is that of the decisive moment – the idea that there is a particular window or point in time in which the significance of an event becomes such that it has to be captured by the image (Ferrell and Van de Voorde, 2010). While Ferrell and Van de Voorde apply this concept to the photographer, can it also be applied to the killer who produces media around the homicide they commit? Is their understanding of the context in which their crime is being committed so unique to them that the images they produce are windows into the 'dynamics of power and transgression in the immediacy of a situation or an event'? (Ferrell and Van de Voorde, 2010, p 46).

It can be argued that networked media has further facilitated the proliferation of the image, and the centrality of the visual, which is turn is changing the context of violent crimes like homicide. Cultural criminologists appear to be at the cutting edge of sense making around networked media and crime. For the past 20 years, they have embraced some of the key themes around mediatisation, even if they have not explicitly used this terminology. In departing from the work of orthodox criminology, they address 'media' as opposed to '*the* media', looking not just at unidirectional representations but at multidirectional consumption and production in a series of perpetuating loops and spirals. There are notable parallels between the cultural criminologists – researching crime in media - and the mediatisation scholars – conceptualising lives in media. Therein lies potential to bring these two strands of enquiry together to make better sense of media in homicide in the 21st century. It is argued that a cultural criminological approach to the study of media in homicide can be enriched by mediatisation and related concepts.

Media in homicide: from celebrity to school shootings

This section examines the few studies exploring homicide perpetrators' use of media. Some scholars have pointed to the killer's pursuit of celebrity status. Penfold-Mounce (2009) notes that several perpetrators have targeted high-profile victims in a bid to acquire fame for themselves, pointing to the killers of musician John Lennon, Swedish Foreign Minister Anna Lindh and actress Rebecca Shaeffer as illustrative in this regard: 'the aim of the men was to gain celebrity status, in what can be described as a parasitical way, by feeding off the celebrated status and glamour of their victims' (2009, p 25). In addition, Gekoski has noted the actions of serial killer Colin Ireland, who telephoned *The Sun* newspaper to boast that he had murdered five gay men in a 'desire for infamy and identity in an otherwise unremarkable life' (1998, p 247). Serial murderers the Zodiac Killer and Dennis Rader (often known by his self-assigned moniker BTK – Bind Torture Kill) are other examples of killers who courted mainstream media, writing letters to media organisations, taunting the police and boasting about their involvement in multiple killings. These perpetrators were using mainstream media in a particular way in relation to the homicides they committed. As consumers of media, it could be argued that their knowledge of media influenced their behaviour, enabling them to manipulate it to secure attention and fame for themselves. It is clear that these studies are important in breaking the homicide-in-media mould, beginning to examine what perpetrators are *doing* with media, as opposed to what media are doing with perpetrators.

The school shootings literature is pushing this theorising even further forwards. Scholars working in this field are carving out a promising approach encompassing key concepts around mediatisation and cultural criminology in their analysis. Use of media by perpetrators of school shootings has long been acknowledged as a worthy focus of scholarly attention following the 1999 shooting at Columbine High School in the US state of Colorado, during which Eric Harris and Dylan Klebold killed 13 people before taking their own lives (Cullen, 2009). Networked media was particularly important for Harris, who developed his own website, making threats and sharing violent fantasies (Larkin, 2007, 2013; Muschert, 2013). Columbine is believed to be a watershed moment in school shootings, not least because of the media left behind by Harris and Klebold. Notable were the so-called 'basement tapes', recordings in which they justified the shootings, bid farewell to their parents and shared their thoughts about a 'revolution of the dispossessed' (Larkin, 2009). In the years since Columbine, there have been numerous school shootings and the question around what the perpetrators were doing in relation to media has been a central one for a handful of scholars in this field.

These scholars have considered media from various angles in relation to school shootings. They have largely dismissed claims by other social scientists that there is a cause-and-effect relationship between consumption of violent media content and school shooting perpetration (Ferguson, 2008; Sitzer, 2013). Furthermore, they have also begun to move beyond the question of representation in terms of how school shootings are depicted in the news media. The concept of the school shooting as a cultural script is a central one for these scholars. Cultural scripts can be understood as strategic and behavioural options for young people in their attempts to resolve the social problems they experience (Newman et al, 2004). Newman and colleagues (2004), drawing on the cases of three school shooters – Michael Carneal, Mitchell Johnson and Andrew Golden – argue that the script in which mass homicide is an option emerges only after various other scripts have been explored by the perpetrators: 'They did not "snap" so much as build toward their crimes as the less violent options failed to produce the results they wanted' (2004, p 149). Newman et al describe that having tried and failed to resolve their problems of low social status, exclusion from peer groups, and weak masculine identities, 'the boys came up with a dramatic solution: the indiscriminate shooting of their classmates and teachers' (2004, p 151). In so doing, they drew on the scripts of masculinity and adolescence and applied them to their own situations in a dysfunctional and antisocial way to create a new script – the school shooting cultural script, which Newman et al argue is a 'powerful explanation for the recent spike in these highly publicized shootings' (2004, p 154).

The school shooting cultural script has come to represent not only a solution but also an organising schema around which later shooters went on to structure their massacres. Therefore cultural scripts are both textual and performative in nature. The perpetrators' use of media has become crucial in performing the cultural script – they will draw on a range of textual, audio and visual devices to demonstrate that their actions are part of a wider movement and are not simply the behaviours of a 'crazy young loner' (Paton and Figeac, 2015, p 235). For example, they refer to a range of cultural products in the media they produce, such as the music of specific bands, games, television shows and masculine discourses (Kiilakoski and Oksanen, 2011). They also use other specific reference points – for example, picturing themselves posing with guns and creating videos of them shooting these weapons. This also extends to attire – the black baseball cap worn backwards was a style adopted by Virginia Tech shooter Seung-Hui Cho and Jokela shooter Matti Saari (Paton and Figeac, 2015). Sandberg and colleagues (2014) argue that Anders Breivik's 2011 killings in Norway paralleled the school shooting cultural script in several respects, notably his YouTube video and manifesto, which echoed the behaviour of the Columbine, Virginia Tech, Jokela and Kauhajoki shooters – even though he tried to distance himself from this and frame his actions as those of a political terrorist.

As this field of study has progressed, the focus is now very firmly on the multidirectional processes at work in the media practices of the shooters around the cultural script:

> ... the shooters (as producers of new media content) often post text and / or videos prior to their attacks. However, shooters (as consumers of new media content) often view and / or participate in blog posts and web videos, often shrines or tribute sites erected to discuss the most infamous school shooters of the past ... (Muschert, 2013, p 270)

Of particular relevance is the work of Kellner (2008), who developed the term 'media spectacle' in relation to his analysis of school shootings. Media spectacle is defined as

> ... various forms of technologically constructed media events that are produced and disseminated through the so called mass media, ranging from radio and television to the Internet and the latest wireless gadgets. (Kellner, 2008, p 3)

Unlike Guy Debord's 'society of the spectacle' (1994), Kellner's media spectacle is not a unidirectional one, consumed by a passive, alienated spectators. Kellner presents the media spectacle as highly contested, with different forces using it to further their own agendas. Kellner's media spectacle therefore gives rise to the possibility of the school shooter as an active agent in the crafting of the spectacle. There is considerable overlap here with the notion of the prosumer (Ritzer and Jurgenson, 2010) and the practical, performative photographic spectacle identified by Carney (2010). Indeed, Kellner explores in some detail the actions of Virginia Tech shooter Seung-Hui Cho in shaping the media spectacle that emerged around the 2007 shootings, in which Cho killed 32 people and injured 19 before taking his own life. Kellner's analysis is particularly unique in his simultaneous consideration of the socio-cultural position in which Cho found himself and the media practices he developed around his shooting. Kellner describes Cho's narrative as one of violent masculinity, which had emerged in response to his struggle in reconciling Korean pressures to succeed with the hedonistic elements of hegemonic masculinity running through US culture. Kellner posits that what Cho was *doing* in relation to media were key indicators of this. For example, discussing the contents of Cho's multimedia package sent to NBC, Kellner notes:

The material made it clear that Cho was planning to carry out a plan that he himself had constructed as the massacre at Virginia Tech. One of the photos in which Cho posed with a hammer in his hand reprises the Korean 'Asian Extreme' film *Oldboy* (2004), which itself is a revenge fantasy ... much of the iconography in the photo gallery quotes poses in films by Hong Kong action director John Woo, as in the images where Cho holds two guns in his hands or points a gun at a camera.... The shy nerdy student was suddenly aggressively staring into the camera with cold and calculating eyes, tightly holding guns, wearing a black baseball cap backward, fingerless black gloves, and a black t-shirt under a khaki photographer style vest. Cho's construction of a violent masculinity is apparent.... Since Cho was apparently not able to construct a normal student and male identity, he obviously resorted to extremity and exaggeration. (Kellner, 2008, pp 39-40)

School shooting scholars have also explored the more recent case of Elliot Rodger, noted earlier in relation to cultural criminological analysis. It is argued that there are clear continuities between Rodger's behaviour in relation to media and that of previous school shooters at Columbine, Virginia Tech and Jokela in terms of the communication of a self-narrative through video and text, in which the themes of entitlement, superiority and injustice are clear (Schildkraut and Elass, 2016).

Exploring this has led school shootings scholars to identify several themes that are consistent with Couldry's media practices. For example, in terms of searching, Larkin (2009) notes that as internet access has grown, it has become easier for school shooters to access information about previous school shootings during the planning phases of their own attacks. In relation to showing, they produce their own media packages or 'audiovisual montages', which they use to 'sign their crime and flaunt its premeditated nature' (Paton and Figeac, 2015, p 236). Paton and Figeac (2015) provide a useful overview of the nature of some school shooters' media packages and methods used to show them (see Table 3.1).

From the table, we can see that school shooters are increasingly bypassing the traditional gatekeepers in their showing practices and going straight to their intended audiences. Kiilakoski and Oksanen describe this in relation to Pekka-Eric Auvinen, who killed eight people at a school shooting in Jokela, Finland in 2008: 'Auvinen connected

Table 3.1: Overview of school shooters' media packages

School shooters	Multimedia package contents			Means used to distribute multimedia packages
	Videos	Photos	Written texts	
Eric Harris and Dylan Klebold, 1999 – USA	2	12	Yes	Blogs created. 'Basement tapes': videos left in Harris' home.
Bastian Bosse, 2006 – Germany	2	15	Yes	Videos broadcast via Bosse's blog. Emails sent the night before to friends.
Alvaro Castillo, 2006 – USA	4	0	Yes	Multimedia package sent by postal package to a local newspaper.
Seung-Hui Cho, 2007 – USA	1	43	Yes	Multimedia package sent by postal package to NBC.
Pekka-Eric Auvinen, 2007 – Finland	60	12	Yes	Videos broadcast via YouTube and Rapidshare.
Matti Saari, 2008 – Finland	5	11	No	Videos broadcast via YouTube, IRC-Galleria and Rapidshare.
Wellington Oliviera, 2011 – Brazil	4	8	Yes	Multimedia packages found in Oliviera's backpack. Videos broadcast by O Globo TN channel.
Total	78	101		

Source: Adapted from Paton and Figeac (2015).

directly with his audience by using social media. His connection with the public *thus involved no mediators*' (2011, p 256, emphasis added). Therefore school shooters are taking control in terms of what they include in their message and when these messages are released. They post this material to social media platforms on which users are able to recycle and recirculate the original posts – for example, through the sharing function on Facebook and the retweet option on Twitter (Schildkraut and Elass, 2016). However, Kiilakoski and Oksanen do not discount a role for media organisations in the showing process, arguing that it was not Auvinen alone who created a spectacle but a news media that celebrates the 'lone anti-hero' (2011, p 256) and places less of an emphasis on the victims. This is the embodiment of remediation, in which older media and newer media coexist, reshaping and refashioning each other (Bolter and Grusin, 1999). In addition, Sitzer argues that school shooters are acutely aware of the newsworthiness of their actions and are always able to count on news desks disseminating the material they provide to them (Sitzer, 2013). Kellner also drew similar conclusions about Virginia Tech shooter Seung-Hui Cho, who was 'media savvy enough to know that NBC (or any other television network) would broadcast his material' (2008, p 42).

Presencing practices are also clear among school shooters in terms of their active profiles on social networking sites. They use the same platforms and applications as their peers. Not only do they use the same tools, but they also adopt similar presencing styles. In his analysis of Seung-Hui Cho, Kellner notes that symbols of everyday presencing were evident in the multimedia package Cho sent to NBC:

> ... Cho's videography and picture posing replicated the form of young people's postings on sites like MySpace or Facebook, while his video is similar to the kinds of postings young people put out on YouTube. (2008, p 43)

In addition to presencing, the school shootings literature has also noted a media practice that might be described as 'absencing', in which the perpetrators immerse themselves in 'phantasy' worlds of extreme violent media prior to an attack (Robertz, 2004). In so doing, they visualise themselves as vengeful aggressors and identify with violent role models from previous massacres. Therefore it could be argued that when considering homicide perpetrators' use of media, both presencing and absencing practices are worthy of attention.

Lastly, in relation to 'archiving', all the school shooters discussed have created a dark repository of video, image and text, through which they believe they will attain immortality and become inscribed within the collective memory (Newman et al, 2004). The fan following of school shooters plays an important role in maintaining this archive and passing on elements of their legacy. An example are 'the Columbiners', a diverse group of individuals, some of whom advocate violence and aim to emulate the shooters while others treat them as teenage poster boys, expressing a desire to date them (Schildkraut and Elass, 2016). The affordances of networked media have given the killers' archive a new significance. This point is well illustrated by O'Hagan, who states that while there have always been killers who have left writings behind – notably Jack the Ripper and the Manson 'family' – today's killers 'carry the wherewithal in the pocket of their jeans. All they needed was a smartphone and a set of grievances, and the world was theirs' (2015, p 6).

Couldry's point that media practices are inherently complex is also evident when further exploring school shooters. A key example in this regard is provided by Sumiala and Tikka (2011), who identify three features of communication in the media practices of school shooters: 'circulation' of violent texts, 'remediation' of these texts across different types of media and 'sharing' through the exchange of materials, which in turn leads to the establishment and maintenance of online relationships with like-minded others. In addition, the literature exploring the fan communities that develop around school shootings (Böckler and Seeger, 2013; Oksanen et al, 2014) draws attention to the continuities between the archiving practices of past school shooters and the searching practices of their followers, a minority of whom go on to play out the same cultural script in their massacres. Pekka-Eric Auvinen had searched the archives created around Columbine and showed this in the media he produced around his killings – using the same music by industrial rock bands as the Columbine killers had admired and drawing on similar themes in the cultural script as Eric Harris did in his diaries – for example, violent misogynistic pornography (Kiilakoski and Oksanen, 2011). Archiving practices are therefore not an end point; rather, they are very much the school shooting subculture's embodiment of the loops described by the cultural criminologists (Ferrell et al, 2008, 2015), which in turn become part of wider spirals of social phenomena that provide the structural framework in which the cultural script of the school shooting develops – hegemonic masculinity, for example (Connell and Messerschmidt, 2005; Muschert, 2013). Adherence to the cultural script is very much about belonging – belonging to a subculture – which is demonstrated throughout all four media practices.

It is clear that the school shooting literature is an incredibly rich repository of cases and examples of the media practices of homicide perpetrators. There are clear parallels between the behaviours of the perpetrators, Couldry's conceptual framework of media practices and cultural criminology's loops and spirals. Couldry's framework therefore may be usefully applied to homicide perpetrators beyond school shooters.

Broadening the landscape

Criminology is far from ignorant of newer media and the ideas underpinning mediatisation, as evidenced in the work of the cultural criminologists. Despite this, criminological insights into what those involved in homicide are doing in relation to media are significantly underdeveloped – the only promising ideas emerging from the empirical work of the school shooting scholars and the conceptual and theoretical contributions of the cultural criminologists. This is not particularly surprising, given the conceptual difficulties of reconciling a face-to-face and embodied crime with networked media that continue to be conceived as virtual and disembodied by many criminologists. However, it is time to push the boundaries and engage with questions of media as *practice*. In the second decade of the 21st century, it is increasingly apparent that people's lives are lived in and through media (Deuze, 2012). These people will inevitably include the perpetrators of homicide. What is needed is a coherent and systematic approach to investigating what those involved in homicide are doing with media. This needs to go beyond the relatively rare event of the school shooting to encompass other homicides that fall outside of this limited schema. Bridging the gap between mediatisation and cultural criminology may enable criminologists to mark out a more distinct territory in which to consider media in homicide. Not only that, it would allow for the development of innovative methods and tools to investigate these phenomena. In the next chapter, the author outlines the approach taken to studying media in homicide in this book, which attempts to do this very thing.

FOUR

Approach to the study

Introduction

Thus far, the author has explored a range of concepts, theories and ideas that exist around the intersection of media and homicide. They hold significant potential for generating insights into the phenomenon of social media homicide confessions. However, the bodies of literature from which these concepts have emerged remain relatively separate, occupying different spheres and sub-disciplines of the social sciences. There is clearly much to be gained from bringing concepts together and this chapter describes the way in which they have been amalgamated into a guide developed by the author to assist in the analysis of the cases in this book. This guide, called Ethnographic Media Practice Analysis for Criminology (or EMPAC), enables both an analysis of individual experiences and the broader contexts within which these lived realities exist. Within this chapter, the author outlines the ontological, epistemological and methodological underpinnings of this guide and describes the rationale for the selection of the three cases to which EMPAC has been applied.

The cases

The cases examined within this book are the murder of Jennifer Alfonso, the Janzen familicide, which claimed the lives of Shelly, Emily, Laurel and Randy Janzen, and the murder of Charles Taylor. Approaching social media homicide confessions at the case level is appropriate given the usefulness of case studies to explore the 'How?' and 'Why?' questions, particularly when the topic of focus is a pressing issue within contemporary social life (Yin, 1994). A case focus enables the researcher to explore deeper meanings and experiences within cases as well as the broader context within which these cases are located (Simons, 2009). As the aim of this study was to develop further insights into social media homicide confessions and build better frameworks within which to situate future research, an information-oriented approach to the selection of cases was required (Flyvbjerg, 2006). This approach intends to maximise the usefulness of the knowledge that can be gleaned, and, as such, cases are selected on the basis of researcher expectations about the nature and extent of information they contain. Given the need to broaden insights into media in homicide beyond school shootings, Flyvbjerg's maximum variation technique was deployed in choosing cases for analysis. The aim of this technique is 'to obtain information about the significance of various circumstances for case process and outcome' (Flyvbjerg, 2006, p 230). Therefore while all the cases needed to involve a homicide, the author opted to include cases that featured different *types* of homicide involving different socio-demographics, victim–offender relationships and circumstances. The murder of Jennifer Alfonso was a 'domestic' or 'intimate partner' homicide. The Janzen case was a 'familicide'. Categorising the murder of Charles Taylor is challenging – as will be explored in Chapter Seven. However, whether Charles Taylor's death is termed a 'revenge homicide' or the first murder in a 'spree killing' that thankfully did not materialise, it is distinct from the other two cases. An additional criteria for case selection was that the perpetrator had confessed to the killing on social media, and, in so doing, had created and shared content in relation to the homicide. Selecting cases that met this criteria involved drawing on the author's personal knowledge of cases from her previous research and setting up content alerts on internet search engines to identify relevant cases as details about them emerged. All three cases prompted considerable comment in relation to the perpetrators' use of media, spawning column inches in newspapers and debate within networked spaces like Reddit, Twitter and Facebook. Debate often focused more on the fact that the perpetrator had confessed on social media than on the killings themselves. Social media was commonly problematised as having contributed to the fatal outcome. The spirit of Wall's 'transformation test' (2007) was clear as people considered whether these killings would have happened if social media was taken out of the equation and adopted positions on this topic around 'cause and effect'. As such, the Alfonso, Janzen and Taylor killings can be described as critical cases – cases of strategic importance in terms of media in homicide and homicide in media (Flyvbjerg, 2006). Popular understanding of these cases was characterised by technological determinism, the idea that technology essentially changes us and compels us to behave in particular ways. Making these particular cases the focus of an academic study was therefore important as it opened up the possibility of a more holistic understanding of them – moving the debate on from cause and effect towards experience and meaning.

Ontology: understanding media in homicide

It is necessary to explain the ontology – or view of the social world – that was adopted in this study as this provides the basic foundation for the research. The author approached the subject matter from the view that there is not an external social world 'out there' that exists independently of us and can be subjected to objective, detached enquiry. Rather, the social world is a construction (Berger and Luckmann, 1966; Couldry and Hepp, 2017) in which individuals are active in creating names, concepts and labels used to make sense of the social world and their experiences of it. As such, this study proceeds from a nominalist as opposed to a realist ontology (Burrell and Morgan, 1979) and echoes the outlook of cultural criminologists in emphasising the continuous generation of meaning in which the screen scripts the street and the street scripts the screen in a series of loops and spirals (Hayward and Young, 2004).

To put ontology in the context of this study, those involved in homicide have adopted, adapted and tailored the media they use, resulting in a unique personalised polymedia (Madianou and Miller, 2013). They have made a series of choices around which media to utilise in their confessions and which to discard, based on a range of reasons and justifications, such as practices among their peer group and the affordances of the different technologies in meeting their communicative and performative needs (Baym, 2010). Derek Medina and Randy Janzen confessed on Facebook. So too did Amanda Taylor, who also confessed on Tumblr and Instagram. What these individuals were *doing* in relation to media – or their media practices (Couldry, 2012) – was diverse and varied. The media lives (Deuze, 2012) in which media are invisible and taken for granted (Baym 2010; Chambers 2013) originate in the thoughts and actions of individuals, who make choices in relation to the media they draw on. Realists might argue that choices are proscribed as the individuals have a limited choice of apps and media from which to craft their mediascape, which can only be used in the ways envisaged by their designers. While this may indeed be true to a degree, the author was of the view that it was not so much the media itself that was the focal point of this study. While the media was clearly important, this study was more focused on how individuals were using and *experiencing* media in relation to the homicides they were involved in. What did it mean to them? What did it represent in terms of their social relationships and identities? How were they using it in relation to meaning making? How was it used to construct and make sense of their own social realities?

Epistemology: approaching media in homicide

Having established the view of the social world that this study proceeds from, it is now necessary to outline the approach to understanding that social world – or epistemology – adopted in the study. How could the author begin to understand the social media confessions and communicate this knowledge to others? What forms of knowledge could be obtained? For example, was there a search for what was true and what was false? The author's response to this question is 'No'. This study was not about establishing truth or falsehood in the same way that it does not subscribe to criminological theorising that separates the online and the offline. Such dichotomies are a key bugbear for cultural criminologists who challenge positivism and argue for creative and novel approaches to understanding a world that is increasingly difficult to categorise. As Ferrell and colleagues explain, 'Understanding this world requires researching it on its own terms, on the terms of representational dynamics, symbolic discourse and stylistic ambiguity' (2015, p 210).

The author did not intend the study to be replicable to such an extent that other scholars could redo it and test the 'reliability' of the findings. Rather, it could be described as 'anti-positivist' in its aims to explore the subjectivities of social media confessions and generate insights into the experiences of the individuals involved (Burrell and Morgan, 1979). This involved attempting to explore the realities of these individuals. Mediatisation scholars have emphasised the strengths of such approaches, arguing that we should seek to understand from the *inside*:

> Mediatized worlds ... are the level where mediatization becomes concrete, where people use media in specific contexts and with specific interests and intentions and by virtue of this can be analyzed empirically. To give some examples: while it is impossible to research the mediatization of a culture or society as a whole, we can investigate the mediatized world of stock exchange dealing, of schooling, of the private home and so on. Analyzing these 'socially constructed part-time realities' as mediatized worlds means researching empirically in what way their communicative construction is shaped by various media, as well as how this communicative construction changes. (Hepp and Krotz, 2014, p 8)

As such, the study engaged with the question of 'narrative' by exploring the stories told by the individuals involved within these realities. Individuals tell stories about their lives through oral, written and/or visual means (Atkinson, 1997; Atkinson and Delamont, 2006; Riessman, 2008) and media practices are an important mechanism for storytelling in the contemporary social world. Through the confessions, homicide perpetrators were telling others about their lives. They represented, in the words of cultural criminologists Aspden and Hayward, 'the cultural trail that individuals leave behind, the transgression, the flawed decisions, the cultural and personal artifacts of a life lived' (2015, p 237). Their stories were revealing in terms of what they conveyed not just about perspectives but also about identities. As Bruner states, 'In the end, we *become* the autobiographical narratives by which we "tell about" our lives' (2004, p 694, original emphasis). This gave rise to several questions. What narrative identities were evident in the confessions? What cultural, subcultural or counter-cultural narratives underpinned these stories (Atkinson and Coffey, 2003; Bamberg and Andrews, 2004)? What social roles were evident in their presentations of themselves? The author drew on the dialogic/performance technique to inform the approach to these personal stories, described as follows:

> Attention expands from detailed attention to a narrator's speech—what is said and/or how it is said—to the dialogic environment in all its complexity. Historical and cultural context, audiences for the narrative, and shifts in the interpreters' positioning over time are brought into the interpretation. Language—the particular words and styles that narrators select to recount experiences—is interrogated, not taken at face value. (Riessman, 2008, p 137)

The homicide confessions explored within this research did not reveal an *essential self* but enabled insights into the performance of a *preferred self* – how they *wanted* to be known by the stories they told (Goffman, 1959; Riessman, 2001). As such, they are also revealing in terms of what they tell us about the culture in which the perpetrators created and told them (McAdams, 2006). Research into the narratives of violent offenders provided additional points for consideration. Of particular note was the work of Brookman (2015), who identified complex, shifting and conflicting narratives in her study with violent offenders. Brookman identified 'action narratives', in which offenders concentrated on the crime they had committed, and 'reflection narratives', in which they focused on themselves, their lives and identities. However, she argues that researchers should acknowledge and embrace this complexity in and around these narratives and warned against trying smooth over the 'bumpy contours' and being careful to pay particular attention to the 'narrative flotsam and jetsam' (2015, p 225).

Methodology: investigating media in homicide

The ontological and epistemological positioning of this study had clear implications for the methodology. What tools and techniques would be most appropriate for making sense of the social media confessions of homicide perpetrators? How could such a study generate insights into what was unique to individuals while at the same time considering the broader social and cultural context of their lives *in* media (Deuze, 2012)? How could the study deal with the rich narrative 'flotsam and jetsam' (Brookman, 2015, p 225) running through Facebook status updates, Twitter feeds, videos and photographs alongside the content embodied in more traditional, orthodox sources? Reassurances and practical pointers emerged from the work of cultural criminologists who have faced similar challenges. In relation to the type of methods required, they argue,

> A criminology of the contemporary world requires methods wired for image production and for producing styles of communication more literary or artistic than 'scientific'. Today, criminals, law makers and law enforcement agencies all make their own media, creating websites, circulating images and otherwise paying attention to the politics of communication. In studying them, we must do the same. (Ferrell et al, 2015, p 210)

As such, cultural criminologists call for 'trashy methods, methods ragged around the edges, methods not fully conceptualized or completed' that suggest 'intellectual life and disciplinary vitality' (Ferrell et al, 2008, p 161). They argue that sources such as those noted previously are often considered 'unworthy of serious scholarly analysis' and consigned to the 'intellectual dustbin' by orthodox criminologists (Ferrell et al, 2008, p 158) but are vital in accessing sites of transgression, ambiguity and victimisation in the 21st century. A cultural criminological approach to this study therefore allowed the author to embrace newer, fluid and flexible forms of content – for instance, social media postings – as well as the more traditional sources such as media reports and court transcripts.

While cultural criminology has often been associated with long-term ethnography, in which researchers immerse themselves within the community they are studying, cultural criminologists acknowledge the practical challenges of academia that make this approach a difficult one to sustain and the characteristics of everyday lives that have altered and shifted amid newer media, and hence require a different and more flexible account. They propose a broader repertoire of investigative techniques, such as instant ethnography, to capture shifts in speed and tempo where crime can come and go in an instant, and where 'a single "decisive moment" can mean everything – and can change everything' (Ferrell et al, 2008, p 182). Instant ethnography is described as 'the ethnography of performance' (Ferrell et al, 2008, p 180) and has clear implications for generating insights into 'performance crime' (Surette, 2015a). The decisive moments where perpetrators captured an image that related to the homicide or uploaded text or a comment to accompany it were important to understand. What narratives were evident in this content? To what extent was it consistent with their wider media practices and archive? There are significant parallels between these thoughts and questions and virtual ethnography, which emphasises continuity between online and offline and the subsequent need to engage in a more flexible manner with the networked nature of social life (Hine, 2015; Kozinets, 2015). Virtual ethnography acknowledges the internet's enmeshment in the rhythms of daily life; it is embedded, embodied and everyday (Hine, 2015). This is as true for homicide perpetrators as it is for everyone else. Criminologists are beginning to adopt virtual ethnographies, in which they explore the content that emerges around crime in newer media and locate this within broader social contexts and communities. Indeed, the school shootings scholars noted in the previous chapter have analysed school shooter content disseminated via networked media and hard copy as well as the reports of official inquiries into the events. Further examples outside of the school shootings literature includes Lane's study of Harlem (2016) and Milivojevic and McGovern's (2014) exploration of social media activity around the rape and murder of Melbourne woman Jill Meagher.

As such, an analysis of the confessions was important but it was also necessary to explore their broader setting. This extended to the social media archives of which they were part and other, wide-ranging, sources that would enable a rich, 'thick description' (Geertz, 1973) of each case. Therefore both content and context were key to developing a methodological approach towards the media practices of individuals involved in homicide. Cultural criminologists draw attention to the potential of ethnographic content analysis (ECA), which facilitates an analysis of both. ECA is not a rigid method as such but a 'methodological sensibility' (Ferrell et al, 2008, 2015). It is a reflexive approach 'used to document and understand the communication of meaning' (Altheide, 1987, p 68) and approaches texts as changeable, connected and multifaceted rather than static, isolated and unitary. The text and its meanings are considered to be an inherently cultural and ongoing process, and, as such, this approach allows for unique sets of data to unfold around each case, rather than attempting to source particular 'types' of data. Different tools and techniques can be applied to different cases according to need. As such, ECA studies unfold in a reflexive rather than a linear manner, engaging with the possibility of some pre-structured categories but not being dogmatic in their application. ECA also stresses the importance of context, emphasising questions around the broader cultural and social structures that form the backdrop to the individual, complex and unique cases. Individuals and events are positioned within their wider landscape, locating the nuances and subtleties of transgressive situations within larger flows of meaning (Ferrell et al, 2015).

This approach appeared well suited to research within a context characterised by convergence, remediation and prosumers, where the lines between readers and writers, actors and audiences, producers and consumers have become considerably blurred. It's fluid and malleable nature made it particularly appealing to explore not just what social media homicide confessions looked like but also how meaningful and significant they were, appreciative of both scale and nature.

Drawing on the principles and values of ECA, the author devised a framework to guide the analysis of each case – termed Ethnographic Media Practice Analysis for Criminology (EMPAC). The framework is a series of themes, terms, words, questions and ideas that were considered when exploring the confessions in their wider context (see Figure 4.1).

EMPAC brought together the relevant concepts from media and communications studies, cultural criminology and narrative criminology that had been central in mapping out the conceptual landscape of this study. It was intended to be a flexible tool and there was no proscribed process in terms of how it was used in relation to each case, nor any set order in which to apply concepts. EMPAC was applied, reapplied and revisited as new sources and materials came to light and fresh insights emerged within each case.

Figure 4.1: EMPAC

PRESENCING

Presence to others – Spaces – Places – Institutions – Organisations – Subcultures – Groups – Cultural scripts – Absences – Belonging – Membership – Access – Acceptance – Exclusion ...

SHOWING

Showing oneself – Showing others – Being shown by others – Roles – Characters – Narrative – Identities – Performances – Statuses – Audiences – Consistencies – Inconsistencies – Control – Gatekeepers – Aims – Outcomes – Representation – Misrepresentation ...

CASE DETAILS

Rich description – Detail –Sequence – Timeline – Victim – Perpetrator – Context – Sense-making – Prominence – Significance – Explanations ...

ETHNOGRAPHIC MEDIA PRACTICE ANALYSIS FOR CRIMINOLOGY (EMPAC)

SOURCES

Social media – Extracts – Sections – Complete – Partial –Screenshots – Mainstream media – Criminal justice – Popular debate – Public – Restricted ...

ARCHIVING

History – Repository – Linkages – Fractures – Absences – Voids – Public – Private ...

NATURE AND SCALE

Text – Image –Video – Where? – Length – Original – Copy – Created – Shared – Who? – Object/subject – How many? – Proportions – When? – Prominence – Significance – Central – Marginal ...

SEARCHING

Search enabling – Tagging – Identifying – Following – Followers ...

FIVE

The murder of Jennifer Alfonso

The murder

On 8 August 2013, 26-year-old Jennifer Alfonso was killed by her husband, 31-year-old Derek Medina, in the kitchen of their Miami townhouse. The couple had argued upstairs and Jennifer had thrown small items at him, including a towel and a tube of mascara. Derek claimed that Jennifer told him she was going to pack her things and leave that evening. He went to the closet and took out his gun. He removed it from its holster and threatened to shoot her if she did not stop throwing things at him. She stopped and went downstairs to the kitchen to make breakfast for her daughter, who was staying with the couple at the time. Derek returned the gun to the closet, followed Jennifer downstairs and continued the argument, later claiming that she was punching him during this altercation. Derek then left the kitchen and went back upstairs, retrieving his gun from the closet before returning downstairs to the kitchen. Seeing Derek with the gun, Jennifer picked up a knife. Derek alleges that Jennifer said, 'Yeah, you're not going to kill me, blah, blah, blah, you're a pussy' (Miami Dade Police Department, 2013, p 10). He took the knife from Jennifer and put it in a kitchen drawer. He claimed that Jennifer punched him several times. Derek then turned the gun on Jennifer and shot her eight times, emptying the clip of his firearm, causing 21 entry and exit wounds.

Movements around the murder were captured on home security video, which was shown to the court during Derek's trial (CCV, 2015a). The camera is positioned overhead, facing into the entrance to the kitchen, where the sink can be seen on the right and the dining area and hallway to the left. Jennifer is standing at the sink, washing dishes. Derek walked down the hallway and into the kitchen. There were a few movements after this; shadows could be seen on the kitchen counter top. Derek then walked out of the kitchen and into the hallway. It appears as though he was struck by Jennifer's arm as he did so. He turned around and went back into the kitchen. He is then seen from behind, backing up into the hallway. He appeared to flip his middle finger at his wife as he walked further into the hallway and out of shot. He returned and re-entered the kitchen area, disappearing out of sight of the camera again. He is then seen to step backwards. A plume of dust particles appeared in front of the camera – the result of changed air pressure following the discharge of the firearm. There were several further plumes of dust following this. He then walked out of the kitchen and retrieved his phone from the hallway. He walked back towards the kitchen again and looked towards the floor at Jennifer – who at this point was either dead or dying. He took a picture on his phone and placed the phone in his pocket. He then picked up his hooded sweatshirt from the dining area, put it on and walked towards the front door. He hesitated, picked up his baseball cap and zipped up his hooded sweatshirt. He exited the house, locking the door after him, leaving Jennifer's daughter in the property with her dead mother.

Derek posted the picture he had taken of Jennifer on both his and her Facebook profiles. The post remained on Facebook for at least five hours until site administrators took it down, at which point it had been viewed and shared thousands of times (Benn, 2013; Sutfin, 2015). In the photograph, Jennifer is on the floor in the corner of the kitchen. She is lying face up, her legs bent underneath her as if she had fallen backwards while on her knees, her head resting against the bottom kitchen cupboards. On his own Facebook page, Derek posted the photograph with the caption 'Rip[1] Jennifer Alfonso' (Medina, 2013a). This was followed by another post:

> Im going to prison or death sentence for killing my wife love you guys miss you guys takecare Facebook people you will see me in the news my wife was punching me and I am not going to stand anymore with the abuse so I did what I did I hope u understand me. (Medina, 2013b)

Following the murder, Derek drove to his aunt and uncle's house. He then went to South Miami Police Department accompanied by his father, telling the officer at the desk, 'I have to turn myself in' and 'I just shot and killed my wife' (CCV, 2015b). On 25 November 2015, Derek was convicted of second-degree murder and child neglect and sentenced to life in prison.

Jennifer's murder was an intimate partner homicide, or IPH as it is commonly referred to by criminologists (Hough and McCorkle, 2017). When men kill women, the suspect and victim are often in – or have been in – an intimate relationship with one another (Brookman, 2005). A common precipitating factor in cases of IPH is often the separation or impending separation of the couple following a relationship saturated with and shaped by the perpetrator's controlling and abusive behaviour (Polk, 1994; Campbell et al, 2007; Stark, 2007; Dobash and Dobash, 2015). However, these dynamics were largely absent from international media reports of Jennifer's murder. Coverage followed a well-established pattern that devalued IPH (Dowler et al, 2006), treating the homicide as a one-off event where an otherwise 'normal' perpetrator 'snaps' and loses control in a moment of madness (Adams, 2007; Dobash and Dobash, 2009; Monckton-Smith, 2012; Monckton-Smith et al, 2014). The fact that Derek had posted on Facebook was at the very the centre of the story, if not the story itself (see, for example, Anon, 2013; Elks, 2013; Williams, 2013). Without the social media element, it is unlikely that this killing would have made headlines outside of Miami. Local and international media branded Derek the 'Facebook Killer' (see, for example, Evans, 2013; Ortega et al, 2013). The visual spectacle (Jewkes, 2015) created by the image of Jennifer's body and the accompanying post ensured this murder reached a threshold that made it worthy of a place in the news in contemporary photographic culture (Carney, 2010). In addition, the newsworthiness of the story was elevated by the appeal to 'conservative ideology' (Jewkes, 2015) – the topic of Facebook providing fodder for those who problematise social media as detrimental to the moral fabric of society. Despite what media coverage suggested, neither the murder nor the Facebook post came 'out of the blue'. Within this chapter, the author examines Derek's Facebook homicide confession in context to shed further light on the case. This is important because while the literature around intimate partner abuse is well established and that around IPH continues to grow, little is known about the social media practices of those involved.

The sources on which this case study draws are wide ranging. They include the media that Derek produced himself, including a small section of his Facebook profile, his YouTube archive and his personal website. Derek's full Facebook profile is not included – the account was removed following Jennifer's murder. While several screenshots of the page on the day he killed Jennifer were available through general internet searches, the full Facebook account is not. It could be argued therefore that the data on which this case study draws is incomplete. However, the author would argue that having every relevant perpetrator-produced media item within the analysis – while desirable – is not necessary for the purposes of this study, which is to generate insights into Derek's media practices, identifying key themes and narratives, documenting and understanding the communication of meaning (Altheide, 1987). Also included in the analysis are the artefacts that Jennifer left behind, including extracts from her diary and an instant message exchange with a friend on the morning of her murder. In addition, it was important to explore online memorials created for Jennifer by her friends and family. Such content represents important counter-narratives when considered alongside the stories of murder told by perpetrators. In addition, a range of publicly available items relating to Derek's arrest and trial have been used to reconstruct the case and access the voices of a range of different people affected by the killing. Such items include Derek's sworn statement to police and video footage of the trial available on several YouTube channels. Articles from local newspapers were also accessed and analysed as many included interviews with individuals who knew Derek and Jennifer. The following section sets the scene in describing the background of Derek and Jennifer's relationship, contextualising the murder in relation to the relevant literature on intimate partner abuse and IPH.

Context

Jennifer Alfonso was born in December 1986, the daughter of Carolyn and Tony. She grew up in Miami. Jennifer gave birth to her daughter when she was 16 and left South Dade High to attend a school with day care facilities for young parents. Jennifer was in a relationship with her daughter's father and the family lived together for four years before they separated. Jennifer and her daughter's father agreed that her daughter would live with him and have visitation with Jennifer every other weekend (CCV, 2015c). Jennifer was described as a devoted mother. A co-worker recalled, 'Her daughter was her pride and joy' (Ovalle, 2013a). Her stepfather reported that 'she was always smiling, always laughing, making jokes … always playing with her daughter' (Ortega et al, 2013). Since the age of 16, Jennifer had not only been a mother but had been a working mother. She worked as a waitress and was described as a loyal and committed employee at branches of Denny's Restaurant in Miami. Louis Schwartz, a regular who ate at one of the restaurants two or three times a week with his wife and mother, said: 'We would say, "Let's go see Jennifer", not "Let's go to Denny's". She had a certain glow to her. A beautiful person. She really loved her daughter and always talked about her family' (Benn, 2013).

Derek was born in March 1982 and attended Coral Gables High School in Miami, graduating in 2001. He claimed to have a qualification in Business Administration from Florida National University (Miami Dade Police Department, 2013). It is claimed that Derek moved from job to job every few months (Ovalle, 2013a), but at the time of Jennifer's murder he was working as a front desk supervisor at The Gables Club, an exclusive residential apartment complex in Miami. While working there, Derek rubbed shoulders with wealthy and successful individuals, parking their expensive cars and answering queries (Ortega et al, 2013). A pastor at a church Derek attended as a child described him as a 'complex and multidimensional person', but tempered this statement by adding 'just like everyone else'. He noted that from age 12, Derek volunteered at the church with his grandfather: 'The stories talk about him as if he's an ogre. I don't know him that way' (Solis, 2013). Derek and Jennifer went to a service at the church in May 2013 for a Father's Day event, where they had coffee with the congregation afterwards (Solis, 2013). This depiction of Derek as 'just like everyone else' – a churchgoer, a husband and a grandson – creates a picture of him as an ordinary guy, an 'average Joe'. Research on homicide perpetrators comparing men who kill their female partners with men who kill other men suggests that the former do indeed blend in in this way (Dobash and Dobash, 2015). They are more likely to have a formal educational qualification, be married and employed (Thomas et al, 2011). Their backgrounds are less problematic, and as such, do not fit the stereotypical image of the abuser – an alcoholic, criminal and/or mentally ill individual (Adams, 2007). What Derek does share with other abusers, though, is his *performance* as an ordinary guy: 'they display to the outside world a different kind of behaviour to that at home and some people find it difficult to believe that someone they know in public can be a domestic violence abuser' (Richards et al, 2008, p 14).

Derek's family supported this depiction of him and claimed in newspaper interviews (although not at trial) that Jennifer was the aggressor. However, others would tell a different story, shattering this image in recalling alleged incidents of deviant, antisocial and criminal behaviour. One former friend claimed that Derek pulled his firearm on a woman who had accidentally spilled beer on Jennifer at the Mayhem Music Festival in 2011 (Ortega et al, 2013). The friend commented in another article: 'None of us knew he had a gun. I don't even think his wife knew. At that point I was like, "This is it. I'm not dealing with this guy anymore"' (Benn, 2013). Another former friend claimed that Derek had threatened to kill him and someone else via Facebook (Ovalle, 2013a). Stalking behaviour was also reported by a man who was on the same softball team as Derek in 2010 (Benn, 2013; Ortega et al, 2013). Derek allegedly made videos of the team playing softball on occasions when he was not included in the team: 'The next day or whatever, Derek posts a video on Facebook of people playing softball, and – guess what? It was us.... We didn't even know he was filming us. It was creepy' (Benn, 2013). A further incident is described in a newspaper interview with Marcos Avellan, a Miami gym owner (Benn, 2013). Derek went to a martial arts class at the West Miami Dade gym and became aggressive when an instructor tried to help him by correcting his stance. Avellan described Derek's disproportionate reaction, stating that he posted a series of videos on YouTube recreating a fight with the instructor. Furthermore,

> He then went as far as to buy a title belt and even engraved the name of the instructor on the belt, claiming he was awarded the belt for defeating the instructor.... It was because of these crazy videos that I remember him by name to this day. He was definitely off his rocker. (Benn, 2013)

These accounts suggest that Derek's behaviour was extremely narcissistic. Individuals with narcissistic personalities are characterised by a grandiose sense of their own self-importance, preoccupied with fantastical thoughts of considerable success, achievement, status and power (Raskin and Terry, 1988). They also lack empathy in their inability to see things from another person's perspective (Raskin and Terry, 1988). Their capacity to tolerate criticism or defeat is very limited and they expect others to treat them favourably, but are not willing to reciprocate this preferential treatment (Raskin and Terry, 1988). Narcissism would continue to characterise Derek's behaviour throughout his relationship with Jennifer and the events of 8 August 2013.

Jennifer and Derek met when Jennifer was working at Denny's. Jennifer's mother Carolyn recalled this as happening in 2010 (CCV, 2015c), but Derek claimed it was much earlier in September 2009 (Miami Dade Police Department, 2013). Derek claimed they were married on 25 January 2011 (Medina, 2011a). Carolyn stated that Jennifer married Derek on a holiday in Puerto Rico and she only discovered that the wedding had taken place on their return (CCV, 2015c). This secretiveness around the wedding provides evidence of Derek's early attempts to isolate Jennifer, a key indicator of coercive control in which abusers attempt to destroy their victim's relationships with their family (Stark, 2007).

After Jennifer moved in with Derek, Carolyn confirmed that there were several breaks in the relationship. Derek would throw Jennifer out of the house they shared and drive her to Carolyn's home with her belongings. Jennifer and Derek would reconcile after a few days and Jennifer would return to the home she shared with him (CCV, 2015c). Their first marriage ended in 2012 when Derek filed for divorce. Reports claim that the divorce cited irreconcilable differences, and Derek was awarded their major assets – a 2006 Hummer vehicle, a 1972 AMC Javelin car and property in Tampa (Benn, 2013). These episodes are clear examples of Derek exerting control, a central element of intimate partner abuse. However, current cultural understandings of abuse revolve around the 'violence model', which positions isolated violent incidents resulting in visible physical injury as 'real' abuse (Monckton-Smith et al, 2014). This is a small net to cast. It does not capture the coercive controlling behaviour, the 'everyday terrorism' (Pain, 2014) characterised by psychological and emotional abuse. Experts argue that coercive control is *the* most significant risk factor for IPH (Stark, 2007). Following their separation and divorce, Jennifer stayed with Carolyn and saved up enough money to live in a condo that belonged to Carolyn's husband. Throughout this period, Jennifer continued to work as a waitress.

Jennifer and Derek remarried in 2012. Carolyn had not known that they had been seeing each other again and did not know they were getting married (CCV, 2015c). Derek's aunt also testified at trial that neither she nor anyone else on Derek's side of the family were aware of their second wedding (CCV, 2015d). This is suggestive of further attempts by Derek to isolate Jennifer from her family. They moved to a townhouse at South West 67th Avenue in Miami. The townhouse is one of several on a small development in South Miami close to a busy intersection that has a 7-11 convenience store and a large Walgreens pharmacy. Jennifer's feelings at this period in her life were captured in a diary. The diary is entitled 'The mind of an insane woman' and extracts from it were released to the media at the time of the trial (Alfonso, 2012). The extracts began during the period following the move to the townhouse in May 2012 and Jennifer's words are revealing about the couple's relationship. Throughout the diary, Jennifer becomes increasingly questioning of her behaviour and appearance, suggesting that Derek's influence and control over her is the cause of considerable anxiety and unhappiness. Early sections of the diary retain traces of a strong, independent woman: 'Crap … I wish everyone could just be happy!! Fucking impossible. Derek told me that I'm never happy for him in anything and everything … coming from the man who married me twice … I think maybe he woke up in a crabby mood. Still, no excuse' (Alfonso, 2012, p 4). However, later sections are increasingly self-doubtful – Jennifer berates herself using negative labels and terms, such as insane, sourpuss, crazy bitch, my jealousy issues. These words and terms are labels applied exclusively to women's 'deviance' and form part of gendered discourses (Lees, 1997; Tanenbaum, 2000). Jennifer's use of these words to describe herself suggest that someone else has applied these labels first. Given the contextual details provided thus far regarding her relationship with her husband, it could be argued that Derek may well have been the origin of these put-downs. Jennifer also quoted lyrics from Bottom (Alfonso, 2012, p 7) – a song by the band Tool about reaching 'rock bottom', or one's lowest point. She tried to reassure herself that she was good enough for Derek, stating that 'he could have whoever he wants' (Alfonso, 2012, p 8). The final section of the diary is the most downbeat. Jennifer described her efforts to stay slim: 'I've been good at keeping the weight off since me and Derek got back together' (Alfonso, 2012, p 9) – suggesting she was doing this *for* Derek. She also described a constant state of fatigue: 'All I want to do is sleep. I wonder if I'm depressed or if I'm just lazy?' (Alfonso, 2012, p 10). She then went on to express her anxiety about not keeping the house clean enough. The diary extracts document the increasing state of chronic fear (Monckton et al, 2014) that Jennifer appeared to be experiencing at this point, adapting her behaviour, language and narratives to Derek's rules.

Throughout their relationship, others observed how Derek became increasingly controlling of and abusive towards Jennifer. Her job at Denny's was a particular point of contention. Her co-workers stated that Derek tried to get Jennifer to quit her job as he did not like her working nights and added that Jennifer would turn up to work with bruises (Ovalle, 2013a). Cathy LaBella, a former co-worker, tried to convince Jennifer to leave Derek during the breaks in their relationship, but 'He would always come back, begging her ... come back ... She would say that he was going to change. She was in love with him' (Ovalle, 2013a). Cathy's statements suggest that Derek was also engaging in stalking behaviour – not letting her speak on the phone and always waiting for her outside work: 'One time, he went storming in, looking for her, telling her to get outside' (Ovalle, 2013a). Trying to force Jennifer to lose or quit her job is evidence of Derek's further attempts to isolate her. Work was a safety zone (Stark, 2007) for Jennifer, one where she had support and recognition in her role as worker – an important part of her identity and personhood. Stark describes the aim of such isolation attempts: 'His hope is to make who and what she is who and what she is *for him*' (2007, p 262, original emphasis).

Jennifer's regular employment at Denny's can also be interpreted as another type of threat for Derek. Focusing on Latino couples, Klevens emphasises the importance of culture as a key determinant of how abuse is defined and responded to (Klevens, 2007; Klevens et al, 2007). The concept of machismo – depicting a traditional male role of a dominant, virile, head of household and sole breadwinner (Stevens, 1973) – is often evoked to explain abuse within Latino couples. Klevens (2007) argues that this is important but its relevance is more nuanced – and indeed, such explanatory models simply serve to lessen the abuser's culpability as they support deterministic models of abuse that the offender 'can't help it' and it is 'just the way men are'. Rather, Klevens (2007) claims *role strain* is a more accurate description of the factors that may be unique to abuse in Latino couples and cited various studies in support of this. These encompassed a study suggesting that Latino women who earned more than their male partners were at greater risk of abuse (Perilla et al, 1994) and another highlighting the importance of gender role changes and instability (Morash et al, 2000). Indeed, for a narcissist like Derek, Jennifer's employment compromised the degree to which he could present himself to others as the dominant head of the household – a role more consistent with the power and control he sought in his relationship with Jennifer.

As noted previously, separation or the threat of separation has been noted by several scholars as a key risk factor for IPH (Polk, 1994; Campbell et al, 2007; Stark, 2007; Dobash and Dobash, 2015). Jennifer's announcement that she was going to leave Derek on the evening of 8 August 2013 was something new. The previous separations were events that Derek had been in control of. He had initiated their divorce in 2012, he had thrown Jennifer out of the house on numerous occasions, he had decided when she would return. However, the tables had now been turned – in announcing her intention to leave him, Jennifer had taken control away from Derek. Dobash and Dobash (2015) describe how this type of separation is viewed differently by victim and abuser:

> Many of the women saw separation as the ending of an intimate relationship while men did not. Instead, these men viewed separation as inappropriate and unacceptable and as a challenge to their ongoing possession of, and authority over, their woman partner. (2015, p 63)

Derek's perceptions of Jennifer as subordinate to him and as someone he was in control of was evident in the language he used during his sworn statement to police following her murder (Miami Dade Police Department, 2013). When asked by the detective, 'Do you live with her [Jennifer] in the home?', Derek replied, 'Yeah, she lives with me. I'm the owner there' (Miami Dade Police Department, 2013, p 5). In addition, Jennifer's daughter is completely excluded from this dialogue.

When asked whether they have children together, Derek replies in the negative, not even mentioning her. In using this language, he is asserting his control, the house is *his*, not *theirs,* she lives *with* him, they do not live *together.* They are not equal, he is in charge and Jennifer is dependent on him; in asserting his ownership of the house and omitting his step-child from the narrative, he is tackling role strain, presenting himself as the dominant head of the household (Perilla et al, 1994; Morash et al, 2000; Klevens, 2007).

The home was an important locus of control for Derek. Neighbours claimed that the shutters were always closed on the windows to the house (Ortega et al, 2013). Derek also installed security cameras throughout the residence. His use of cameras in the house was a further manifestation of his control over Jennifer. The content he uploaded to Facebook after killing her was posted to both his and Jennifer's accounts. This suggests that Derek knew the login and password details for Jennifer's Facebook account and was likely monitoring her activity on this site too. On the day of the murder, he followed her from room to room. These behaviours are all examples of pre-homicide stalking behaviours *within* a relationship (Monckton-Smith et al, 2014).

Sadly, Jennifer's murder was not the first IPH to affect the Alfonso family. In 1986, Jennifer's grandmother, Mercedes Alvarez, was shot and killed by her husband Manuel Alvarez at a house less than two miles from the home Jennifer shared with Derek (Benn, 2013). After driving from Texas to Miami, Manuel shot Mercedes in the chest, killing her, before turning the gun on himself. Two generations on, Jennifer would also be killed by her partner, with one journalist reflecting: 'The shooting wasn't unusual by South Florida standards' (Rabin, 2014).

Life in media

Manuel Alvarez and Derek Medina were both abusers. However, Derek *lived* in media (Deuze, 2012) and as such, *abused* in media. He used 21st-century networked technology to show himself and others and create a sense of presence in social and cultural spaces. He told these stories drawing on a range of narrative identities and roles. These practices are revealing about the abuser he was. Within this section, the author draws on the Ethnographic Media Practice Analysis for Criminology approach described in Chapter Four to explore Derek's media practices and consider what they imply for our understanding of Jennifer's murder.

The archive

The media archive Derek left behind is a mixed repository, encompassing a range of different spaces (Couldry, 2012). It included a YouTube channel, a personal website entitled 'Emotional writer' and screenshots of his Facebook profile. The YouTube channel is the most extensive part of the archive and forms a significant proportion of the content analysed in relation to this study. At the time of writing, it contained 138 videos, uploaded between May 2011 and August 2013. The shortest is nine seconds, the longest is 13 minutes and 59 seconds. March of 2013 was the most prolific month in relation to Derek's uploads to YouTube – he posted 22 videos in this month. In relation to his activities on Facebook, Miami Herald journalist Evan Benn (2013) described Derek as a heavy Facebook poster, but one who had only 164 friends – stating that average number of friends per user is around 245. Benn also noted that Derek had more YouTube videos than he had numbers of views before Jennifer's death – there were fewer people looking at his videos than there were videos. In addition, Derek appears to have been the only individual commenting on these videos before Jennifer's murder.

The author arranged his videos into seven broad categories corresponding to their content: playing sports; watching sports; socialising; motors; family; books; and other. Derek's activity on YouTube could be described as erratic. In some months he posted nothing, in others he uploaded a small number of similar videos on a specified topic and in others he posted numerous videos on multiple topics. His interest in different pastimes also appears to vary dramatically. 'Motors' was a very prominent topic between October and December of 2011 when he uploaded several videos of a mini pocket bike and his 1972 AMC Javelin car. After this the topic never appeared again. Videos around the theme of 'socialising' appeared only in August 2011, where he uploaded footage of himself and Jennifer attending social events and going out with friends in a group. This included a video of the 10-year reunion of his high school graduating class (Medina, 2011a) and another of him jumping around in the mosh pit at the Mayhem Festival (Medina, 2011b, 2011c) – the same event where he allegedly pulled a gun on a fellow festival goer (Ortega et al, 2013). Six self-published books are the topic of several videos posted between February and August 2013. Watching sports features prominently in February, March and June of 2013. From September 2012 the content of the videos becomes more disparate as the 'other' category emerged in prominence.

Jennifer is heard or seen in around one fifth (n=31, 22%) of the videos. The proportion of videos she appeared in per year increased from 28.3% (n=17) in 2012 to 41.8% (n=23) in 2013. The topics of the videos she appears in also become more diverse with the passage of time. Derek appears to be showing Jennifer off to others in the earlier videos, drawing attention to the fact she is married to him – for example, the video of his high school 10-year reunion, on which he comments: 'Our ten year reunion woth my wife', 'Jan 25 2011 I got married' (Medina, 2011a). However, in later videos, she is either the one behind the camera – Derek issuing instructions to her as she films him practising sports – or is pictured sitting next to him in the crowd at sporting events. Derek's increasing surveillance and monitoring of Jennifer becomes clear throughout the media archive. The videos provide a window into his escalating control over her as the footage changes in nature and tone. The shrinking of Jennifer's physical personal space is stark when contrasting the 2011 'socialising' videos with later videos of the couple at sporting events. In the former, Derek's focus appears to be on communicating the fact that he and Jennifer are at the biggest and best parties and events in town; often the camera is on the crowd and he appears keen to emphasise his presence among the young, exciting groups of people out and about in Miami (see, for example, Medina, 2011d). However, in the latter, the focus had shifted very much towards Jennifer. They were always sat or stood next to one another and Derek regularly panned the camera around to focus on himself and Jennifer, 'showing' that they were together and that she was with *him*. Jennifer's smiles appeared to become more forced with each video he posts (see, for example, Medina, 2013c, 2013d).

The manner in which Derek labelled and presented his YouTube videos is indicative of the level of status he conferred upon himself. He often included his own name in the titles and used uppercase text. A video of him playing basketball is titled 'DEREK MEDINA 10/10 THAT'S 100 PERCENT SHOOTING FROM THE FIELD' (Medina, 2012a). Another is of him training in a boxing ring, and is labelled 'derek medina training with the temp boxing trainer BEFORE PRO EXHIBITION FIGHT' (Medina, 2012b). The use of the third person creates a sense of importance, almost as if someone else has made and posted the video *about* him. His videos are very rarely titled using the first person, as is the case for many personal home videos individuals put up on YouTube. As such, Derek separates his videos from those posted by others. The way he presents the videos appear to be an attempt to make them – and indeed *him* – more worthy of attention. As the subject of the video, he is someone we *should* look at.

It's not enough for him to present himself as he is – just a man casually shooting hoops on a basketball court and training in a boxing ring. His presentations of self are grossly enhanced, elaborated and exaggerated. Within the next sections the author explores the prominent narratives within the YouTube archive, their broader cultural contexts and the media practices of showing, presencing and archiving that are evident within them.

Derek Medina, 'Renaissance man'

Derek showed himself in a range of diverse roles and identities throughout his YouTube archive but the most prominent was 'the sportsman'. This included videos of him engaging in a variety of activities including athletics, basketball, pool, golf, baseball and boxing and watching several other sports – tennis, basketball and baseball. Derek always portrayed himself as 'the winner' and the content of the videos rarely lived up to what is suggested by their titles. One, entitled 'DEREK MEDINA WINNING THE GOLD' (Medina, 2011e), consists of footage of him running laps of an athletics track with a group of other men who vary in age, shape and size. The video is therefore not of a prestigious sporting event or even a serious race, there is no medal ceremony or even acknowledgement that he has 'won' – as the title might suggest. The same is true for other videos. In relation to those of him playing basketball, he is not playing in organised games or matches but shooting hoops on a public basketball court in a neighbourhood or park, using language that accords them much more significance and importance. Furthermore, Derek even appears to be cheating during some of these activities – the person keeping time at the athletics track shouts at him to 'run outside the cones' on more than one occasion (Medina, 2011e). The identity of the accomplished sportsman carries much kudos in mainstream American culture and this is an identity Derek appeared keen to communicate to others. The titles of his videos often included self-proclaimed statuses, such as '*APA* pool player' (Medina, 2012c), '*pro* exhibition fight' (Medina, 2012b, 2012d, 2012e) '*pro* basketball player' (Medina, 2011f) '*semi pro* basketball player' (Medina, 2012f, 2013e, emphasis added). Derek always appeared to accord himself an elevated status; it was not sufficient just to be someone who enjoyed these sports but someone who was among the *best* at them.

Derek's interest in one particular sport – boxing – appears to have been a significant one at the time of Jennifer's murder. On 6 August 2013, just two days prior to her death, he uploaded two videos, both entitled 'Work hard play hard' (Medina, 2013f, 2013g). In the video, Derek was in a gym, wearing a black suit, white shirt, black tie and training shoes. He kicked and hit a punch bag. The second video began with Derek urging someone in the gym to film him. He shouted, 'Julio, Julio! Record me man – one more time, one more round' (Medina, 2013g), suggesting that Julio was reluctant to record him and was simply humouring him. Indeed, the video cut out while he was still kicking and hitting the punch bag. Through this video, Derek shows himself at a gym in the company of other men – a masculine, tough environment – creating the impression that he has a presence there, is part of a boxing culture and belongs to this group. In her opening statement at trial, the prosecutor made reference to Derek's identity as a boxer. Her first words were 'Twenty-five and out' (CCV, 2015c), referring to his self-proclaimed record as someone who had never lost a fight. The accuracy of this statement is difficult to establish. It was something Derek was sure to include in the police interview after killing Jennifer. When asked by a detective how long he was an *amateur* boxer, he responded, 'Since 2004. 2007 I started *professional*' (Miami Dade Police Department, 2013, p 16, emphasis added).

Derek also attempts to edit his sports videos by creating videos of existing videos, in which he omits segments where he is not performing well – for example, only including basketball shots that he successfully makes. These practices of refining and retouching online images of oneself, essentially engaging in selective self-presentation, are characteristic of narcissistic personalities (Fox and Rooney, 2015). Videos of him attending sporting events – baseball and basketball games feature heavily in his archive – suggest that it is important for him *to be seen* to have a presence at these events. Jennifer – and sometimes her daughter too – accompanies him to several of these events. In a video of the family attending a baseball game in June 2012, Derek repeatedly calls down to the players in the bull pen, urging them to wave (Medina, 2012g). They do so, apparently quite reluctantly and in a half-hearted way. 'That's cool, we got their attention,' Derek says (Medina, 2012g). At other games, he often comments on the status of the team in various leagues and championships, saying, for example, '*We* are number two in the country' (Medina, 2013h, emphasis added), thus presenting himself as part of the team's following, part of these sporting cultures and communities.

Derek self-published six books in the period February to July 2013. These books are short but have lengthy titles, some of which are littered with grammatical and spelling errors. Examples include *How I saved someone's life and marriage and family problems thru communication* (Medina,

2013i) and *World just ask yourself why we are living a life full of lies and how I an emotional writer made all of my professional dreams come true blocking society's teachings* (Medina, 2013j). The identity of the writer was an important one for Derek, one which he displayed in an overt way in a range of spaces. Notable among these was his website 'Emotional writer' (Medina, 2013k). For the most part, this website simply listed and described the books – there were many images of their front and back covers. He appeared to be showing the books on the website as if to *prove* that they existed. He badged them all as 'self-help' titles. The identity of the self-help writer and the characteristics usually associated with this – gentleness and mindfulness, for instance – stand in stark contrast to the impression of Derek created by the comments of his former friends and acquaintances noted previously in this chapter.

Derek rarely referred to himself in the first person on this website – he used the third person most of the time. He also depersonalised Jennifer in this space. His final book (Medina, 2013i) appears to include material relating to their relationship. He says of the book, 'The author discusses how James … saved his marriage after getting divorced and remarried to the same person' (Medina, 2013k). However, he does not refer to himself in the first person – instead referring to a character called James – and does not mention Jennifer by name at all. In a book about ghost hunting, he does something similar, this time calling himself 'the author' and referring to Jennifer as 'his wife' (Medina, 2013k). The only time the first person is used is when Medina is being defensive about his books, for example, in the following passage, justifying why they are so short:

> My goal is for you, the readers, to open up your eyes and change for the better. My goal is for the readers to realize what life they are living. If I could pick up the phone and call every single person in the world and tell them my messages I would if it was possible, but I am expressing to the world my messages by writing thru my books. I only write thru emotions. That's the only way I will write. Please understand why I write short novels. When it's an urgent message and a life threatening situation you expect the messages to be quick and fast. I hope these books touch your spirit.' (Medina, 2013k)

He did not talk about the inspiration for the books, which one might expect to see on a writer's website. He never talked about where the ideas for particular titles came from, why he felt compelled to write particular books, the story of a book's development or any other contextual information. It could be argued that the content of the books was not important for Derek – what mattered was to *show* the world that they existed and that he had written them, providing *evidence* of his status as a writer. His narcissism is evident in his choice of the self-help genre.

Derek posted 10 videos on his YouTube channel about his books. He frequently addressed an audience in these videos, saying things like 'thank you fans and I hope you enjoy the books' (Medina, 2013l), 'you guys' (Medina, 2013m), 'don't forget to go to emotionalwriter.com' (Medina, 2013n) – as if speaking to a community of readers. However, as was the case on his website, detailed description of the content or context of the books is absent. Even in a video entitled 'The world needs to read this book' (Medina, 2013n), he doesn't say *why* this is the case. However, he does emphasise the expected impact of his books, stating in one video: 'The third and fourth book to me are the two new books that are definitely going to help the world out in so many ways' (Medina, 2013m). He also creates the illusion of a having a publisher or team around him by using collective terminology – 'the book that *we* are promoting' (Medina, 2013n). The YouTube videos on the topic of the books have a strong instructional tone to them. They are screen captures of websites on which the books are available and in audio, Derek tells people what they will see if they scroll down and what to click on to reach the payment page. He is keen to mention the name of the sites on which the books are available – Amazon, and Barnes and Noble. It appears important to him to show others that he has a presence on these websites alongside other authors, which gives him an air of legitimacy and accords him a similar status to other writers. One point that Derek *is* keen to emphasise, however, is the speed at which he has written the books. One video is entitled '6 books created in 6 months by author Derek medina' (Medina, 2013o). Much like the identity of the sportsman, it is not enough simply to be a writer; rather, he has to present himself as a prolific and efficient writer. Derek is seemingly unaware of his poor level of written English and mispronunciations and misspellings of various words and terms in the videos about his books and on his website.

Derek was also keen to display his identity as a writer through other means. In one video, where he was observing a debating club at a local university, he panned the camera around to focus on his clothing (Medina, 2013p). He was wearing a hoodie with stitching that read 'Writer' on it, to which he pointed with his finger. That he felt the need to wear such a garment to 'prove' himself is revealing – it is not enough to simply go along to the debate and introduce himself verbally as a writer. Indeed, nowhere in any of the four videos of him attending the debating club does he ever actually *say* anything. However, the videos fulfil a function: Derek is not only showing himself as having a presence within an academic environment – somewhere he considers it important to *be seen* to be – but is presenting himself as an intellectual among other intellectuals. The debate videos were not the only media in which Derek would wear such an item. In the home security footage on the day of Jennifer's murder, Derek is seen exiting the house through the front door. The hooded sweatshirt he is wearing has the slogan 'writers rock' on the back of it. Derek's identity as a writer – and more importantly, his creation of a presence to others as a writer through networked media – is an important strategy for him in addressing role strain (Perilla et al, 1994; Morash et al, 2000; Klevens, 2007), creating the illusion of the machismo head of household that had been threatened by Jennifer's role as the regular and consistent breadwinner.

A screenshot of Derek's Facebook timeline covering the day of and days preceding Jennifer's murder suggests that he was also keen to show himself as a 'family man'. The profile picture is of him, Jennifer and Jennifer's daughter sitting around a table in what appears to be a restaurant overlooking a marina. All are looking at the camera and smiling, and Derek is leaning towards Jennifer. The family appears to be in the middle of dinner, as all have plates of food and cups in front of them. However, Derek the writer is also clear, as inset into the profile picture is an image of the cover of one of his books. As such, he is showing himself on Facebook as *both* an author *and* a family man. Updates and photographs posted to his profile on 7 August all appear to relate to time spent with family in the same location as the restaurant in the profile picture. There are further pictures taken in the restaurant. These included images of food, entitled 'Curry heaven at the marina' (Medina, 2013q) and the family sitting at a dining table. Other pictures are of birds flying, and boats moored in the marina. The latter image is entitled 'Our view' (Medina, 2013r). It appears to be an idyllic but exclusive location – it has the feel of a members-only club. There are two additional pictures, one of Derek and Jennifer sat on sun loungers, and one of Jennifer and her daughter standing up next to a sun lounger. Derek captions these images 'Summer fun' (Medina, 2013s). The impression Derek creates in these sections of his Facebook timeline is of someone living the good life. He presents himself a successful author who provides for his family and enables them to enjoy the finer things in life – the very embodiment of the roles associated with machismo. As such, through these images and captions, the spectator is given the sense of access to an idyllic family lifestyle. Derek often includes the word 'marina', so no one is in any doubt that he is at a prestigious, exclusive and upmarket location. In so doing, he is strongly shaping how the spectator should interpret the images and in turn, make assumptions about the lifestyle that he and his family live.

The YouTube channel in the weeks before Derek killed Jennifer also include footage of the family at the marina. However, these videos are far more revealing in terms of the function his family served for him. One video is titled 'Summer 2013 sailing camp at our yacht club' (Medina, 2013t) and most of them consist of Derek panning the camera around the marina, filming boats and houses on Star Island, a well-known Miami neighbourhood where American celebrities have homes. Derek is quick to point this out, stating: 'That's Star Island over there', and 'There are dolphins there too'. In part of the video he focuses the camera on a red boat moored out in the bay and says, 'You see, my boat over there ... our boat, the family boat' (Medina, 2013t). Very little time is spent on Jennifer and her daughter; the camera only points towards them for a few seconds before going back to the surroundings of the marina. These videos suggest that it is important for Derek to be seen to have a presence at the yacht club and to communicate this to others, verbally confirming that he had legitimate access a prestigious and exclusive location. He is showing himself as someone who is wealthy and successful, inviting viewers to witness this suggestion of a privileged life. The videos are not of him showing himself as a family man but as a successful family man living the American dream for whom the family are an important prop in his performance.

YouTube posts further back in his archive include videos of Derek, Jennifer and Jennifer's daughter engaging in various activities together. This includes a video of going to a fun fair (Medina, 2011f, 2011g, 2011h) and one of Derek and Jennifer's daughter playing the video game Call of Duty (Medina, 2012h, 2012i). In the latter, Jennifer's daughter can be heard saying 'Don't cheat!' to Derek as they have a shoot-out (Medina, 2012i). The earlier portrayals of family life are mundane and everyday, the latter grandiose in comparison. This is perhaps indicative of an increasingly narcissistic and exhibitionist pattern of behaviour in Derek. What he excludes from the family videos is also of interest. He and Jennifer married twice but nowhere is there any footage of either wedding or anniversary celebrations.

There are several overlaps in the selves that Derek showed through his media archive. Within the 'family' category of videos, there is considerably more overlap with other topics than is the case in relation to other categories. An example is the funfair video (Medina, 2011f). The footage shows Derek throwing a basketball towards a hoop trying to get it in and win a prize. He comments on the video, 'I played pro basketball and now Im teaching my step daughter the fundamentals of shooting a basketball' (Medina, 2011f), emphasising his sportsman identity. A further instance is a video in which he visits his grandmother, entitled 'My 89year old grandma is my number one fan of my 6books' (Medina, 2013u). In the video he has copies of his books, which he shows to his grandmother. When he points the camera to her chest of drawers, all of his books are displayed on top of it. As such, the impression created is that it is not enough for Derek to simply be seen to be a family man, he must show himself to others as a family man who is also an accomplished athlete and writer, distinct from other fathers and husbands, *better* than them. The family for Derek appears simply in its role of reinforcing his narrative identities and performances of self – he appears as the star, the family simply as the support act.

Murder in social media: 'Renaissance man' and 'victim'

Turning to examine Derek's confession in the context of his 'Renaissance man' presentation of self, he continued to show himself as a sportsman and a writer but also crafted another narrative identity – that of victim. This involves a shifting the type of family man he showed himself to be from a successful breadwinner living the American Dream to a battered, disempowered husband.

However, Derek was not the only one on Facebook on the day of the murder. Jennifer and her friend Kelly were exchanging Facebook instant messages on the morning of 8 August 2013. These messages were shown at trial (CCV, 2015e) and assist in giving Jennifer's perspective as a victim – a voice not often heard in IPH cases (Monckton et al, 2014). The messages represent a counter-narrative, challenging the ways in which Derek showed himself and Jennifer through media in relation to the murder. Kelly testified that she worked with Jennifer at Denny's restaurant and the two communicated on a regular basis via Facebook messenger (CCV, 2015e). In the messages exchanged with Kelly during the morning of 8 August, Jennifer told of her frustration that Derek had let her down – she told Kelly that he had promised to wake her and her daughter up so the family could watch a film together and he did not do so. Jennifer also told Kelly that she had sent a text message to Derek because she did not know whether or not he was in the house. Jennifer shared with Kelly her anxiety as to why Derek did not wake her up: 'Its stupid shit like this that makes me think crazy shit you no … like it doesn't do anything now but later on it will eat away at my brain' (CCV, 2015e). She said that she wanted to spend more time together as a family. The two friends reflected on Derek's behaviour and how he would have reacted if Jennifer had done the same; Jennifer stated that 'he would be really pissy' (CCV, 2015e). Kelly gave Jennifer advice to tell Derek that she was disappointed. Jennifer agreed, but noted that she would have to approach the subject in a certain way so as not to aggravate Derek: 'I just have to be not pissed when I tell him' (CCV, 2015e). Jennifer was therefore aware of how she needed to manage herself around Derek, modifying her behaviour to fall in with his rules and expectations. Later in the exchange, Jennifer reported that Derek was in the house: 'He just woke up … he came in the room … and then he walked out and didn't say anything' (CCV, 2015e). Jennifer then told Kelly that she was going to take a shower and reports that she was feeling better afterwards. However, the next messages Jennifer sent to Kelly indicated that the couple had argued: 'We fought', 'He doesn't give a shit', 'He called me a bitch LOL', 'He said I was inconsiderate' (CCV, 2015e). Kelly tried to reassure Jennifer, told her everything would be okay and that and that she loved her. Jennifer said she loved Kelly too. The last text message in the exchange seen in court was from Jennifer, who said: 'I feel like I want to leave' (CCV, 2015e).

Derek's performance on the day of Jennifer's murder began not on Facebook but in front of the home security cameras. It is not so much what is seen in the footage that is enlightening but what is *concealed*. The murder itself is not seen on the video footage. At trial, the prosecutor emphasised that Derek knew *exactly* where all the cameras in the house were and that he was acutely aware that full footage of the murder would not be captured (CCV, 2015b). As such, it could be argued that Derek was controlling the narrative around the homicide already. In choosing *not* to show it on video camera, he was concealing the reality of the act from those who would come to judge his behaviour in relation to it. He was also simultaneously silencing Jennifer. Derek created a spectatorship void – in not allowing anyone to *witness* him killing Jennifer, he created a blank slate on which to craft his own narrative.

However, the narratives created in the Facebook posts that followed were wholly inconsistent. The image he posted of Jennifer is one that signals victory, power and patriarchal control. It was not sufficient for him to write about what had occurred; he had to 'show' and prove it. The text 'rip Jennifer Alfonso' (Medina, 2013a) is a dark and final pronouncement, factual and detached. Derek did not refer to her as his wife or use language suggesting any emotion, regret or remorse. The photograph was taken from an angle that looked down on Jennifer; she is an object within the image, humiliated and vulnerable. The photograph has a heavily gendered feel to it. Jennifer is in the kitchen, a stereotypically 'female' space in the home, and as such, she is cast in a subordinate role, Derek in a dominant one. The narrative that Derek crafted contained both action and reflection narratives (Brookman, 2015). He commenced with reflection, about what was going to happen to him – that he was going to prison or would receive the death penalty for killing his wife. He then drew on his fantasy identity as a writer in acknowledging his followers. Only after this did the action narrative emerge, in which he presented the homicide as wholly justified. He then reverted back to reflection, presenting himself as his wife's victim rather than her killer. His narcissism was evident in such heavy emphasis on the reflection narrative in the immediate aftermath of a homicide. There was no hint of regret, sadness or concern for anyone but himself and what others would think of him. The contrast between the image and the text is striking in its inconsistency. Considered alongside the wider contextual knowledge of the couple's relationship, the image speaks louder than the words. Jennifer's identity as the victim and Derek's as the aggressor is compelling, despite Derek's attempts to claim that the reverse was true. Social media provided one of the final opportunities for Derek to show himself and Jennifer in an unedited, unfiltered manner. However, once he entered the criminal justice process, these opportunities would no longer exist. While he admitted to killing Jennifer, he continued to try to claim the victim role and drew on techniques of neutralisation, minimising the homicide, deflecting responsibility, blaming Jennifer and lacking empathy for her and their family (Sykes and Matza, 1957; Dobash and Dobash, 2009, 2015).

Derek would appear at first glance to be an anomaly in taking a picture and posting it online. Most perpetrators leave the scene immediately after killing their intimate partner (Dobash and Dobash, 2015). Those who remain attempt to cover up the crime by destroying the body and a small number engage in sexual acts with the body (Dobash and Dobash, 2015). However, it is not so much the specific act of taking the picture and sharing it online that is important here, but what the act *represents* – a continuation of Derek's abusive and controlling pattern of behaviour. What had changed is that Derek had shifted the objective through which he sought to achieve his aim of control. Rather than seeking to possess Jennifer, he turned his attention to punishing her for expressing her intention to leave him and *showing* her family that he had done this and was in control, clearly aware that they were among the audience of his and Jennifer's Facebook accounts. This phenomenon is well summarised by Dobash and Dobash:

> ... acts in which men attempt to possess women and 'keep' them ... may be followed by acts of revenge when possession, control and authority are lost ... a man decides to 'change the project' from attempting to keep her within the relationship to destroying her for leaving it. (2015, p 39)

Having changed the project, and captured this 'decisive moment' (Ferrell and Van de Voorde, 2010) in an image, Derek performed the role of the victim to other audiences. A colleague from The Gables Club who usually took over from Derek when his night shift ended testified at trial that he received a call from Derek on the work telephone on the day of the murder. Derek apologised that he would miss work later and told him that he had killed Jennifer (Ovalle, 2015a). The colleague stated 'he said he couldn't take it anymore and she was punching him and he killed her' (Ovalle, 2015a). Derek's victim identity was performed again at his aunt's house. He drove there after the murder and told her and his uncle what he had done, adding that 'she [Jennifer] was abusing me' (Miami Dade Police Department, 2013, p 14). He asked his aunt to call his father and stepmother, 'so I could, you know, say goodbye before I go to the police station' (Miami Dade Police Department, 2013, pp 14-15). The selfish nature of these acts highlight his preoccupation with own needs – saying goodbye to relatives – rather than ensuring that emergency services attended the scene, where his stepdaughter was locked in the house with her deceased mother. Derek was, however, aware of the importance of *appearing* to have empathy and concern for others. In his sworn statement he said he posted the image on Facebook because he wanted Jennifer's family to know about what had happened. His attempt to present this act as borne out of concern for Jennifer's family is not a convincing one; he stated 'So the family would know and be notified and they could rush over there to get my ~~stuff out~~ stepdaughter' (Miami Dade Police Department, 2013, p 13; Derek altered 'stuff out' to 'stepdaughter' and initialled the change).

During his time with detectives, Derek continued to blame Jennifer for her own murder. This is far from unusual – in the aftermath of IPH, abusers often attempt to manipulate others, most notably the criminal justice professionals they encounter (Monckton-Smith et al, 2014; Dobash and Dobash, 2015). Derek presented Jennifer as irrational, claiming that her ranting preceded the killing and she was 'trying to agitate and push me' (Miami Dade Police Department, 2013, p 8). He also claimed that she threatened him, saying that she hoped he would die and that 'she'll get someone to kill me' (Miami Dade Police Department, 2013, p 11). He continued to emphasise that Jennifer was unpredictable and a threat to his safety. Derek's defence team attempted to reinforce the image of her as a dangerous woman, claiming that she had taken alpha PVP – a drug with the street name 'bath salts' – before the argument on the day of her murder (Rabin, 2014; Ovalle, 2015b). Derek claimed that Jennifer had attempted suicide in the past and that he thought she would do so again. He drew on this as a justification for remaining in the house after the argument. When asked by detectives whether he had ever called 911 on any of the previous occasions, he said no (Miami Dade Police Department, 2013, p 11). Derek continued to try to present Jennifer as unstable and violent by providing a contrasting image of himself as a calm and collected. Reporting his reaction to her plan to leave, he stated: 'And then she said she was going to leave me at midnight when I go to work ... and I said go right ahead I don't have a problem with that' (Miami Dade Police Department, p 8). Later in the interview he further built his victim identity by emphasising the ongoing nature of her alleged abuse towards him. This was a continued nurturing of the seed that he planted in the Facebook post: 'I am not going to stand it anymore with the abuse' (Medina, 2013b). In saying this, he presented himself not just a victim but a *long-suffering* victim. He said when asked that he had never called the police when Jennifer was violent towards him before because 'I figured I had to solve it on my own. I dealt with this for four years and I never had to call the cops. We've been able to resolve it. I didn't know if was going to get to this' (Miami Dade Police Department, 2013, p 18). He also presented himself as a victim of the criminal justice system, writing on the statement that 'I feel the court system is corupted' (Miami Dade Police Department, 2013, p 22). However, other points he made during his police interview served to undermine his self-proclaimed victimhood as another well-used narrative resurfaced – that of sportsman. His description of killing Jennifer is almost victorious, as if reporting a win: 'Everything that was in there hit her. The full round' (Miami Dade Police Department, 2013, p 16).

Murder in mainstream media: identity management

Derek was remanded in custody and pleaded not guilty to second degree murder in a court hearing on 29 August 2013 (Ovalle, 2013b), further expressing the victim narrative of an abused husband. In the days and weeks following his arrest, others around him assisted in showing him in this role. At a bail hearing in October 2013, Derek's defence attorney claimed Derek was a battered husband, commenting 'Battered spouse syndrome.... It doesn't only apply to women' (Ovalle, 2013c). Derek's family also painted Jennifer as the aggressor, saying in a newspaper interview that she 'pushed him to the point of insanity' (Benn, 2013).

It is interesting to consider these comments in light of Monckton-Smith et al (2014), who note that there is a hierarchy of victimisation among abuse victims. Those killed by their partners attain the lowest status – they are silenced, their voices and narratives drowned out by those of the perpetrator and his advocates. However, strong counter-narratives emerged from Jennifer's family, friends and others affected by her killing. Within days of her death, a Facebook memorial page was set up, which included a large number of pictures of her and tributes from people who had known her as well as those who had not (Ortega and Dixon, 2013). As a victim, she may have been silenced by her death, but social media provided an opportunity for the secondary victims of her murder – her friends and family – to create on her behalf an ongoing positive presence to others. This was joined by a video tribute posted on YouTube (SoFlaRocks, 2013), a montage of images showing Jennifer with family, friends and colleagues. The soundtrack of the video is the song Bittersweet Symphony by The Verve. The description of the video reads as follows:

> This is Lou S. I was friends with Jennifer Alfonso and made this video of her for her family and friends. She was so cool and gorgeously beautiful with an awesome soul. She would light up any room she walked into with her smile and presence. She didn't deserve the tragic end she received. She was loved by everyone who knew her. Only 26 years old. Her 10 yr old left without her Mommy. (SoFlaRocks, 2013)

These online tributes present Jennifer as much more than a victim of IPH – the way she had been shown to others by Derek in the Facebook post. These counter-representations depict her as a mother, a daughter, a sister, a friend and a colleague. The tributes also directly challenge the portrayal of Jennifer as an aggressor that had been voiced by Derek, his family and his legal team. While those affected by homicide once were reliant on the cooperation of mainstream media to tell their loved one's story (Rock, 1998), in Jennifer's case social media enabled them to do so in the way they chose, not constrained by editorial concerns of newsworthiness (Yardley et al, 2015).

Other key insights into the abusive relationship emerged in the aftermath of Jennifer's death. Ortega and Dixon (2013) reported on Jennifer's wake and spoke to relatives about the white clothes Jennifer and others were dressed in: 'The colour had been requested by Alfonso herself. According to one of her sisters ... Alfonso had long feared that her husband, Derek Medina, might do her harm.' This supports work by victim advocates claiming that those experiencing domestic abuse are the often the best risk assessors as to the level of danger they are in (Richards et al, 2008). The victim identity was ultimately an unsuccessful one for Derek. His characterisation of Jennifer as dangerous, violent and out of control was shattered during the criminal justice process. No trace of drugs was found in her blood and at trial the judge did not allow the defence to pursue the claim that she was high at the time of her death (Ovalle, 2015a, 2015c). The judge also declined the defence's request to use two experts to support Derek's claim of battered spouse syndrome (Ovalle, 2015c).

In the period of incarceration between his arrest and trial, Derek was a narcissist losing power over his own self-presentation. He was aware of his status as an iniquitous criminal celebrity (Penfold-Mounce, 2009). He was not just a murderer who had breached a legal code, but a murderer who had breached a moral code through the exhibitionist act of posting a picture of Jennifer's body on Facebook, inspiring loathing and disgust across the world. His actions in early 2015 suggest he was desperately seeking to turn the media's attention on himself again. In January 2015, he appeared in court and made a bizarre request for a bench trial rather than a jury trial. This was denied. At the court appearance, reporters noted that he had also drastically changed his appearance to 'long dark locks and a bushy mountain-man beard' (Ovalle, 2015d). However, by the start of the trial in November 2015, the beard and long hair had gone and Derek was wearing a suit (Ovalle, 2015a).

With Derek's credibility as a victim destroyed, by the time the case reached trial, Jennifer's status as a victim came into the spotlight. Here, criminal justice actors evoked stereotypical discourses of domestic abuse, questioning the degree to which victims of coercive control are 'real' victims. Dominant discourses present the perfect victim as someone who is a stranger to the physically violent 'big bad' perpetrator (Monckton-Smith et al, 2014). The perfect victim is meek and traumatised, engaging in respectable activities, blameless and compliant with the criminal justice process (Monckton et al, 2014). The court was shown home security video footage from June 2012 (CCV, 2015f). The camera was positioned on a living area where there was a sliding door out onto a patio or terrace. Derek was standing by the sliding door and grabbed Jennifer, pulling her sweater as she went to walk out of the door. Jennifer struggled out of his grip and pushed him out of her way as she exited the room through the sliding door. When asked about the relationship by the prosecutor (CCV, 2015d), Derek's aunt stated that she had never seen a physical confrontation between them but that she had seen injuries on Derek in the past. Jennifer was therefore presented as less than the 'perfect victim' – she was alleged to be 'violent', she defended herself, she was 'difficult' and 'stroppy', she lived with her abuser and did not report him to the police.

The last attempt by Derek at trial to enhance his newsworthiness (Penfold-Mounce, 2009; Jewkes, 2015) occurred when his life sentence was handed down. A local reporter described the events as follows:

> Medina refused to apologize or even look at the tearful relatives of his former wife. Instead, he bizarrely implored President Obama to 'focus on corruption' and announced plans to 'sue the world'. 'Basically, I didn't get a fair trial', he said, 'Only God knows the truth.' (Ovalle, 2016)

This final statement was testament to Derek's narcissism: his failure to accept defeat, his desire for preferential treatment and his continued lack of empathy for Jennifer and her family. The Derek described by the prosecutor in her opening statement was now clear for all to see: 'This was a defendant who was all about him. His rules. His way. He wins. He shoots when he wants and he leaves when he wants. And he tells the world about it on his terms' (CCV, 2015b). Unfortunately this knowledge came too late to save Jennifer Alfonso's life.

Intimate partner abuse and homicide in media

As a narcissist, Derek was extremely concerned with how other people saw him; to be was to be seen, and indeed, individuals with narcissistic traits and behaviours are likely to spend much more time on social networking sites than those without (Buffardi and Campbell, 2008; Mehdizadeh, 2010; Ryan and Xenos, 2011; Carpenter, 2012). The media practices he engaged in enabled him to show himself in the ways that he wanted others to see him and perform narrative identities that conferred him with status, superiority and importance. This was as true for his general media practices as it was for those he engaged in in relation to Jennifer's murder.

Derek showed himself as a sportsman, writer and family man, creating a continuous presence to others on his YouTube channel, personal website and Facebook profile. However, these identities and selves were grandiose exaggerations, consistent with his narcissistic leanings towards fantasies of success, achievement, status and power (Raskin and Terry, 1988). Derek appeared to be experiencing a consistent crisis of being (Ferrell et al, 2015), in which he desired and performed – but did not live or experience – those social roles accorded status in contemporary American culture. He marginalised himself from friends and acquaintances who concluded he was odd and strange, distancing themselves from him when his behaviour transgressed moral, social and legal boundaries. Therefore *who* Derek was showing himself *to* was an imagined audience of people who were interested in his life, a following whom he later came to call his 'fans' as he attempted to perform the role of the writer. Derek was largely ignored – there was no one to see him, no one interested in the increasingly bizarre representations of himself he posted online. Derek also showed Jennifer through media, but only in ways that would support his self-presentation as a successful family man, the embodiment of machismo. Jennifer was a prop in Derek's performance, one that he had to be in constant control of as she was a threat to his enactment of the successful family man. Nowhere did he present her as the regular breadwinner or head of the household, even though these were roles she likely fulfilled. Couldry (2012) has argued that the media practice of showing is testament to the dissolving boundaries around private life. Derek's showing practices represent something altogether different. For him, showing was about *constructing* boundaries around his fantasy self and his real self; showing was about presenting who he wanted to be seen as rather than who he actually was.

When seen in the context of media practices, we see Derek for the 'abuser turned murderer' (Dobash and Dobash, 2009, p 216) he was. There was evidence of an escalation in his monitoring and surveillance of Jennifer in his YouTube archive as she appeared in more of his videos, emphasising a sense of ownership and 'showing' her to be 'his'. The things he did with media were manifestations of his narcissism and controlling behaviour. All of this challenges the dominant stereotypes of IPH as events that occur 'out of the blue' when men 'snap'. In this way, the murder and the posting on Facebook that followed it cannot be presented as a one-off event but a continuation and exacerbation of an established history of grandiose narcissistic exhibitionism and coercive control. When Jennifer expressed her intention to leave him, Derek regained control first by killing her, and second, through showing others that he had done so by posting the picture of her body on Facebook. This decisive moment (Ferrell and Van de Voorde, 2010) – one where he 'changed the project' (Dobash and Dobash, 2015, p 39) from possessing her to destroying her – was an event of such significance for him that it had to be captured by an image. The image therefore is a window into the 'dynamics of power and transgression' (Ferrell and Van de Voorde, 2010, p 46), where far from losing control, an abuser is *asserting* control. Sending out a message to those he knew would see the picture – Jennifer's family and friends – Derek communicated that he had succeeded in isolating her and taking her away from them, something he had been attempting to do for some time (Stark, 2007). Derek wanted to be fully in control of the narrative, so ensured that the homicide was not captured on the home security camera. Jennifer's murder cannot be simply described as a 'performance crime' (Surette, 2015a) enacted for the camera; the reality was more nuanced that this. Her murder was the precursor to a spectacle, in which Derek created media to support his performance as a victim. Jennifer was not the focus or subject of the Facebook confession; rather, this was all about Derek. He created and shared the macabre image in order to continue what he had been doing for many years – placing himself centre-stage.

In the following chapter, the author explores another homicide committed within the family context that was followed by a social media confession. However, the perpetrator in this case killed three members of his family and posted his confession before going on to take his own life – something that we could argue Derek would have been highly unlikely to do, given his narcissism and the priority he placed on maintaining his fantasy self. While Derek's media practices were grandiose, exaggerated and all about having a presence, those of the perpetrator considered in the next chapter appear to stand in direct contrast to this.

Note

[1] Throughout this chapter, grammatical errors and misspellings are left as they appear in the original source.

SIX

The Janzen familicide

The homicides and the suicide[1]

On Tuesday 28 April 2015, 19-year-old Emily Janzen was fatally shot twice in the head by her father, 50-year-old Randy, in the Rosedale family home located in the Canadian province of British Columbia. Later that same day, Randy killed his wife, 56-year-old Laurel, also shooting her twice in the head. One week after these killings, on Tuesday 5 May, he travelled to the Langley home of his sister Shelly – a 40-minute, 60-km drive on the Trans-Canada Highway from Rosedale. Shelly, who was 53, had just returned home from a shopping trip and her bags were still over her shoulders. Similar to the manner in which he had killed Emily and Laurel, Randy shot Shelly twice in the head. He covered her body with several layers of blankets before leaving the house. Two days later, on Thursday 7 May at around 12 noon, Randy's Facebook friends noticed a status update on his profile. It read:

> Over the last 10 days, I have done some of the worst things I could have ever imagined doing. First to do with my dear sweet loving daughter Emily. The best little girl two parents could ever hope for. She was talented and smart and filled out hearts with her laughter. She was always willing to help with a smile even when she was feeling lousy. Emily excelled at so many things but slowly had to stop almost everything because of the migraines. (But when it effected[2] her beloved singing it took a part of her soul). She has been very ill with migraines that have plagued her since Elementary School. This has caused her to miss two years at UBC, which completely broke her heart. I don't think anyone really knew how much pain Emily was in on a daily basis and the severe depression that these migraines caused her. Emily watched her friends from high school move on with their lives, while hers was spent wretching into a puke tray and hours at the Emergency rm. Since Oct/Nov her migraines have escalated to excruciating again and I just could not see my little girl hurt for one more second. She

had shown unimaginable strength through a lot of migraine pain over the years and always seemed try to look on the bright side and always loved talking about things: 'When I get better lets do this and lets do that.' I wish sweetheart [sad emoji]. Emily had tried everything to get better but nothing seemed to help her. I took a gun and shot her in the head and now she is migraine free and floating in the clouds on a sunny afternoon, her long beautiful brown hair flowing in the breeze, a true angel. Then I shot Laurel, because a mother should never have hear the news her baby has died. Then a couple of days later my sister Shelly, because I did not want her to have to live with this shame I have caused all alone. Now my family is pain free and in heaven. I have great remorse for my actions and feel like the dirt that I am. I am taking full responsibility for my actions of these murders. So sorry to anyone I have hurt. Rest in peace my little family [emoji blowing a heart kiss]. Love Daddio xoxo. (Cited in Pynn, 2015)

Having seen the post, friends of Shelly went to check on her. On arrival, they noticed stacks of newspapers piled up outside the house – Shelly was a delivery agent for a number of local publications. Concerned at what they had found, they called the police, as did others who had seen the Facebook post. By 4.30pm, the Janzen family home on Llanberis Way was surrounded by police. Officers later saw a man they believed to be Randy inside the house and attempted to make contact with him. Calling out through bull horns, they repeatedly asked him to come outside. Following a four-hour stand-off, neighbours reported hearing gunfire. The gunfire was likely to have come from the long barrel gun that Randy used to shoot himself in the forehead. The house then caught alight and a large fire consumed the structure. Emergency services entered the home but had to retreat given the severity of the fire. They did, however, see a body wrapped in a sheet on the floor before they exited – it would later transpire that this was Laurel. The fire was so severe that it was not until three days later that officials from the Identification and Disaster Response Unit of the British Columbia Coroners Service were able to enter the home.

Following the deaths, the coroner released reports in relation to the four victims (British Columbia Coroners Service, 2015a, 2015b, 2015c, 2015d). The reports confirmed Emily, Laurel and Shelly's deaths as homicides by multiple gunshot wounds to the head (British Columbia Coroners Service, 2015a, 2015b, 2015c) and Randy's as suicide by self-inflicted gunshot wound to the head (British Columbia Coroners Service, 2015d). Within the report relating to Randy, the coroner noted that the Facebook post and the police response to the deaths provided a clear timeline of the events (British Columbia Coroners Service, 2015d). The coroner also stated that Emily did indeed have a medical history of chronic migraines, which were a source of family stress and a potential motive for the homicides (British Columbia Coroners Service, 2015a, 2015d).

These events can be described using the term 'familicide' or 'family annihilation'. Definitions vary, but it is broadly described as a homicide incident in which multiple members of a family are killed – commonly by the male head of household, who kills his female partner and their biological children (Dietz, 1986; Wilson et al, 1995; Cooper and Eaves, 1996; Websdale, 2010; Liem et al, 2013; Fox and Levin, 2015; Hough and McCorkle, 2017). Further definitional contributions identify sub-types – 'familicide-suicide' or 'family annihilation-suicide' – within which the perpetrator commits suicide shortly after the familicide (Marzuk et al, 1992; Harper and Voight, 2007; Websdale, 2010). Liem and Reichelmann (2014) note that familicides have primary victims – who are the main target for the act – and secondary victims, 'killed because they are seen as extensions of the primary victim or because of their physical closeness to the primary victims' (2014, p 54). While Emily appears to have been the primary victim and Laurel a secondary victim, the Janzen familicide is unusual in that Randy killed Shelly too. It is rare that extended family members are targeted in these incidents (Yardley et al, 2014) – and when they are it is because they happen to be in the location where the killings occur and as such are *available* to him at the time he acts' (Hough and McCorkle, 2017, p 90, emphasis added). Shelly was not spatially or temporally close to the killings of Laurel and Emily.

On the whole, familicide is a very rare type of homicide. Wilson et al (1995) explored homicides within Canadian families over a 15-year period and noted that only 2% were familicides. The same scholars reported an average four cases a year in Canada and three in England and Wales (Wilson et al, 1995). However, while numbers remain low as a proportion of all homicides, some researchers suggest that the phenomenon is on the increase (Websdale, 2010; Yardley et al, 2014). Familicide is a largely male-perpetrated act and the literature identifies two types of perpetrator, who sit at opposite ends of a familicidal spectrum (Websdale, 2010). First, there are 'livid coercive hearts' (Websdale, 2010) – abusive individuals with a history of violent and controlling behaviour. Their female partner or former partner is often the primary target, the killings carried out in circumstances where the perpetrator feels she is slipping out of his control. Livid coercive characteristics appear in other perpetrator typologies – for example, 'accusatory' (Wilson et al, 1995; Wilson and Daly, 1998), and 'self-righteous' and 'disappointed' (Yardley et al, 2014) – and in instances of 'spousal revenge' (Liem and Reichelmann, 2014) and 'murder by proxy' (Frazier, 1975. At the other end of the spectrum, Websdale (2010) describes 'civil reputable hearts', who appear to be the antithesis of livid coercive hearts. They have not been outwardly aggressive or coercively controlling. As such, their actions elicit a shocked reaction within their communities, who struggle to reconcile the respectable, conforming, upstanding family men they knew with an individual capable of committing such a heinous act. Despondency and depression are common among these perpetrators, who see themselves as the sole provider and protector within the family. They are more likely to commit suicide after the familicide and believe their actions are a merciful way of 'saving' their families from lives of anticipated suffering initiated by real or perceived threat to family life. Civil reputable characteristics have been identified in 'paranoid' (Yardley et al, 2014), 'despondent' (Wilson et al, 1995; Wilson and Daly, 1998) and 'despondent husband' (Liem and Reichelmann, 2014) types of perpetrator, and in cases of 'suicide by proxy' (Frazier, 1975).

The Janzen familicide made headlines locally, regionally, nationally and internationally, the story appealing to multiple news values (Jewkes, 2015). The number of victims, the relationship between the victims, the manner in which they died and the Facebook confession all ensured the story met thresholds of newsworthiness. Emily, Laurel and Shelly were ideal victims (Christie, 1986), innocent and undeserving of their fates. The homicide deviated significantly from cultural norms and expectations (Pritchard and Hughes, 1997; Lundman, 2003; Gruenewald et al, 2009, 2013). It was an unexpected event ending the lives of people in the mainstream as opposed to on the margins, living regular, low-risk lifestyles – simply going about their daily business. Images of the Llanberis Way home in flames surrounded by emergency services provided graphic imagery and visual spectacle. The Janzens were the embodiment of the middle-class, respectable Canadian family. This provided a sense of proximity and risk – they could have been anyone's neighbours, colleagues or friends. Family photographs and snippets about their lives enabled mainstream media to individualise those involved, particularly Emily, a talented singer and the child of the family, even though at 19 she was legally an adult. The tone of mainstream media coverage varied. International media tended to simplify and vilify Randy. The UK's *Sunday Mirror* described him as '*crazed* Randy Janzen' (Sassoon, 2015, emphasis added) and the *New York Post* wrote about him as 'a *deranged* Canadian man' (Strum, 2015, emphasis added). However, local and regional press adopted the more sympathetic tone identified by Monckton-Smith (2012) in coverage of cases where a perpetrator is believed to have killed out of love. They presented Randy very much as a civil reputable heart (Websdale, 2010). The familicide was described as tragic, sad and heartbreaking (Bucholtz, 2015a; Eagland and Saltman, 2015; Bolan, 2016). Randy was described as a 'desperate' man, Emily a daughter who was '*shot* by her father' rather than 'killed' or 'murdered' by him (Henderson, 2015, emphasis added). Randy's status as an upstanding and respectable man was bolstered by this coverage, some of which drew on a narrative of mental ill health, one journalist arguing that mental illness 'can cause otherwise fine people to do irrational and awful things' (Bucholtz, 2015a). Such coverage has the effect of locating responsibility for the killings as something external to the perpetrator and beyond their sphere of control (Monckton-Smith, 2012).

The Facebook confession appeared to be the focal point of the stories in international mainstream media and was the factor that first drew the author's attention to this case. It could be argued that were it not for the Facebook confession, the case may not have been reported outside of Canada. Many multiple killings like the Janzen familicide are locally newsworthy, but few are covered more widely, the killings requiring increasingly novel and unusual features to achieve national and international exposure (Duwe, 2000). In this chapter, Emily, Laurel and Randy's social media practices are examined to generate additional insights into the significance of networked media in their lives. While the literature around familicide is well established, the media practices of those involved in these acts have not been explored in detail. If such cases are to be better understood in the context of contemporary networked culture, there is a need to capture what those affected by such crimes *do* in relation to networked media – both in general as part of their everyday lives and specifically in relation to the familicide that ends those lives.

In relation to the sources on which this case study draws, events surrounding the killings have been reconstructed using the aforementioned reports from the British Columbia Coroners Service. Local newspaper reports have been used to develop insights into the local context of the familicide, particularly in terms of the family's links to and activities within the local community. In terms of social media, Randy's Facebook post is explored in detail. His Facebook profile is still publicly available (apart from the confession, which was taken down after the events of 7 May) and is therefore also included in the analysis. In addition to this, the social media archives of Emily and Laurel were central to the analysis in this case for three reasons. First, they helped in exploring Randy's engagement with them on social media; his comments and 'likes'[3] are still visible on their memorialised profiles. Second, the archives enabled the author to tell the story of these women as more than simply the victims of familicide. They shed light on Emily and Laurel's interests, hobbies, talents, worries and aspirations, enabling us to see them as the complex, multidimensional people they were rather than simply the victims of a newsworthy familicide. Third, the social media archives were useful in considering the extent to which the ways Emily and Laurel showed themselves in social media were consistent with the narrative in Randy's confession. The media archives analysed for the purposes of this chapter consisted of Emily and Laurel's memorialised Facebook profiles, Twitter and Instagram accounts, as well as Laurel's YouTube account and her family history page on genealogy.com. Unfortunately, autobiographical archives to this level of detail and nuance are not available for Shelly Janzen, who appeared not to have a social media presence; interviews with friends and colleagues given to local newspapers are therefore the sole source of information about Shelly's life. The next section explores the individual, familial, local and structural context of the Janzen family.

Context

In April 1959, Laurel Janzen was born Laurel Cusiter, the daughter of William Cusiter and Evelyn Annabelle Myers (Laurel-E-Janzen, 2016a). William Cusiter was born in 1917 in Aberdeenshire, Scotland and travelled by ship to Canada as an infant with his family in August 1919 (Laurel-E-Janzen, 2016b). Laurel's mother Evelyn was born in 1922 in Kamsack, Saskatchewan. Laurel had two brothers, one of whom died in infancy (Laurel-E-Janzen, 2016b). Evelyn married again in 1966 and Laurel had two half-brothers as a result of this relationship (Laurel-E-Janzen, 2016c).

Randy Janzen was born in Langley, British Columbia in 1965, three years after his sister. Randy and Shelly were the children of Henry Janzen, a Ukrainian migrant, and Katharina Hooge, whose family helped establish the Bethel Mennonite Church in the local area in 1936 (Sinoski et al, 2015; Tamminga, 2015; Fayerman, 2016a; Laurel-E-Janzen, 2016d). Henry and Katharina were famers (Fayerman, 2016a). Randy and Shelly's formative years during the 1960s and 1970s were spent on 66 Avenue in Langley, which was described as an 'idyllic rural area' during this period (Bucholtz, 2015b).

Shelly never left home, living with her parents her whole adult life. When Henry died in July 2004 (Laurel-E-Janzen, 2016e), Shelly moved to the Langley house with Katharina. Shelly cared for Katharina until her death in August 2014. She was a member of the congregation at Bethel Mennonite Church. Pastor Philip Wheaton had known the family for several years and last saw Shelly at church on 26 April 2015. He commented that she was a quiet, loving and gentle woman (Sinoski et al, 2015; Fayerman, 2016a). Brian Jones, a childhood friend of Randy's, described Shelly as 'quiet, shy and somewhat reclusive' (Kane, 2015). An animal lover, she had worked as a pet groomer for 15 years at a local kennels and was known to donate her tips to animal rescue causes (Sinoski et al, 2015; Fayerman, 2016a). A church administrator recalled that 'Shelly had a gentle spirit. She was a real giver to people and to animals' (Tamminga, 2015). In her work as a newspaper delivery agent, her employers described her as reliable and trustworthy (Bucholtz, 2015a). Shelly had arthritis and was hearing-impaired, which, Philip Wheaton claimed, 'seemed to wall her off from people a bit' (Fayerman, 2016b). Although she was quiet and introverted, she appeared happy and contented with her life – she had a small group of people 'who truly invested in her and who she deeply cared for in return' (Sinoski et al, 2015). Philip Wheaton did, however, allude to the somewhat isolated nature of the Janzen family, at least on Randy and Shelly's side, telling reporters that when he was arranging Shelly's funeral he had difficulty establishing a next of kin because all of her immediate family members were deceased (Sinoski et al, 2015).

As a young man, Randy enjoyed music and from the 1980s to the early 2000s was the lead singer in a band called Marauder (Sinoski et al, 2015). In a photograph of the four band members from the mid-1980s, Randy has long, wavy hair that comes past his shoulders. He is smiling, as are the other band members. However, Randy stands out from the others in several ways. He is standing up straight with his arms at his sides while other members of the band are leaning or crouching against the wall behind them. In contrast to Randy, they have their arms crossed or their hands resting on their knees, or they are gesticulating at the camera. Randy's expression appears more serious than that of the others, and he is more focused on the photograph being taken. Like the others, he is wearing a t-shirt and jeans, but his clothes are a darker shade and his jeans do not appear faded or worn like those of the other band members. In addition, he is the only member of the band wearing smart leather shoes rather than white trainers. A fellow band member, Shane Dwight, recalled his and Janzen's time with Marauder in a newspaper interview following the familicide. He remembered Randy as mature, responsible and paternal: 'When they were in the band, Janzen was seen as a "big brother" figure, someone who always wanted to help fix problems' (Sinoski et al, 2015). Brian Jones recalled a gregarious man (Kane, 2015), not just of good character but of *superior* character: 'He was so gentle. He never hurt a fly his whole life. When we were all young and getting in fistfights, Randy didn't do that... He wasn't a monster' (Anon, 2015). Randy's maturity, consistency and reliability are also alluded to in reports of his working life. He had been employed at a local sawmill for around 35 years and made a good living from this job (Eagland and Saltman, 2015). The picture that emerges of a young Randy Janzen is one of a mature and responsible man. He appeared to command the respect of his peers while still being included as one of the crowd, striking a balance between being admired for his upstanding moral character but not perceived as self-righteous or condescending. No one talking about his early years to the local newspapers reported odd, unusual or abnormal behaviour. Randy's Facebook profile, while giving away very little about his life, does include a few details of his interests. In relation to sport, he liked the BC Lions football club and the Vancouver Canucks ice hockey team. He also liked Leah Pells, a Vancouver-born former track and field Olympian. In relation to music, he liked the musician and producer David Foster – who also hailed from British Columbia – bands including Hellyeah, Chickenfoot and Playing for Change, and Star 98.3FM, a local, light-rock music radio station. The music-related likes also show a clear overlap with Emily's musical interests and activities – the Chilliwack Cultural Centre, Chilliwack Academy of Music and the University of British Columbia's School of Music and Opera Ensemble. He also liked books by the author Mitch Albom, including *The five people you meet in heaven* (2003), and the Rick Hansen Foundation, a local organisation dedicated to improving the lives of people with disabilities.

With regards to Laurel's history, very little is known. The local newspapers devoted many column inches to the lives, interests and characteristics of Randy, Shelly and Emily, but did not explore Laurel's life to the same level of detail. This is perhaps not surprising, given the prominence of Randy and Shelly's family in establishing a local church and Emily's activities as part of the local performing arts community. However, Laurel's absence in effect casts her as a supporting actor – Randy's wife and Emily's mother but nothing else, simply playing a walk-on part in the story of her own homicide. However, social media archives provide a window into her life beyond these ascribed roles and identities.

A black and white photograph posted to Emily's Instagram is entitled 'My mom in the real breakfast club circa '74 #detention #breakfastclub #mymomwasbadass' (EmilyJanzen_1, 2014a). In the picture, Laurel, who would have been around 15 at the time, is sitting around a table in a library with three classmates who are all turning to face the camera. They are all smiling and one of them is holding up their middle finger. Laurel is looking across at one of them with a look of amusement on her face; her hair is neatly styled and she is wearing smart, fashionable clothes. Laurel's interest in fashion and beauty is evident in her own social media archive too; she posted pictures of the nail polishes and shoes she had purchased on shopping trips along with images of her colourfully manicured nails. Cooking and gardening were also among her interests – she shared images of meals she had prepared and the herbs and flowers that were growing in her garden. Laurel also appears to have had passion for animals – there are many posts about Sophie, the family's golden retriever dog, in and around the family home and out on walks. Genealogy was also an interest, with posts referring to the family history research Laurel had conducted on social media. Laurel's strong and assertive personality comes across in the numerous memes she reposted, including 'Tell the negative committee that meets inside your head to sit down and shut up – Ann Bradford' (cloudsinmycoffee59, 2015a), 'Seek respect, not attention, it lasts longer' (cloudsinmycoffee59, 2014a) and 'All great changes are preceded by chaos' (cloudsinmycoffee59, 2014b). Laurel identified a range of her favourite musicians on Facebook, including The Beatles, Lisa Fischer, The Tenors, David Bowie, REM and Chris Isaak. She listed the films Pulp Fiction, The Party, A Streetcar Named Desire, Annie Hall and the Johnny Depp film Cry Baby among her favourites. She liked the television shows Modern Family, Parks and Recreation, Hells' Kitchen, Who Do You Think You Are? and Antiques Roadshow. She included John Steinbeck's *East of Eden* and Kathryn Stockett's *The Help* on her Facebook list of books, alongside titles by Mitch Albom – an interest she shared with Randy.

Laurel and Randy met in the mid-1980s. Shane Dwight recalled that Randy was in his late teens or early twenties when the couple first got together (Kane, 2015). He remembered Laurel as a striking and beautiful woman, who was a few years older than Randy and working in a bar at the time (Kane, 2015). It is thought that they married in the early 1990s (Eagland and Saltman, 2015). There are few records of their relationship during this period, but one exception is a photograph Laurel posted to her Instagram and Facebook account in July 2014 with the comment, '#tbt[4] #1992 #mediterrean #barcelona #ladyinred #the love boat' (cloudsinmycoffee59, 2014c). Emojis of a heart, ship and anchor follow the comment. The comment seems to suggest that the picture was taken during a special holiday, perhaps a honeymoon cruise. In the picture, Laurel and Randy are dressed in smart evening wear – Randy in a black dinner suit and Laurel in a glamorous, knee-length red dress. They are standing together at the bottom of a carpeted blue spiral staircase. The picture appears to be of the type taken by cruise ship photographers of guests on their way to dinner or drinks in the evening. Laurel is holding Randy's arm, which is placed at his side; the other is holding onto the handrail of the staircase. Both Laurel and Randy are facing the camera, smiling. Randy's hair is still long, as it was in the aforementioned photograph with Marauder. Laurel's hair is also long, and fashionably styled in keeping with the trends of the early 1990s.

In 1995, three years after this photograph was taken, Randy and Laurel purchased the family home on Llanberis Way (Eagland and Saltman, 2015). Online images on the Google Maps website (www. google.com/maps) show the Janzen house as a detached residence with a double garage and a long driveway, framed on either side by a tidy garden with several trees and shrubs. Llanberis Way is filled with similar large houses and bungalows with well-kept gardens. There is considerable space around each property and the houses are neither too close together nor too far apart. This creates a sense both of proximity and privacy – a place where people might engage with neighbours through a wave or a 'good morning', but where they also have the option of keeping themselves to themselves. This was the impression created by neighbours in newspaper interviews following the familicide; they described the Janzen family as nice, quiet people who went out to work every day and had a daughter in school (Sinoski et al, 2015). Many homes along the street have recreational vehicles, sport utility vehicles, caravans or basketball hoops in the driveways. Children can be seen riding their bikes and residents tending to their gardens or engaging in home improvement work at the front of their houses. The street feels distinctly middle-class and family-oriented. The area was described by local news media as a tranquil, 'good community' (Bucholtz, 2015a) situated on an 'idyllic no-through street, backed by the former Minter Gardens site and tucked in a forested area filled with tall cedar trees' (Peters, 2015).

In 1996, the year after Laurel and Randy purchased the family home, Emily was born. Pictures of her as a child in social media archives tell the story of a small but happy family. There are several pictures of Emily and Laurel together when Emily was a toddler; in one she is holding a daisy up to Laurel's nose for her to smell (EmilyJanzen_1, 2014b), and in another she is sitting on Laurel's lap as the sun streams through a living room window (cloudsinmycoffee59, 2014d). A picture posted to Laurel's Instagram in July 2014 is accompanied by the comment '#tbt #2002 #buildingcastlesinthesand #cultuslake', followed by sunshine, sunglasses and heart emojis (cloudsinmycoffee, 2014e). Emily, who would have been five or six years old in 2002, is sat cross-legged on the sand at Cultus Lake, a popular leisure destination in British Columbia. Emily is wearing a yellow bikini and has a child's spade in her hand. Randy is crouching down next to her, wearing shorts, sunglasses and a red and green baseball cap with the word Arctec on it (the name of a welding equipment and supplies company in British Columbia). Randy's hair is close-cropped, different from the long hair he had in earlier photographs. In front of Emily and Randy is a sandcastle, and they are both looking at the camera, smiling – perhaps at Laurel, who may have been taking the picture. Later pictures of Emily as an adolescent show a happy, slightly overweight, smiling girl wearing glasses. It was around this time that she developed her interest in music. Fourteen-year-old Emily appeared in an item for a local television station, in which she explained that she began to sing in church choirs at around the age of eight (SuperLola59, 2011). At age 12, she joined the Chilliwack Academy of Music and began receiving vocal coaching from Paula Quick, who also appeared in the television segment and had the following things to say about Emily:

> I will never forget seeing this little, bouncy little, at that time – somewhat chubby – little girl, with a ponytail at the top of her head just bounding down the stairs to our meeting room and I think, 'Oh – isn't she delightfully cute?' As soon as she opened her mouth and started to sing we realised the lunchbox just landed.' (SuperLola59, 2011)

In her teenage years, Emily blossomed into a tall, slender and elegant young woman with a growing passion for the performing arts. Within the aforementioned television piece, Paula Quick praised both Emily's talent and work ethic, while Emily talked about her interest in musical theatre and opera, expressing her desire to study the latter at university:

> Musical theatre is such a love of mine and then opera – I don't know – I feel a bit more comfortable singing opera – it

comes a little more easily to me and its similar to musical theatre in that its acting out a story and singing in a different style…. I'd really like to go the university to study like for Operatic Studies. So that's where I'm looking right now, making sure I get good grades so I can get scholarships and stuff to get to a good music school. (SuperLola59, 2011)

This dream was on its way to being realised in April 2014, when Emily was offered a place with the September 2014 cohort of the Opera Performance course at the University of British Columbia, something she proudly shared on her Facebook profile with the comment 'Life couldn't be better' and a smiley emoji (Janzen, 2014a). Shane Dwight suggested that Emily inherited her vocal talents from her father (Eagland and Saltman, 2015) and seemed destined to become a famous opera singer (Kane, 2015). Dwight further commented that Randy was a 'kind and loving family man', who 'loved his daughter more than anything and was so proud of her' (Sinoski et al, 2015).

After her death, the local arts community paid tribute to Emily's 'beautiful voice' (Eagland and Saltman, 2015). A former bandmate described her as 'amazing', recalling a standing ovation she received after one of her performances (Woo and Kane, 2015). A friend shared plans that she and Emily made about performing and travelling together: 'It breaks my heart to know we'll never perform together again or live in London with all of our dogs and drinking our tea like we planned' (Crawford, 2015). The arts community commented on Emily's pleasant and magnetic personality as well as her artistic talent: 'She was a very kind spirit, very giving. Everyone would rally around her because she had that personality very warm and inviting, generous' (Fumano, 2015). A fund was set up in Emily's memory to assist students pursuing a performing arts education – the Emily Janzen Memorial Bursary Fund (Indiegogo, 2016).

Emily's dreams of moving out of Chilliwack to study at the University of British Columbia (UBC) in Vancouver never materialised. Randy claimed in his Facebook confession that this was wholly due to debilitating migraines, which had worsened in the six months prior to the killings. Randy also claimed that Emily had experienced migraines since elementary school, which in Canada spans the age range six to 12. Others were aware of Emily's difficulties with this type of pain. Her former bandmate recalled Emily being unwell during practice a couple of times a month: 'She just sort of took Tylenol or Advil to relieve the pain…. She wouldn't stop. In between, she would say she had a headache, and then start playing again' (Woo and Kane, 2015).

In relation to how Randy coped with Emily's illness, insights from those in his social circle are somewhat limited. Shane Dwight had not actually seen or spoken to him for around a decade, only keeping in touch with him via social media. However, Brian Jones confirmed that he was very distressed by Emily's health: 'It consumed him. It really did. He couldn't stand to see her suffer' (Anon, 2015b). As is often true in relation to civil reputable familicide perpetrators, Brian Jones found it difficult to reconcile the Randy he knew with the man who killed his family, saying that he never knew Randy to own a gun or be physically violent towards his family (Anon, 2015b). Co-worker Raymond Norfolk also gave interviews to the local press. His comments are of interest because as a work colleague of eight years' standing (Woo and Kane, 2015), he is likely to have interacted with Randy on a daily basis and as such, his remarks may provide more detailed insights into his behaviour than those who spent time with him socially. Norfolk claimed that Emily meant the world to her father and that Randy talked about her constantly (Eagland and Saltman, 2015) – a similar observation to those made by others. However, commenting on Randy's behaviour at work, Norfolk painted a picture of a man prone to mood swings: 'He was a funny guy, but he was a rollercoaster too. He was depressed, and then one minute he was up. And then he was down' (Eagland and Saltman, 2015). The coroner noted that Randy had reported stress and trouble sleeping to his family doctor in 2014: 'Mr Janzen attributed this stress to the ongoing care of his daughter and her battle with chronic migraines' (British Columbia Coroner's Service, 2016d, p 2). Aside from this detail, however, Randy's medical history was described as 'limited' (British Columbia Coroner's Service, 2016d, p 2). There was certainly no record of him expressing feelings about harming himself or others, and he was not receiving any psychiatric support at the time of his death (British Columbia Coroner's Service, 2016d). Raymond Norfolk did, however, recall Randy expressing suicidal feelings at work in relation to Emily's health problems: 'He kind of talked about it. If she ever goes, he's done. "Why bother being here? There's nothing left in my life"' (Eagland and Saltman, 2015).

The civil reputable perpetrator embodied

The picture that emerges of the Janzen family from the outside looking in is one of the middle-class respectability often associated with civil reputable familicide perpetrators (Websdale, 2010). These perpetrators are likely to be white men, often in their thirties or forties (Liem, 2010; Liem and Reichelmann, 2014). Randy's sociodemographic characteristics are consistent with this, albeit at the top end of this age bracket. Liem and Koenraadt (2008) compared familicide perpetrators with perpetrators of single domestic homicides and filicides. They found that familicide perpetrators were more likely to be older men who were married and were less likely to have a record of violent offending than the other two groups – very much like Randy. Websdale (2010) notes that civil reputable perpetrators like Randy go unnoticed; they fit neatly into the social order, are seen as respectable and responsible, are employed in well-regarded occupations and fulfil their traditional gender roles. Therefore, socio-demographically, Randy *looks* very much like the general sketch of a familicide perpetrator and appears to fit with some of the civil reputable characteristics described by Websdale.

Randy's behaviour at the crime scene suggests that he engaged in the civil reputable practice of 'killing with care' (Websdale, 2010, p 212). He used just enough violence to end his victims' lives and there are suggestions that he cared for the bodies of Shelly and Laurel by wrapping them in sheets. Websdale stated that such men may kill family members while they sleep and this could well have been true in relation to Emily. Her body was found at the back of the home on the ground level and she appeared to have fallen from the upper floor during the structural collapse of the house; the coroner suggested that she was lying horizontally with her torso facing up at or around the time of death (British Columbia Coroners Service, 2016a). This gives rise to the possibility that she may have been lying down in her bedroom when she died. Therefore his offence and post-offence behaviour also locates Randy on the civil reputable rather than the livid coercive side of the familicide spectrum.

A range of explanations are offered for the acts carried out by familicide perpetrators. Wilson et al (1995) argue that their actions are due to a 'proprietary conception of his wife and family' (1995, p 289), a feeling of ownership over them and as such, a sense of entitlement to decide their fates. Wilson et al's 'despondent' type of familicide perpetrator views familicide as 'an act of mercy or rescue' (1995, p 288). Liem and Reichelmann (2014) argue that a loss of control over the family and family life are key motivating factors for these men. They also identify a subset of *despondent husbands*, whose perceived inability to look after their family leads to despondency, depression and finally a familicide driven by pseudo-altruistic reasons. Yardley et al (2014) identified 'paranoid' perpetrators, who were driven by the fear that an external threat – real or imagined – would destroy their family, and believed that by killing their family they were protecting them from such a fate. From these contributions, we may therefore interpret Randy's decision making on behalf of others as something he saw as part of his family role – that of provider and protector, the one who believed he knew what was best for his family.

The small body of work exploring homicide-suicide also offers insights into the Janzen familicide. One such contribution is that of Stack (1997), who drew on the two 'currents' of lethal violence identified by Henry and Short (1954): homicidal and suicidal. Exploring homicide-suicides in Chicago, Stack argued that these events represent perpetrator attempts to address their central anxiety – not being able to live with or without the victim. Stack claimed that the homicides were a way of overcoming a sense of powerlessness and the suicides resulted from the guilt that ensued afterwards. Randy's actions could be interpreted in this light – unable to bear to see Emily suffer but equally unable to carry on without her – as he had suggested to Raymond Norfolk. Harper and Voight (2007) draw on Agnew's (1992) thesis of personal strain to argue that homicide-suicides demonstrate 'conflict intensity structures' (2007, p 310), including excessive dependence, assumed responsibility, unequal relationships, hostility and precipitating crises like illness, divorce or financial ruin. Assumed responsibility appeared to be evident in Randy's character as someone who had long taken it upon himself to look after other people and do what he considered best for them – from playing the role of the big brother to his bandmates in Marauder to taking the ultimate decisions about his victims' fates in 2015. In relation to familicide-suicides specifically, Harper and Voight claim that the perpetrator feels a sense of failure because particular goals or needs have been blocked. Their families have either contributed towards the failure or will become the victims of the failure's consequences. Randy indeed seemed to feel that there was a failure – a failure to solve Emily's health problems – but whether he felt that this failure was *his alone* is debatable. One other interesting study is that of Liem et al (2009a) around filicide-*para*suicide, where perpetrators had killed their child and made a serious attempt to end their own lives. In such cases, because older men's self-concept is well established in middle age, they have difficulty responding to life-changing events. They become despondent and depressed, keeping their troubles to themselves and not displaying outward aggression to loved ones prior to the filicide. Liem et al (2009a) also argued the perpetrator's relationship with the victim was characterised by high levels of dependency, to the extent that the perpetrator often considered the victim as part of the self, not as an autonomous individual. As such, the perpetrator's actions are an attempt to protect the self-concept.

When reconsidered in light of this study, the comments reported earlier that Emily was 'everything' to her father and that he loved her 'more than anything' can take on new meanings, suggesting a heightened degree of enmeshment where Randy's sense of self did not simply overlap with Emily's but began to map onto it.

The aforementioned theses are helpful in considering what type of familicide perpetrator Randy was and offering tentative explanations for his actions. However, in terms of why he chose to kill his family – when thousands of other men in similar situations to him have not – there is not yet a conclusive answer. Many parents have children who experience chronic and severe ill health. Many of these parents describe their children as being everything to them and loving them more than anything. However, very few of these parents kill their children and other family members and take their own lives. How was Randy different? The key to this question may lie within Websdale's (2010) unique analysis focusing on the emotional styles of familicide perpetrators. Emotion is often an uncomfortable topic for criminology, particularly given its historically positivistic tendency to quantify in order to explain (Young, 2011). However, Websdale (2010) points to the importance of management of identity, which necessitates the unpicking of a complex web of individual, family, community and cultural factors. Civil reputable perpetrators in particular expend considerable emotional energy in managing others' impressions of them and their families. They are driven by powerlessness, brought about by the accumulation of shame. This emotion – alongside alienation and humiliation – is experienced in a visceral and amplified manner by familicide perpetrators. While livid coercive perpetrators mask these emotions with anger, violence and aggression, civil reputable perpetrators repress and internalise them, conforming to modern social expectations that one should limit and control displays of acute emotion, particularly in public. The shame they experience leads to social disconnection and a nominal sense of self. Websdale argues that civil reputable perpetrators have often experienced rigid, authoritarian parenting as children. Randy was raised in a farming family who had helped establish the Bethel Mennonite Church. Some behavioural expectations would have applied here, even if they did not encompass the aforementioned parenting styles. The values and norms of respectability, morality, traditional gender roles and a strong work ethic would seem important for life on a farm as a descendant of a church founder. Randy may have been isolated to a degree in his adult life – at least from *some* sources of emotional support. He had not seen or spoken to Shane Dwight for many years and both of his parents had died, his mother most recently in August 2014. There did not appear to be kinship links and he was no longer a member of the church community. This may well have been the backdrop against which Randy lived a life 'full of tension and apprehension about the future, often quietly worrying away [his] days' (Websdale, 2010, p 176). The ongoing repression of emotion and impression management work is a form of 'emotional constipation' (Websdale, 2010, p 224) for civil reputable perpetrators, which creates difficulties in coping with potentially significant issues that loom over the family. Heightened levels of shame and acute social isolation combine to create the toxic conditions in which familicide becomes the only remaining flight option for these men.

Websdale's thesis is valuable because it helps develop insights into Randy as a man who may have *looked* like the thousands of respectable and upstanding fathers in our local communities but who *felt* in a different way. His feelings of shame, humiliation and isolation were more significant in nature and extent, and the unique combination of these emotions may have led to the writing of a lethal script. However, one key element of the broader context in which these events occurred remains unexplored – networked media. How did Randy become so isolated and keep his acute emotions so hidden in an era in which we are supposedly constantly in touch, connected and visible? The next section explores the media lives of Randy, Laurel and Emily in an attempt to consider how their practices could shed further light upon the familicide and help broaden insights into civil reputable familicide perpetrators.

The Janzen's media lives

Randy, Laurel and Emily all had social media profiles, and as such, engaged in the media practices of showing, presencing and archiving within broader cultural and structural contexts. This section considers what they *did* in relation to this media, the stories they told about their lives and the extent to which their lives were connected through it. In so doing, the author hopes to explore the fine detail of the family members' complex narratives and as such, situate the familicide in a broader cultural and structural context. This section is divided into subsections exploring practices around different social media platforms.

Instagram

Laurel began posting images to Instagram in November 2012 and posted 134 images between 23 November 2012 and 20 April 2015. The final three images Laurel posted on Instagram were of the family's golden retriever dog Sophie sitting on a lawn (cloudsinmycoffee59, 2015b), Emily and Sophie wearing Vancouver Canuck's t-shirts (cloudsinmycoffee59, 2015c), and a picture of flowers, a greetings card, chocolates and gifts, accompanied by a comment thanking Emily for her birthday presents (cloudsinmycoffee59, 2015c). Emily posted 175 images on Instagram between 12 January 2013 and 23 April 2015. The final images in Emily's archive are a picture of her with a friend in Dr Seuss-style theatre make-up (Emily Janzen_1, 2015a), a mirrored selfie of her wearing a new hat bearing the slogan 'NEAT DUDE' (Emily Janzen_1, 2015b) and a then-and-now-style image of her as an adolescent alongside a more recent photograph (Emily Janzen_1, 2015c). As such, the final pictures posted to Instagram by Laurel and Emily appear routine, upbeat and fun loving, with no indication of what was to come.

Emily features heavily throughout Laurel's Instagram archive, appearing or being tagged in a quarter of all posts. Laurel also features in Emily's archive and is referred to in around one tenth of her posts. Mother and daughter were following each other's accounts and frequently liked or commented on them. Both of their profiles include images of them together – Emily as a baby with Laurel, mother and daughter on birthdays and Mother's Days – and of gifts Emily bought for her mother.

Laurel's first posts in 2012 relate to Emily singing and acting, including a picture of Emily performing on stage, her arms outstretched as she sung, and one of her singing solo at a church Christmas service. This is similar to a relatively small number of videos Laurel uploaded to YouTube between May 2010 and August 2013; all were of Emily singing and acting at a range of performing arts events, concerts and workshops. Emily's earlier posts also refer to her singing and performing, but coverage of this topic tapers off during 2014 and 2015. Both Laurel's and Emily's posts became increasingly diverse and extensive over time; individual topics came to the fore and faded into the background at different times. Laurel's archive included content relating to Emily's migraines, cooking, fashion, pets and family occasions. Emily's archive included selfies – which many others liked and commented on – and images of pets and food, and pictures showing her with friends or taking exercise. Emily's Instagram tells the story of her journey through many milestones of young adulthood, including her first legal drink, her high school graduation ceremony and her prom.

One key point of note was that more than a third (n=48, 35.8%) of Laurel's Instagram posts could be classed as memes. These memes are sometimes humorous and inspirational; as well as those mentioned earlier in the chapter, examples include 'I can't keep calm, it's my daughter's birthday' (cloudsinmycoffee59, 2015e) and 'Talking about our problems is our greatest addiction. Break the habit. Talk about your joys – Rita Schiano' (cloudsinmycoffee59, 2013a). However, most of the memes Laurel posts relate to the harmful or negative behaviour of other people. Examples include: 'Some people create their own storms, then get upset when it rains' (cloudsinmycoffee59, 2014f); 'I don't hate you, I'm just disappointed you turned into everything you said you'd never be' (cloudsinmycoffee59, 2014g); 'Never push a loyal person to the point where they no longer give a damn' (cloudsinmycoffee59, 2014h); 'Women should empower each other instead of being so hateful and envious of one another' (cloudsinmycoffee59, 2015f). Four memes also make reference to Emily's migraines. On one about the failing of people to respect those with invisible disabilities, she comments '#preachingit' (cloudsinmycoffee59, 2014i). On another, which reads 'HOPE: Hold On Pain Ends', she comments 'Get better Emily [heart emoji]' (cloudsinmycoffee59, 2013b). In relation to the meme 'The struggle is part of the story', Laurel adds '#mygirl #staystrong #gonnagetbetter #hangin' (cloudsinmycoffee59, 2014j). In contrast, Emily only mentions migraines once with reference to a novelty pill box that a friend gave to her for Christmas. The box is shaped like a macaroon, one of Emily's favourite treats: 'Macaroon pill case for a very sick emmy #earlychristmaspresent #mybestfriendrules #adorable' (EmilyJanzen_1, 2014c). Food increases in prominence throughout 2014 and 2015 as a key topic in Emily's posts. She shares her liking for cakes and fast food as well as healthy salads, smoothies and organic foods, sharing her excitement on days when she indulges in the former: 'Cheat day is the best day – Chocolate covered strawberry inspired Nicecream!' (EmilyJanzen_1, 2015d). Emily's posts of her with friends in 2014 and 2015 become increasingly reminiscent in nature. One example is an old picture of Emily with two friends at a performance, all wearing similar outfits. She writes 'Throwback with my two sopranos #tbt #idaho #2011 #lovethem', to which several friends reply, one stating 'OMG I MISS THIS AND YOU TOO' (EmilyJanzen_1, 2014d).

Randy's appearances in Emily and Laurel's Instagram archives are few and far between. He only appears in four of Laurel's posts. A video shows Randy and Sophie the dog lying on a sofa (cloudsinmycoffee59, 2015g). Randy can be identified by the tattoos on his forearm, but his head is out of shot as the video focuses on Sophie, who is playing with a chew toy. Two images have been mentioned previously in this chapter: the 1992 picture of Randy and Laurel on a cruise (cloudsinmycoffee, 2014c) and the 2002 picture of Randy and Emily on the beach at Cultus Lake (cloudsinmycoffee, 2014e). The other image, posted in June 2014 – and indeed the only one to include all three family members – appears to have been taken in the family's rear garden (cloudsinmycoffee59, 2014k). Emily is wearing her prom dress and is standing between Randy and Laurel; Laurel has her arm around Emily's waist and Emily's hand is on Laurel's shoulder. Randy appears less tactile. There are two mentions of Randy in Emily's Instagram archive. In November 2013, she posted an image of a bunch of flowers, commenting 'My dad knows how to cheer me up #hospital #sucks #flowers #daddysgirl' (EmilyJanzen_1, 2013a). The only picture of Randy in Emily's archive is an image of her and Randy sitting in the front seats in a car; both are smiling and Emily is holding a pack of macaroons. About the image, she commented '… on my cheat day eating macaroons with the father' and goes on to state that they had bought them from a local shop (EmilyJanzen_1, 2014e). Perhaps not surprisingly, this image received several comments after the familicide from people who do not appear to have known Emily: 'This guy is her dad and he killed her', 'Really?', 'That's scary'. However, one of Emily's friends was quick to respond and shared her own views and memories of Randy:

> … her dad was a really nice guy honestly. He was just sick. But he wasn't always that way. I knew him and he was so gentle and kind … I know he has no right [to kill her] Emily was some of my closest friends and I get it but he's not as big of an ass as you may think. (EmilyJanzen_1, 2014e)

Twitter

Given the large volume of content in and around Laurel and Emily's Twitter accounts, Chorus TweetVis software (Brooker et al, 2016) was used to explore trends and patterns and identify content of interest to this research. Laurel began tweeting on in March 2012 and sent a total of 1451 tweets between then and 25 April 2015. Her tweet volume varied over this time period. She sometimes tweeted very little; for example, in a 12-week period in the winter of late 2012 and early 2013, she only sent seven tweets while during the same time frame during the summer of 2013, she sent 218. Sentiment analysis (Brooker et al, 2016) suggests that Laurel's tweets up until the summer of 2014 were largely positive in nature; however, during and after this period, they were mostly negative. Laurel had 47 followers and was following 235 other accounts. The accounts she followed covered a broad range of topics, but the most recent additions included those of people writing about experiences of trauma, Huffpost Women (the *Huffington Post's* women's interest blog), singer Lisa Fischer, migraine bloggers and support organisations, television subscription service Netflix, the American newsmagazine television programme 60 minutes and actor Brian Cranston. Laurel's last tweets were all retweets,[5] one being a humorous comment from the Twitter account of the Netflix television series Unbreakable Kimmy Schmidt (laureljanz, 2015a) and the other from two accounts on the topic of migraines (laureljanz, 2015b, 2015c). Laurel also liked a wide range of tweets posted by others between 24 and 25 April 2015, including a post by Chelsea Clinton, daughter of the former US President Bill Clinton, about different types of coffee, a CBS news item about television personality Bruce Jenner and a tweet including a trailer of the film Black Mass starring actor Johnny Depp.

Emily's Twitter feed began in February 2012, around the same period as Laurel's. She sent 3,080 tweets between then and 26 April 2015. The number of tweets she sent increased significantly in September 2013; prior to this she was only sending an average of three or four tweets per week, but from September 2013 she sent between 12 and 46 per week until she died. Sentiment analysis (Brooker et al, 2016) suggests that Emily's tweets were largely positive in nature. She had 184 followers and was following 297 other accounts. Her followers were largely individuals as opposed to organisations. The accounts she followed included those of her Chilliwack friends and a wide range of actors, musicians and television presenters, and also included humorous accounts like Emergency Cute Stuff, a Twitter feed featuring pictures of animals. Emily's final activities on Twitter included a retweet of a humorous post from the Kardashians Reactions feed (emmers_janzen, 2015a), several tweets relating to a Vancouver Canucks ice hockey game she appeared to be watching (see, for example, emmers_janzen, 2015b) and a few funny tweets relating to a doctor Emily thought was attractive, such as 'I want to bite my docs bum and that's bad' (emmers_janzen, 2015c) and 'Doctors shouldn't allowed to be so damn SEXY' (emmers_janzen, 2015d). Emily also liked several tweets including one by posted by an artist friend, two posted by online comedian Matt King and tweets relating to the Canucks game.

Emily and Laurel did not follow each other on Twitter and did not appear to communicate via this medium either.[6] While Laurel included Emily's username in 57 tweets, the reverse was not true and most of Emily's Twitter conversations happened within a small group of friends; hence, there does not appear to be the same degree of interconnection between Emily and Laurel's Twitter accounts as was seen on Instagram. This is perhaps not all that surprising, given the broad range of differing interests that Emily and Laurel tweeted about compared with the Instagram posts, which appeared to focus more heavily on family life.

With regard to overall patterns of usage, a consistently high proportion of Laurel's tweets contained links to other websites, suggesting that she was sharing information that she thought others might find interesting or useful. A smaller proportion of Emily's tweets contained URLs, or website addresses. The early part of Laurel's archive from mid-2012 to spring 2013 includes tweets about Emily's musical performances, competitions and trips. However, after this point, Laurel's mentions of Emily tend to focus on her migraines. 'Migraine' and words relating to it are among Laurel's most frequently used words on Twitter and there are many retweets from accounts offering migraine information and support. However, other tweets are in Laurel's own words and describe numerous episodes of illness and her frustrations during these periods. Illustrative examples are provided in chronological order below.

> Back in the ER. Day 13 of a migraine from hell (laureljanz, 2013a)
>
> Really missing @emmersjanzen #sad #ChristmasAgony #ER #packed no doctors #lovemyfamily #bestrongemily (laureljanz, 2013b)
>
> My daughter has had a #migraine for 11 months. Don't know what else to do #sadtweets #chronicmigraines #stop (laureljanz, 2014a)
>
> So lost. My daughter has suffered #daily #migraine #headaches for 515 days #broken (laureljanz, 2015d)
>
> Watching someone I love in unbearable pain everyday for 18 months and I feel helpless #migraine #weneedhelp @FraserHealth (laureljanz, 2015e)

By contrast, Emily did not use the migraine hashtag, and expressed feelings about her migraines in a different manner. She rarely used the word 'migraine', instead using terms like 'sick' and 'healthy', including humour and sarcasm in her posts on the topic and focusing on the impact of the migraines on her everyday life and friendships. Examples of Emily's tweets regarding her migraines are as follows:

> Being sick is just so blaaaahhh (emmers_janzen, 2013a)
>
> I. Hate. The. Hospital. I. Am. Fed. Up. Meh. (emmers_janzen, 2014a)
>
> I'd love to be healthy annnnnnytime now (emmers_janzen, 2014b)
>
> WHY AM I ALWAYS SICK HOLY MOLY (emmers_janzen, 2014c)
>
> Being sick and having no one is the best life to live I highly recommend (emmers_janzen, 2015e)
>
> I need this life to be over (emmers_janzen, 2015f
>
> I'm so tired of people making me feel guilty for being too sick to hangout. Do you think I want to sit at home or in the hospital all day? NO (emmers_janzen, 2015g)
>
> Whenever I start to feel sorry for myself, I just thank God I'm still alive. I complain about all the pain, but at least I'm here to feel it (emmers_janzen, 2015h)

Local news media reported heavily on Emily's migraine-related tweets after she died, particularly those with a depressive tone. However, there was much less focus on Emily's other tweets, particularly positive tweets and those about different topics. On the same day that she was tweeting 'I need this life to be over' (emmers_janzen, 2015f), she was also posting about her dating frustrations – '"I care about you" *has a different girlfriend week later* #ihateboys' (emmers_janzen, 2015i) – and retweeting others' posts about fashion, dogs and food. Prior to this, Emily appeared to be planning for the future, tweeting for example, 'Picking a career is hard af' #whatdoidowithmylife' (emmers_janzen, 2015j) and 'Maybe I should start singing again' (emmers_janzen, 2015k). Emily's most frequently used words on Twitter included 'like', 'love', 'life', 'people' and 'happy'. Emily therefore expressed an upbeat outlook on life through her Twitter account, despite media reports that suggested otherwise. Her tweets are humorous and self-deprecating, and the content includes many of the issues and interests common among women in their late teens.

In terms of Randy's presence on Emily's Twitter feed, there are five tweets that mention him. This is a relatively small proportion of Emily's archive of over 3,000 tweets, but the tweets are all positive and suggest a loving father–daughter relationship, as was the case in relation to Emily's mentions of him on Instagram.

My dad is my bestfriend and I'm so proud of that (emmers_janzen, 2013b)

My dad just said ass tea at taco bell god dad (emmers_janzen, 2014d)

My dad: I discovered youtube like 3 weeks ago. His buddy: What the hell is youtube? (emmers_janzen, 2014e)

Don't know what I'd do without my dad (emmers_janzen, 2014f)

My dad watches vines with me #bestdadever (emmers_janzen, 2014g)

Tweets in which Randy is mentioned also represent a very small proportion of Laurel's Twitter archive, as was the case with her Instagram account. She only appears to refer to him twice, in 2012. One tweet reads: 'Dinner at Deluxe in White Rock with dear hubby. Gorgeous sunset over Semiahmoo and yummy lobster ravioli' (laureljanz, 2012a). The other tweet mentions him by name and describes him using what might be interpreted as disparaging and emasculating language: 'Happy Birthday to my timid little husband Randy Janzen' (laureljanz, 2012b). While Randy appears minimally in both Emily and Laurel's Twitter accounts, Emily's representation of her relationship with him is more recent and positive in nature.

Facebook

Turning to explore the family's Facebook accounts, it is clear that this is the one social media platform where the media lives of Laurel, Randy and Emily linked up. They all had Facebook accounts, were Facebook friends with each other, liked many of each other's posts and occasionally commented on content that the other family member had posted. These interconnections will be explored in this section through a detailed examination of each person's Facebook account.

There are many parallels between Laurel's Facebook and Instagram accounts. The images she posted on Facebook appear to be largely the same images uploaded to her Instagram account. Emily liked many of Laurel's Facebook posts and occasionally commented on them. Laurel very rarely wrote or commented on Facebook, and when she did it was often in direct response to comments posted by friends. For example, Laurel posted a picture of her and Emily in a restaurant on 30 July 2014 (Sinclair Janzen, 2014a). Emily commented 'Love you momma xoxo', and a friend named Lisa stated 'You have a beautiful daughter Laurel!' to which Laurel replied 'Thanks Lisa'. Although Laurel did not post images of Randy on Facebook, he regularly liked the images that she posted. Randy once commented on Laurel's Facebook page too. This was in response to Laurel uploading the 1992 cruise picture to her Facebook page (Sinclair Janzen, 2014b), when he commented: 'My God you are so beautiful Laurel!!' Laurel in turn liked his comment.

Emily's Facebook page was very similar to Laurel's in terms of her posting habits; she tended to post pictures and links rather than text-based status updates, writing in her own words only when responding to comments. Emily's Facebook archive includes many of the same pictures as her Instagram archive and Emily regularly changed her profile picture to her most recent selfie. The pictures she posts with her friends elicit similar comments to those on Instagram in terms of the friends missing each other, particularly around the summer of 2014, when many of them were moving away to start courses at colleges and universities. There is a sense that Emily is a participant in many of the events captured on Facebook and Instagram – for example, graduation and prom – but a spectator in others – notably her friends going on to the next stage of their lives.

Randy and Laurel both liked most of Emily's pictures, as did some of her 505 Facebook friends. Laurel did not tend to comment on Emily's pictures of status updates, but Randy did; indeed, he commented on six of her posts in the year prior to the familicide. Randy posted 'My beautiful daughter!' in response to one of Emily's last selfies (Janzen, Emily, 2015a), an image of her in a green and white spotted dress wearing glamorous make-up. Also in April 2015, in a change from her usual picture-posting practices, Emily posted several links to inspirational stories about people who live with chronic pain and disability as well as a link to an article entitled '16 things people in chronic pain want you to know'. Emily commented on the article, stating: 'This is so important. As someone who has been suffering with chronic pain for over two years, it's 100% relatable' (Janzen, Emily, 2015b). Randy commented in response to this: 'I found this very interesting and informative. I don't think any of us realize how difficult it must be to live every day with pain. I love you Emily and admire the strength and courage you have shown. Stay strong little buddy! xoxoxo Daddio' (Janzen, Emily, 2015b). Randy also commented on a picture of flowers, hot cross buns and a cup of tea that Emily had posted: 'Beautiful way to start an Easter morning!' (Janzen, Emily, 2015c). There were three occasions in 2014 when Randy commented on Emily's posts. One was in response to another of Emily's selfies – 'Emily you are awesome [emoji blowing a kiss]' – to which Emily responded, 'Love ya daddio [heart emoji]' (Janzen, Emily, 2014b). After the death of

Emily's paternal grandmother Katharina Janzen in August 2014, Emily uploaded a picture of herself as a child with Katharina, commenting: 'The kindest soul I've ever known. No one could have made me feel more loved than you. Rest in paradise, Grandma [three heart emojis]' (Janzen, Emily, 2014c). Randy responded, 'She was so proud of you Em and she loved you so much' (Janzen, Emily, 2014c). In April 2014, Emily shared some exciting news on Facebook – 'Accepted to UBC for Opera Performance [smiley emoji] life couldn't be better' – to which Randy, who was the first to post a comment, stated: 'So proud of you Emily!' (Janzen, Emily, 2014a).

Randy's Facebook page was the only social media account that could be found for him. This is not particularly surprising, given that Emily had alluded to his unfamiliarity with mainstream networked media in her 2014 tweet about him discovering YouTube (emmers_janzen, 2014e). Randy had 63 Facebook friends, 17 of whom were tagged as having grown up in the Langley area. Among them was Shane Dwight, discussed earlier in the chapter relation to his newspaper interviews, who had not seen Randy for around 10 years but at the time of writing appeared to live in the local area. Whether he did so at the time of the familicide is not clear, but if so, it adds to the evidence of Randy's social isolation. Randy's profile states that he lives in Rosedale, is from Langley and is married, although, unlike many couples who have their own Facebook profiles, he does not say who is married *to*.

Randy's Facebook profile is not very extensive compared with the well-populated feeds of his wife and daughter. He did not appear to post pictures of Emily and only posted one of him and Laurel, despite being active in supporting their performances of self on their own profiles through likes and comments. There are only a handful of status updates, all of which are changes to his profile picture. The most recent was posted in August 2014 and is a selfie of him and Laurel (Janzen, Randy, 2014a). They are both wearing sunglasses and the reflection of Randy's hand holding a small camera or phone can be seen in the lenses of their shades. The photo appears to have been taken in their rear garden, as there are trees in the background with rays of sunshine streaming through them. Eight people liked the photo, including Emily, but not Laurel. Randy also updated his profile picture two days earlier (Janzen, Randy, 2014b). In the image he is outdoors in what looks like a yard, as there is a shed in the background. The tattoos on his arms are visible – he is wearing a sleeveless t-shirt with the words Novia Scotia and a picture of puffins on it, perhaps a holiday souvenir. He is holding a blue ball and green ball in one hand, has a small white ball in the other and is walking towards the camera. The picture was liked by five people, including Emily and his friend Shane Dwight, but again, Laurel was not among this group. One friend commented on the photo: 'That looks like one serious bocce player! [smiley emoji]'. Randy replies: 'Can you tell that I am not winning?' The post prior to this is nearly two years earlier in July 2012 (Janzen, Randy, 2012) when Randy updated his cover photo to an image of a beach at sunset and the only other post is when the beach picture was uploaded to his profile in 2010.

The status update that Randy posted prior to taking his own life stands in stark contrast to the rest of his Facebook profile. The post is 379 words long, considerably lengthier than any of the other posts or comments he had made prior to this. In addition, the post is largely free of grammatical and spelling errors, which suggests that it has been carefully prepared and read over prior to posting. What Randy did not do in relation to the post is also interesting. Unlike the other perpetrators discussed in this book, he did not post a picture of his victims. Rather, he shielded them from the prying eyes of others. This was consistent with his actions at the crime scene, 'killing with care' (Websdale, 2010) by wrapping bodies in sheets. Furthermore, if the house fire was started by him – something that has not been definitively established – this would also have been served to prevent others from looking at the bodies of his wife and daughter.

Much of the reflection narrative (Brookman, 2015) within the post focused solely on Emily, portraying her a favourable manner. She was presented as childlike – 'little girl', 'sweetheart' and 'baby'. However, she was also portrayed as autonomous – '*Emily* had tried everything'. This created a sense of her as suspended, occupying an uneasy territory between childhood and adulthood. He emphasised the longstanding nature of her illness and used strong words and graphic descriptions, almost as if to counter any dispute as to its significance – 'severe', 'excruciating', 'wretching into a puke tray'. He presented Emily's music as an integral part of her identity and personhood, excluding references to her other interests and passions. He used the first person frequently in both action and reflection narratives: '*I* have done some of the worst things *I could* have ever imagined a person doing', '*I* just could not see my little girl hurt', '*I* took a gun and shot her in the head', '*I* shot Laurel', '*I* did not want her to live with this shame *I* have caused all alone', '*I* have great remorse', '*I* am taking full responsibility' (emphasis added throughout). Emily's migraines were presented as an external threat (Yardley et al, 2014) that no one had any control over, and Randy did not blame himself or others for failing to tackle them. He came across a man who was accepting responsibility for his criminal actions, but presenting them as the justifiable solution to an uncontrollable external threat. His role as the decision maker was also evident in his description of Emily's discussion of future plans, suggesting in comments such as 'I wish sweetheart' that her plans were futile, that she was never going to get better and that she was displaying an innocent naiveté. The fact that her friends had moved on is presented as something of significant magnitude, almost as if it had happened years ago, whereas it had only been a matter of months since some of them had moved away to university or college. The despondency about the situation (Liem and Reichelmann, 2014) was clear. However, it was *his* interpretation of the situation that carried weight; he knew best and furthermore it was his actions that led to the fantasised, dream-like and perfect depiction of her later in the post, with the familicide presented as an act of mercy (Wilson et al, 1995). This hints at the proprietorial characteristics of familicide perpetrators identified by Wilson et al (1995), as does some of terminology chosen by Randy in the post, like '*my* daughter' as opposed to *our* daughter, and '*my* little family' (emphasis added). Shelly was included in this proprietorial conceptualisation of family; Randy perhaps felt a sense of excessive responsibility for her by virtue of her disabilities and vulnerability due to the fact she was living alone for the first time following the death of their mother the previous August. While his actions were wholly disproportionate, a unique combination of heightened shame and isolation (Websdale, 2010) precipitated the familicide – feelings that were also clear in the post.

Randy explicitly used the word 'shame'. Alongside other phrases such as 'all alone', the post seemed to embody the civil reputable perpetrator, wracked with feelings of isolation and alienation (Websdale, 2010). This is further evidenced in the way Randy referred to Laurel. He never referred to her as his wife or to them as a couple, instead using collective terms like 'my family'. He expressed empathy for her as a mother and justified her killing solely in relation to this role. All of this would appear to indicate that, as is true of many civil reputable perpetrators, Randy even felt isolated and alone within his own family (Websdale, 2010).

One might interpret the outpouring of emotion in the Facebook post as entirely inconsistent with the civil reputable familicide perpetrator, someone who adheres strongly to the social norms of repressing and controlling emotional displays, particularly in a public-facing context (Websdale, 2010). However, it could also be argued that the Facebook post is an exercise in impression management (Websdale, 2010). Randy appeared to put significant effort into managing others' impressions of himself and his family, supporting Emily's identity as a talented opera singer and being excessively complimentary towards Laurel in his comment on the 1992 photograph. The Facebook post may have represented an attempt to maintain the positive light in which other members of his family were seen by other people. Randy shows little such concern for others' impressions of him, labelling himself 'dirt' and using the term 'murder' before anyone else has the opportunity to assign this term to the homicides. There is no real sense of Randy's identity or personhood beyond his role as Emily's father, signing off as 'Daddio', a word unique to Emily and Randy's father–daughter relationship. These points further reinforce the ignominy and nominal sense of self that runs throughout the post.

Familicide and life in media

Randy's media practices highlight several important points regarding the significance of networked media in the life of this civil reputable familicide perpetrator. In relation to showing, Randy focused on *showing others* – Emily and Laurel – through commenting on and liking their posts. While the existence of his Facebook profile and his list of friends meant that he had some sense of presence to others in media, the profile was sparsely populated and rarely updated. He appeared more concerned with reinforcing and supporting Emily – and to a lesser extent Laurel – in their showing, presencing and archiving practices. While Randy's Facebook presence may have given the illusion of sociability and a support network, his identity came to centre largely on family roles, particularly that of Emily's father. His media practices strongly indicate a nominal sense of self (Websdale, 2010). While Emily and Laurel's archives are extensive, rich and detailed, enabling powerful insights into their everyday lived experiences, Randy's archive is skeletal in comparison, leaving behind more questions than answers as to who he was.

Much emotional work (Websdale, 2010) was performed in media by Laurel, particularly in relation to Emily's migraines. Laurel regularly expressed her sense of helplessness and vented her frustrations at the perceived failing of local health services on Twitter. She shared this space with Emily, tagging her or referring to in her posts. Instagram was also *their* space, one where Laurel expressed emotion in a more subtle way through reposting memes. In effect, Laurel actively took *ownership* of Emily's illness in media. Furthermore, Emily and Laurel's relationship was highly visible in media, their presence to others as mother and daughter well established through social networking sites.

Randy was largely absent from these networked spaces, a shadowy figure making rare and fleeting appearances, a 'timid little husband'. He was often depicted as a ghost from the past – the man posing for a picture with Laurel on a cruise ship in 1992, the man on the beach with Emily in 2002 – not someone who was viscerally connected and present. Randy and Laurel's relationship as lived through media was blurry and for the most part invisible. While the couple liked and commented on Emily's Facebook posts and offered her supportive words, they did not do the same for each other to such a degree. Did this compound the sense of isolation and alienation that Websdale (2010) has identified among civil reputable perpetrators like Randy? Networked media was not embedded in his everyday life to the same extent that it was for his wife and daughter. While Emily and Laurel were the central actors on the main stage, Randy's role was less visible – at times a supporting actor, but mostly working behind the scenes.

This theme of marginality continued in Randy's familicide post, evident in both the action and reflection elements of his narrative (Brookman, 2015). While the post was expressive and emotive (Aspden and Hayward, 2015), an outpouring of sentiment appearing to contradict the typically restrained and repressed style of the civil reputable perpetrator (Websdale, 2010), it served a key purpose. This was to take some control of the narrative around the events, to show Emily, Laurel, Shelly and himself in accordance with how he thought people should see them before others began to apply their interpretations. The post alluded to broader cultural norms and expectations around young people's life trajectories and milestones – transitions from childhood to adulthood, realisation of potential, achievement and independence. Randy perceived Emily's goals as blocked by her migraines and as such, he ascribed a 'crisis of being' to her (Hayward and Young, 2004). Her talents were untapped, her potential unrealised, she was left behind while others had moved on.

The familicide Facebook post would be the first and last time that Randy would share his shame with others. He chose to post the note on his publicly accessible Facebook page, so one might assume that he anticipated it being seen by thousands of people. It could also, however, be argued that he was not *aware* of the widely accessible nature of what he posted on his profile and assumed that only his Facebook friends would be able to see the post, their searching practices encompassing updates to his news feed. Randy appeared to have a very local focus – his Facebook likes encompassing mostly teams, individuals and organisations from his home province. In this light, it is difficult to present the Janzen familicide as a performance crime enacted for the camera (Surette, 2015a) or the familicide post as a conscious self-marketing exercise within a wound culture (Seltzer, 2007, 2008) where the perpetrator knows that others will be drawn to the trauma and suffering of the victims. His intended audience may well have been limited to local people, colleagues and friends – those with whom he wanted to share his narrative of the familicide and whose impressions of his family he wanted to manage.

Randy's media practices are suggestive of a sense of enmeshment with Emily. Websdale argues that perpetrators like Randy 'view their family members as extensions of themselves as opposed to autonomous individuals' (2010, p 205). He further argues that their 'ontological insecurity and nominal sense of belonging ... made it difficult for them to recognize the autonomy and individuality of others. This is one of the reasons why they were able to murder the ones they professed to love and care for' (2010, p 224). However, the author suggests that this applies somewhat differently in this case. Randy appeared to view *himself* as an extension of Emily. His media practices were mostly premised on reinforcing the self that she was presenting – the opera singer, the successful performer. Randy was raised in an influential religious family, but later abandoned the church. His workmates noted his constant talking about Emily. He was overly dependent on his family role as her father for a sense of his own identity (Yardley et al, 2014). As such, he was living vicariously through her. Her blocked goals (Harper and Voight, 2007) became his blocked goals. The amplified and visceral way in which familicide perpetrators experience emotion (Websdale, 2010) meant that Emily's migraines, in delaying her transitions to adulthood and a successful life as an opera singer, appeared more significant to Randy than they were to Emily. The stunting of her ambitions represented a form existential death for Randy; her disappointment became his devastation, her homicide a form of suicide by proxy (Frazer, 1975).

For Randy, networked media functioned in different ways for different purposes. His general everyday usage of Facebook served the purpose of supporting his family's sense of presence to others through reinforcing their narrative identities. In relation to the familicide, his post enabled him to engage in impression management on behalf of his family, fulfilling his perceived responsibility as their sole protector. The civil reputable characteristics that Randy exhibited are clear within his media practices. The way he experienced networked media offers a unique window into the performance of his narrative identity. It can be argued therefore that such an analysis offers a window into the lives of these very private men. While they blend into the background and go largely unseen, their media practices may reveal their shame, isolation and nominal sense of self and as such, may enable us to access their experiences and sense of being in the world in a way that was not possible prior to contemporary networked media.

Randy's use of networked media appears wholly different from that of Derek, the perpetrator considered in Chapter Five. Randy did very little with networked media, and when he did use it, it was for the purpose of reinforcing and defending the identities of others. Derek used networked media to place himself centre-stage, engaging in elaborate performances of a fantasy self, casting others in supporting roles. As such, the two engaged in different media practices to achieve different outcomes. What does unite them, however, is the culturally and socially rooted nature of their media practices. While Derek called into play the values and behaviours associated with machismo, sports and the American Dream, Randy drew on the role of the protector and provider within a context of Canadian middle-class respectability. In Chapter Seven, the theme of evoking these valued identities continues. The focus shifts to a female perpetrator, Amanda, who killed her former father-in-law and expressed desires to go on a killing spree. The case will highlight the performance of valued gendered identities through networked media prior to, during and following the homicide.

Notes

[1] The term 'homicide' is used rather than 'murder' in this case because murder refers to a legal penalty for homicide rather than the act itself. Randy Janzen committed suicide following the killings and was therefore never subject to criminal justice proceedings. As such, it was not felt appropriate to use the term 'murder' with reference to this case.

[2] Throughout this chapter, grammatical errors and misspellings are left as they appear in the original source.

[3] 'Liking' a Facebook post is a quick and easy way to let someone know you have enjoyed their post without having to comment upon it.

[4] 'tbt' stands for 'throwback Thursday', where people post old pictures on their social media accounts on Thursdays.

[5] Retweets are messages posted originally by another user and shared more widely by others.

[6] People who follow each other on Twitter are able to send direct, private messages to each other but where this is not the case, a person people can communicate with another by including their username in a tweet. The person whose username has been included will receive a notification from Twitter alerting them to the tweet, to which they can reply. These tweets will be visible to all, unless they have placed restrictions on their accounts limiting the people who can view their tweets.

[7] 'af' is often used as the shortened form of 'as fuck'.

SEVEN

The murder of Charles Taylor

The murder

On 4 April 2015, 59-year-old Charles Taylor was murdered by his daughter-in-law, 24-year-old Amanda Taylor and her friend, 32-year-old Sean Ball. Amanda had travelled to Charles' house in Montgomery County, Virginia with Sean, who had picked her up in his car earlier that day. Together, the two had purchased a bayonet-style knife. They also had in their possession a tyre iron, which Sean concealed down his trousers, and various firearms including two pistols and a rifle. The weapons had been stolen from the house belonging to Sean's parents. Amanda later admitted that they had gone to Charles' home with the intention of killing him.

During the visit, the conversation turned to the topic of Rex Taylor, Amanda's late husband, who had committed suicide in August 2014. Amanda blamed Charles for Rex's suicide, firmly believing that he was responsible for Rex's drug abuse, which had become particularly problematic in the two years preceding his suicide. While Charles was sitting on his sofa, Amanda began to stab him repeatedly as she stood over him. Charles reached for the knife and as he did so, Sean swung the tyre iron and hit him five or six times, while Amanda continued to stab him. Charles' autopsy would later reveal that he was stabbed 31 times and suffered blunt force trauma to the head. Some of the stab wounds were so forceful that they went completely through his neck and arm. At a 2016 hearing, Amanda said of the killing, 'it was personal…. Because I wanted Charlie Taylor gone. He made me mad. I felt like he didn't deserve to be here anymore since Rex was gone' (*Commonwealth of Virginia v Taylor*, 2016, p 35).

A photograph of Amanda with Charles' dead body was taken on Sean's phone at the crime scene. Later that day this image was uploaded to Amanda's Tumblr blog and sent to an online friend who ran a serial killers website. Before leaving the scene, the pair also took money from Charles' wallet and told his bedridden father Allen that Charles had hurt his leg and they were going to take him to the hospital.

Following the murder, the two drove to Tennessee, where they spent the night. Amanda posted to her Facebook account early the following morning, 'I proudly did this for Rex. I love my children but charlie[1] killed my husband' (Taylor, 2015a). The pair then travelled to North Carolina. A police officer who interviewed Amanda later claimed that during the drive, 'they had discussed continuing, which she had called a spree ... prior to her husband's death they had discussed going on a murder spree' (*Commonwealth of Virginia v Taylor*, 2015a, p 181). Indeed, the pair had stopped and attempted to purchase ammunition at two separate stores during their journey. Amanda apparently became frustrated with Sean, who did not want to continue. He had taken some of her prescription medication and would not stop mumbling. Amanda described what happened next: 'I shot him in the throat so he would stop talking because he kept lying' (*Commonwealth of Virginia v Taylor*, 2016, p 45). She took a photograph of him on a phone because she did not want to look directly at him (*Commonwealth of Virginia v Taylor*, 2015a). On examining the photograph, she believed that he was dead. She left him on the side of a road and continued driving.

Believing she had killed Sean, Amanda turned once more to social media. One Instagram post featured images of Amanda and Sean in a news story and was accompanied by the following text:

> Everything I did was for the right reasons. I stabbed my father in law to death because he destroyed my husband with drugs ... depression. i wasn't the perfect wife but this was one last good thing i could do for rex i dont care what anyone thinks i loved rex more than the world. This was for you [heart emoji] seans dead, but I finally have closure with rex after charlie. If you keep looking for me more will die. Just let me get to the place rex and i always wanted and ill be free without having to kill more. Till we rot rex, till we fucking rot [heart emoji]. (Cited in Murdock, 2015)

Hours prior to her arrest, she posted a photograph of a hand gun in what appeared to be her lap on Instagram. She included the following text with the image:

> Alright...it's about that time. Im going to go find my husband in Hell and finally be at peace. I love you mom and my beautiful crazies, i know youll give them the life i just couldnt after everything. ([[Cited in]] Murdock, 2015)

Authorities used signals from Amanda's smartphone to establish her location. She failed to stop her vehicle when North Carolina State

Highway Patrol officers requested she do so. A high-speed chase ensued, which ended when police used a stinger device to stop the car. Sean was found at around 7pm later that day on the Blue Ridge Parkway in North Carolina and taken to hospital.

Amanda was charged with several offences, including second-degree murder, and was placed in a North Carolina county jail to await extradition to Virginia. Her second-degree murder charge was later replaced with a first-degree murder charge alongside federal charges in relation to attacking Sean and a probation violation relating to a 2012 felony. She was found guilty of first degree-murder in November 2015. The life sentence for the conviction was confirmed in February 2016, the judge commenting, 'It's evil, what you did.... You are evil personified' (*Commonwealth of Virginia v Taylor*, 2016, p 52). Sean was charged with second-degree murder on his release from hospital. This was later altered to first-degree murder and stood alongside other charges including probation violations. He pleaded guilty and received a prison sentence of 41 years. At the hearing in which he entered his plea, he apologised for the crime and said sorry to his family: 'They've always done their best for me and this is no way to show gratitude for the way they brought me up' (cited in Demmitt, 2016).

Considering the details outlined thus far, Charles' murder might be considered a 'revenge' (Brookman, 2005) or 'conflict resolution' (Polk, 1994). In such cases, the perpetrator has decided that violence is the *only* way to resolve a conflict and makes plans to physically harm the victim (Polk, 1994). In such cases, the victim and perpetrator have often known each other for a considerable period of time, having been friendly at the beginning of their relationship (Polk, 1994). The conflict is commonly a 'slow burn', which builds incrementally over time until one of the parties decides that violence is the only resolution and begins to plan accordingly (Polk, 1994). However, one key characteristic of conflict resolution homicides that the literature consistently reinforces is that such crimes are committed by *men* engaged in criminal subcultures. The male pronoun has become so integral to debate that the notion of a woman committing such an offence appears not have been considered to any significant degree by criminologists. The homicide might also be examined in relation to co-offending – Amanda did not carry out the killing alone, Sean also participated. Literature around co-offending in homicide presents the female offender as a powerless or at least *power-limited* actor, participating under duress and emerging more as a victim than an offender (Browne and Williams, 1989). This would not appear to be an easy fit with the circumstances around Charles' murder, in which Amanda seemed to be very much the dominant partner and expressed a desire to go on a killing spree. Attempting to understand the homicide by drawing on the literature around women who kill is also challenging. Female perpetrators tend to kill their intimate male partners or children (D'Orban, 1990; Brookman, 2005); their crimes very much gendered. It is argued that women are socialised to conform to feminine norms and roles of caring, nurturing, being docile and submissive (Schwartz, 2006a, 2006b), these norms heavily influencing the nature and extent of their violence in such circumstances (Steffensmeier and Allan, 1996; Jensen, 2001). Therefore from the information presented thus far, Charles' murder appears to be a difficult one to reconcile with any single homicide framework or concept.

The difficulty in making sense of this homicide was also evident in mainstream media representations. Local press coverage was largely descriptive, outlining the facts of the case and reporting particular milestones in the legal proceedings. It did occasionally draw attention to one particular element of the case, though – Amanda and Rex's apparent interest in death and multiple murder. They had corresponded with several convicted serial killers during their relationship (see, for example, Korth and Williams, 2015). Turning to examine international press coverage, this 'dark' side of the Taylors became the focal point of the reporting, even eclipsing the fact that Amanda had posted about the murder on social media. The UK's *People* newspaper described Amanda and Rex as 'violence fanatics', their relationship 'far from conventional' (Shortland, 2016). Mainstream media discourse also included attempts to re-feminise Amanda and cast her in the role of the victim, focusing on her late husband's influence on her, describing her 'troubled childhood' and emphasising her feminine roles as a 'mother' and 'widow' (Faberov, 2015; Shortland, 2016).

Perhaps one of the most noteworthy points to emerge from the international press coverage of Charles' murder was the relative *lack* of it. In the previous cases examined, coverage was considerably more extensive, the social media confessions generating considerable comment. The reasons for the relative lack of attention in this case may be due to several factors. Charles' ideal victimhood (Christie, 1986) as an elderly and vulnerable man may have been harmed by Amanda's allegations that he played a role in his son's addiction to prescription drugs and the fact that he lived in an area of economic deprivation. Poor, marginalised men from households in which alleged drug misuse is entrenched are considerably less newsworthy than those who are considered to be more innocent, vulnerable and deserving of victim status – for example, the Janzen women, who embodied Canadian middle-class respectability. In addition, it could be argued that social media was less worthy of comment in general. In the years preceding this murder, social media had become part and parcel of everyday life and indeed, everyday homicide (Yardley and Wilson, 2015). As such, it was no longer *interesting* – it had lost its function in helping a story reach a newsworthy 'threshold' (Jewkes, 2015). Amanda's social media posts were noted in reports of Charles' murder and indeed, without it, his murder may not have generated headlines beyond Montgomery County. However, the author argues that alone, the social media element was no longer sufficient to generate widespread attention. The case needed to appeal to other news values and in the Charles Taylor case, these were not as clear as they were in the other cases examined in this book. In addition, journalistic analysis was limited to descriptive accounts of the social media posts around the murder and did not extend far into the rest of Amanda's extensive media archive. This, combined with the challenges of making sense of this homicide within existing criminological frameworks, make an analysis of what Amanda did in relation to media even more important.

The sources on which this case study draws are court records, newspaper reports and social media archives. Prior to engaging in an analysis of Amanda's media practices, the broader context of Charles' homicide is explored. Records were obtained from the Virginia courts and have been used to describe the facts of the case. News reports from local and national newspapers and television stations were used to develop further insights into the lives of those involved, as some coverage included interviews with friends and family of the victim and perpetrators. The sources in relation to Amanda's media practices include the content produced by Amanda herself via her publicly available Instagram, Facebook and Tumblr profiles. They also include media produced on her behalf by one of her friends, who took over two of her social media accounts when she was incarcerated. While most of the content that Amanda posted in the aftermath of Charles' murder has long been removed from her accounts, descriptions and screenshots of these posts are available elsewhere – online, in court documents and mainstream media reports – and have also been analysed. In addition, the academic literature is referenced throughout this chapter, as richer detail about the experiences of those involved emerges, in an attempt to better contextualise the homicide within criminological frameworks.

Context

Turning to explore the stories of the people involved in the homicide, media reports focused mainly on Amanda and Rex, and to a smaller degree on Sean Ball. Charles was largely absent from the news coverage. In addition, few details of his life were shared at the trials and hearings relating to the case. He played a minor part in the story of his own murder. As such, we know very little about who Charles Taylor was. However, what can be established is that he lived with his elderly father Allen (*Commonwealth of Virginia v Taylor*, 2015a). Allen was in his eighties, in very poor health and had difficulty getting out of bed and moving around by himself (*Commonwealth of Virginia v Taylor*, 2015a). Charles was Allen's caregiver. Their home was on Den Hill Road in the Ellett area of Montgomery County. Images of the house in local news reports show a small detached residence with white wooden boarding and a front porch (Korth, 2015). The neighbourhood in which Charles resided appears distinctly rural. The houses on Den Hill Road are all built on large plots and surrounded by wooded areas, hills and fields. Less than one kilometre further along the road is a gas station with a small convenience store and two churches, North Fork Baptist Church and Trinity United Methodist Church. There are various farms and agricultural businesses in the area and the landscape is broken up by many streams and creeks – the North Fork Roanoke River is to the east of the house. Blacksburg is the nearest town and is roughly eight kilometres away – around a 10-minute drive. The area is rich in cultural heritage, with many local buildings appearing on the National Register of Historic Places, a US government official list of structures deemed worthy of preservation. However, Montgomery County is not without its difficulties. Just under one quarter of people (24.8%) live in poverty, compared with just over one in 10 (11.2%) for the state of Virginia as a whole (United States Census Bureau, 2016).

Amanda was born in Laurel, Maryland and moved to Florida with her mother when she was an infant (*Commonwealth of Virginia v Taylor*, 2015a). Amanda's biological father went to prison before she was born and remained there for 16 years, serving a sentence for a homicide offence. Amanda's mother remarried when Amanda was 18 months old and while in Florida, Amanda's younger sister was born. Amanda joked on Instagram about living in the Everglades, in a comment on a 1995 photograph of her as a four-year-old standing on a backyard jetty: 'I was a straight up swamp baby ... I was crazy stoked when #ahs[2] took place there' (brunette_bomber, 2014a). The family moved to Virginia when Amanda was 10. When her mother had to return to Florida to serve a prison sentence, her uncle looked after Amanda and her younger sister. Recalling this time at trial, Amanda's mother stated: 'When I got back, it just kind of, it was different. She just kind of drifted away from me. I think she was angry at me' (*Commonwealth of Virginia v Taylor*, 2015a).

Amanda began experiencing mental health problems when she was 13 or 14 and was admitted to psychiatric facilities for suicidal and self-harming behaviours (*Commonwealth of Virginia v Taylor*, 2015a). Her mother recalled Amanda's teenage years as difficult. She had been an angry adolescent. Her mother believed that her own drug and alcohol issues had had an impact on her children:

> I drank and I did drugs and I had a lot of problems of my own … I tried to love her and I tried to talk to her … I could tell she needed like a woman, a female figure, a positive role model to talk to, that I couldn't be that for her. (*Commonwealth of Virginia v Taylor*, 2015a, pp 260-1)

Amanda met Rex Taylor at Christiansburg High School and the two started dating during the ninth grade, when Amanda was around 14 or 15 years of age. He was two years older. Amanda spent time at the family home on a regular basis and as such, came to know his father Charles. Amanda said of this time: 'I really liked him a lot. We always had a really good relationship with each other' (*Commonwealth of Virginia v Taylor*, 2015a, p 284). Aged 16, Amanda became pregnant and left school (*Commonwealth of Virginia v Taylor*, 2015a). She sometimes lived with Rex at Charles' house. Amanda drew attention to this time at trial, stating that it marked a turning point in how she felt about Charles:

> He got Rex addicted to drugs … when I moved in with them, I would watch it … Rex and Charlie were more like party buddies than father and son. Rex would be like seventeen years old and his dad would have him scraping up pills for him. (*Commonwealth of Virginia v Taylor*, 2015a, pp 284-5)

Amanda claimed that she would confront Charles about encouraging Rex's drug use. In response, she said that Charles would chastise Rex and pretend to be on Amanda's side, 'but then, behind my back, he would just keep doing it' (*Commonwealth of Virginia v Taylor*, 2015a, p 286). Amanda and Rex married in September 2007, aged 17 and 19 respectively. Amanda's mother said that she put pressure on Amanda to get married: 'I just felt like they had a baby and they should be married so I kind of pushed that on her' (*Commonwealth of Virginia v Taylor*, 2015a, p 262). The family spent several years living with their respective parents before moving to their own home. Amanda gave birth to her second child, a daughter, in November 2012.

Records show that as an adult, Amanda built up a criminal record for felonies and misdemeanours. In July 2010, aged 19, she pleaded guilty to and received fines for public swearing and intoxication and purchasing/possessing alcohol (*Commonwealth of Virginia v Taylor*, 2010a, 2010b). In June 2011, Amanda was released on recognisance and ordered to pay costs in relation to an assault on a woman who was one of her closest friends at the time she was convicted of Charles' murder (*Commonwealth of Virginia v Taylor*, 2011). She joked on her Facebook feed that she had been hungover at the time, 'making it through court still wasted was fun, woo no jail time [smiley face emoji]' (Taylor, 2011a). In September 2011, she was arrested for a felony in relation to possessing items used in the manufacture of methamphetamine (*Commonwealth of Virginia v Taylor*, 2012). She pleaded guilty in August 2012, received a suspended sentence with supervised probation, and paid a fine and costs of over $1,000 (*Commonwealth of Virginia v Taylor*, 2012). She stated later that this charge related to buying a box of decongestant[3] for her boyfriend at the time, who possessed the other items needed to make methamphetamine (*Commonwealth of Virginia v Taylor*, 2016).

Commenting on Amanda's relationship with Rex and the impact it had on the woman she became, her close friend Mariah Roebuck claimed that the couple shared an obsession with death and serial killers (Korth and Williams, 2015). They had written to convicted multiple murderers and established a regular correspondence with one serial murderer and rapist, Paul Runge (Korth and Williams, 2015). Runge raped and murdered a woman and her 10-year-old daughter and admitted responsibility for killing five other women in Chicago in the 1990s. He was described by the assistant state attorney as 'a sexual sadist with no empathy or sympathy for anyone' (Ward, 2011). Rex changed his name on his Facebook profile to 'Rex Runge' in homage to him (Korth and Williams, 2015). Amanda received $1,000 in cash from Runge when Rex died in August 2014 (Korth and Williams, 2015).

Amanda and Rex's relationship broke down allegedly because of arguments and Rex's use of prescription drugs (*Commonwealth of Virginia v Taylor*, 2015a). They separated in April 2014 and had little contact with each other. Following their break-up, Rex went to live with Charles at the Den Hill Road house. Amanda recalled their separation at her trial:

> … we had to because he was just really bad on drugs. And I told him that I couldn't be with him and he couldn't see the kids until he got off everything. [Crying.] And he just didn't have it in him to, we separated, he moved down with his dad. I mean, the drugs there are right there in front of him. He just went, got worse. (*Commonwealth of Virginia v Taylor*, 2015a, p 286)

It was in a shed at the Den Hill Road property that Rex took his own life in August 2014, on the birthday of his and Amanda's eldest child. She firmly placed the blame for Rex's drug use and suicide on Charles. Rex's family strongly resisted Amanda's attempts to hold Charles responsible, arguing that her claims were simply ploys for attention and that 'Rex loved his father' (Jeffries, 2015). Amanda's friend Mariah claimed that there was ongoing hostility between Amanda and Charles, with each blaming the other for Rex's suicide (Korth and Williams, 2015). Amanda's mother also saw a change in Amanda following Rex's death: 'She never grieved over it or anything…. Her eyes just went empty, she changed. It wasn't her. She just hid out at my house. She wouldn't go anywhere' (*Commonwealth of Virginia v Taylor*, 2015a, p 266). Amanda attempted suicide while visiting Rex's grave with friends on 27 March 2015 – the birthday that they shared: 'I was going to stab myself', she stated at trial (*Commonwealth of Virginia v Taylor*, 2015a, p 289). The day following this incident, she was admitted to Saint Albans Hospital, where she received treatment and was prescribed medication. It appears that she did not complete the course of medication. On a trip to Walmart to buy things for Easter with her mother on 4 April, her mother claimed that Amanda asked her to throw the medicine away, which she did (Korth and Williams, 2015). Amanda stated later: 'I didn't like the way they made me feel…. I felt like I didn't have control' (*Commonwealth of Virginia v Taylor*, 2015a, p 290). Her reluctance to take medication was not unusual for Amanda, who had long resisted attempts by friends and family to get help for mental health issues. During her time in prison she stopped taking medication that had been prescribed to her after three or four months, again citing similar reasons for her non-compliance: 'I just didn't feel right. I felt kinda like not all there. Like I didn't have control, you know' (*Commonwealth of Virginia v Taylor*, 2016, p 30). Mariah had also urged her to get help for her mental health issues in the past (Korth and Williams, 2015).

Indeed, Mariah was a constant presence in Amanda's life and would continue to be so, even after Amanda was sentenced to life in prison. She posted status updates on Amanda's social media accounts, which included contact details so that people could write to her in prison (see, for example, Taylor, 2015a, 2015b, 2016).

Sean Ball moved in the same social circles as Amanda and Rex. He had known the couple and other mutual friends for several years. Like Amanda, Sean also had a criminal record, but his past crimes related largely to property offences. For example, records show that in 2010 he faced charges in relation to 24 incidents of burglary, committed in 2009. He pleaded guilty to 10 of these crimes and received a three-year prison sentence (Virginia Courts Case Information, 2016). Sean worked at Applebee's, a chain restaurant in Christiansburg, and lived in the basement of the house belonging to Mariah and her husband Johnny (Korth and Williams, 2015). Sean had been one of the people present during Amanda's suicide attempt at Rex's grave on 27 March 2015. The knife she intended to use to stab herself with had been a birthday gift from Sean (Commonwealth of Virginia v Taylor, 2015a). A phone call to Sean was the second that Amanda made when she was released from Saint Albans hospital on 1 April 2015. Mariah and Johnny had previously declined her request for a lift and a place to stay (Korth and Williams, 2015). Sean left work in the middle of his shift at Applebee's to pick her up. Mariah claimed that Sean was besotted with Amanda but that these feelings weren't reciprocated: 'He loved Amanda so much…. He was in love with her. Completely in love with her. Obsessed with her. He would do just anything for her' (Korth and Williams, 2015). He stayed with her in motels in the days following her release from hospital and sent a text to Mariah and Johnny the day after Charles' murder, saying he was moving to North Carolina (Korth and Williams, 2015). Johnny described Sean as a people-pleaser, someone who was easily led: 'He just wanted to make everyone happy…. He was the kind of person who wanted to do whatever you wanted to do' (Korth and Williams, 2015).

Amanda Taylor through a criminological lens

The information presented in the preceding section enables some insight into Amanda as a homicide perpetrator. Earlier, the author noted the difficulties in conceptualising the murder within existing criminological frameworks simply from the information presented about Charles' murder. Now, revisiting the criminological literature, some answers can be provided. However, at the same time, new questions emerge. A conflict resolution (Polk, 1994) homicide does appear consistent with what is known. Amanda stated that she got on well with Charles when they first met, but the seeds of her dislike for him lay in his alleged role in her husband's drug use – a point that she consistently returned to when justifying her actions. Sean Ball was indeed a co-offender, but the traditional gender dynamics associated with homicide co-offending were reversed in this case. Sean appeared to have been obsessed with Amanda and willing to do whatever she wanted if this offered some chance to gain her affections. As such, Amanda was able to control and manipulate Sean to assist her in the homicide and his failure to do what she wanted resulted in him becoming an incidental victim (Brookman, 2005) as well as a co-offender.

In relation to what is known about women who kill, while Amanda's victim was not her intimate partner or child – as is common in such cases (D'Orban, 1990; Brookman, 2005) – she did share many characteristics attributed to female homicide offenders. Mann (1996) identifies the typical woman who kills as a single mother who has not completed high school, as does Schwartz (2012), who adds that these women are likely to be unemployed and that if they do work, their employment is likely to be in the service sector. Amanda left high school when she became pregnant and was indeed a single parent at the time of the murder. She did not appear to be employed at the time of the homicide, although her social media archive – which is explored in the next section – does indicate that she had worked in the past as a server at a local restaurant during the summer of 2011 (see, for example, Taylor, 2011b). The structural factors of poverty and social disadvantage are something that female homicide offenders have in common with their male counterparts (Steffensmeier and Haynie, 2000a, 2000b). However, when compared with male offenders, they are more likely to come from stable family backgrounds, and to have children and settled living arrangements prior to the homicide (Schwartz, 2012). The comments made by Amanda's mother in relation to her childhood years indicate that the family background was not stable, and, while she did have children, the period preceding the homicide was far from 'settled'. In terms of prior criminality, Amanda's record does appear somewhat consistent with other female homicide perpetrators. Research suggests that around 30% have felonies on their records, that 60% have misdemeanours and that they 'are not immersed in criminal subcultures to the same extent as male homicide offenders' (Schwartz, 2012, p 195).

While the criminological literature helps situate Amanda as a co-offending female perpetrator of a revenge homicide, many questions remain unanswered. Many people feel aggrieved after a loved one commits suicide, but do not kill the person they hold responsible. Many people experience similar adversity to Amanda, but they do not go on to kill either. Indeed, Amanda's younger sister graduated from high school and at the time of writing is a successful college student. Amanda's actions in posting about the murder on social media are significant. These actions and her broader media practices open a window onto the life of an individual who lived *in* (Deuze, 2012) and *through* media. It is to her media archive that the analysis now turns.

Life in media

In this section, the author summarises the key points emerging from an analysis of Amanda's media practices. The first section focuses on the scale and extent of Amanda's media archive. This involves identifying the social media platforms she used, the format of the content she created and shared and her usage patterns over time. The second section explores the key themes and topics of her posts, both within and across these platforms. It is anticipated that this analysis will help shed further light on the significance of media practices for homicide perpetrators like Amanda and enable a more nuanced understanding than can be gleaned from mainstream media coverage or criminological frameworks around homicide.

The archive

Amanda's media archive spans three platforms – Facebook, Instagram and Tumblr. She began posting on Facebook under her real name, Amanda Taylor, in September 2010 when she was 19 years of age. Her profile picture is a selfie and her cover photo is a mirror image of a woman's hand holding a gun; the woman has one finger on the trigger and her nails look sharp and recently painted. In her 'About' section, Amanda states that she lives in Blacksburg, Virginia and works at Elite Hunting and the Umbrella Corporation. This is the first indication of Amanda's interest in horror films, as Elite Hunting is the name of the organisation that features in Eli Roth's Hostel films and the Umbrella Corporation is the sinister pharmaceutical business in the Resident Evil series. At the time of writing, Amanda had around 900 Facebook friends and most appear to have become linked with her since Charles' murder – just under two thirds of her Facebook friends had been added to her account from January 2015. The monthly volume of posts to Facebook varied widely during the time she used it, the most prolific periods being September 2010, August 2011 and December 2012, when she posted over 30 times per month. The quietest period fell between June and August 2012, when she did not post at all. In relation to the type of posts she made, text-based status updates make up the largest category of posts (n=331, 53.1%), followed by photographs she had taken (n=96, 15.4%) and videos from elsewhere on the internet that she had shared through her account (n=84, 13.5%). The remainder of her posts comprise videos she had made, updates to her cover or profile picture, and shared pictures, articles and other material from elsewhere on the internet. The most recent posts have been uploaded by her friend Mariah and include contact details for writing to Amanda in prison and details of a JPay account through which inmates can receive money and messages while incarcerated (Taylor, 2015b, 2015c; 2016).

Amanda began posting on Instagram in December 2012 when she was 21 years old and her archive contains 603 posts. The account was not in her real name; she used the handle 'brunette_bomber'. The image at the top of her Instagram homepage appears to be the head and shoulders of a woman's dead body. Also at the top of her homepage are lyrics from the Lana Del Rey song Serial Killer, followed by two emojis – a heart and a knife. At the time of writing, she had around 1,200 followers. The volume of posts does not follow as sporadic or chaotic a pattern as was true for her Facebook account; her Instagram peaks and troughs are more gradual, increasing and decreasing incrementally. The only month in which she did not post anything was December of 2013 and her most active period was between July and October of 2014, when she posted between 44 and 47 times per month. As is typical of Instagram – which began as an image-sharing site – the vast majority of the posts are still images accompanied by a comment, although there are also 16 videos. As with her Facebook account, the most recent posts have been uploaded by Mariah, the most recent being an image of the April 2016 edition of *Master Detective* magazine, which features Amanda's picture on the cover (brunette_bomber, 2016). The second most recent post is an image of a letter from Amanda's attorney, on which Amanda has penned a handwritten note to Mariah as follows: 'Ah this shit is real rooooo! I'm so nervous dude. Mark your calender I can't wait to see you [heart emoji]' (brunette_bomber, 2015a). The third most recent post is a selfie of Amanda accompanied by a comment informing followers of Amanda's interview with a journalist that was due to air on a local television station (brunette_bomber, 2015b).

Amanda's Tumblr account was active for a little over a month between early March and early April 2015, during which time she made 39 posts to the account, 24 of which were videos and 15 of which were images. A small image of Amanda is on her Tumblr homepage, and, similar to her Instagram, the account was in the name 'Brunette Bomber'. However, her handle was 'letsbindtorturekill'. Bind Torture Kill – or BTK – was the self-titled moniker of serial killer Denis Rader from Wichita, Kansas, who pleaded guilty to the murders of 10 people over a 17-year period (Hickey, 2010). At Amanda's trial, the judge shared his belief that Amanda had planned the murder for around one month (*Commonwealth of Virginia v Taylor*, 2015a), which broadly corresponds with the time she had the Tumblr account. All of the content on her Tumblr blog appears to have been posted by Amanda herself, as the most recent post was dated 4 April 2015 – the day of Charles' murder. This is the only social media account that Mariah did not take over following Amanda's incarceration.

Key themes and events

Having analysed all of the posts in Amanda's media archive, three key themes emerge as particularly significant: family, violent media and self-portraits. These themes are now be explored in turn, including the points at which they overlap and converge are considered. Thereafter, Amanda's media practices around Charles' murder and milestones in the legal proceedings are considered.

Family

By far the most prominent theme on Amanda's Facebook and Instagram accounts was family. This category contained the largest number of posts than any other, and included entries in which Amanda referred to or depicted her children, Rex, her mother, sister and other family members. Just under half (n=268, 44.7%) of her Instagram posts and just over a third (n=221, 35.5%) of her Facebook posts could be categorised under this heading. In relation to her children, she referred to them as her 'crazies' and included a large number of images of them in and around the home. Her posts told a story of a mother doing everyday activities with her children, such as building a gingerbread house for Halloween (brunette_bomber, 2014b), playing with colouring books (brunette_bomber, 2014c), showing the children playing with their Christmas presents (brunette_bomber, 2014d), practising for a spelling test with her son (brunette_bomber, 2014e) and encouraging people to buy the cookies and lemonade that her son was selling at a yard sale (Taylor, 2013a). Amanda also alluded to the structural context of her parenting – one in which her resources were limited – and showed herself as someone who made her children happy despite these circumstances. In one post, she proudly shared an image of her daughter playing a home-made ball pool that she made from items on sale at a supermarket (Taylor, 2013b). However, while these posts are evidence of Amanda showing herself as a mother and having a presence in the home environment performing a traditional gender role, there were very few pictures that included *both* her *and* the children. The pictures she posted were largely of the children alone. At a sentencing hearing she stated, 'That's the only thing I was good at, was being a mom' (*Commonwealth of Virginia v Taylor*, 2016, p 38). At trial, Amanda's mother suggested that while Amanda was proud of her children, she was not proud of herself in her own role as a mother: 'I didn't feel like I was good enough for her and her sister. And I could see that in Amanda sometimes. I feel like she thought she wasn't good enough for her kids, and she was. Her kids loved her more than anything' (*Commonwealth of Virginia v Taylor*, 2015a, p 263).

One of the last images Amanda posted of her children was a photograph of her son sitting on the steps of Charles' house (brunette_ bomber, 2015c; Taylor, 2015d). The posts were dated two weeks prior to Charles' murder – 22 March 2015. The caption reads: 'Spent the day in Ellett Valley visiting his daddy's side of the crazies [heart emoji]' (Taylor, 2015d). After a friend commented that she hoped Amanda's son had a nice time, Amanda replied: 'He had a really good day. Charlie asked if we'd go to church with him this morning so we went down there for that.' Amanda then added that her son was always happy when he was around Rex's relatives. Through these posts, Amanda showed her and her son's relationship with Rex's family to be a positive one. She also showed Charles as a churchgoer, a man of faith, which contrasts starkly with the addiction-enabling drug user she would present later. If indeed the slow-burning rage typical of most conflict resolution homicides was present, there was no indication of it in these posts.

Rex featured less prominently than Amanda's children in her Instagram and Facebook archives. He is mentioned in 14 (2.2%) Facebook posts and 22 (3.7%) Instagram posts, most of which were created in the time before the couple separated. During their time together, Amanda referred to Rex as her husband and her posts about him were always positive, referring to everyday things they were doing together. Amanda presented herself as a wife and mother within a nuclear family unit, proudly showing herself in these roles. December

2012 appeared to be a particularly happy time for her, shortly after her daughter was born: 'I found the perfect match to create this perfect lil family with best husband/father ever' (Taylor, 2012a); 'I'm so thankful for my two amazing kids&husband. Can't imagine life without these 3' (Taylor, 2012b). After Rex's death Amanda posted an old family picture from the previous year of the four of them together (Taylor, 2015e), and also wrote about an appeal to raise money for Rex's funeral through a friend who was selling artwork (brunette_bomber, 2014f). She followed this up the following month, thanking people who had helped and supported them (brunette_bomber, 2014g). There are several Instagram posts in February and March of 2015, in which Amanda reminisces about Rex, including photographs of them together and memories of experiences they had shared. She showed her late husband to others in these posts and presented her memories of him as happy ones; nowhere did she refer to his alleged drug use. In early March 2015, she posted an old picture of him on Instagram playing with former bandmates. This appeared to be a fond memory that was as much about looking to the future as it was about reminiscing:

> I came across this & HAVE to #throwbackthursday it. That crazy in the misfit shirt is my children's dad ... I went through so many years watching him grow into an amazing musican ... Im just thankful to have alot put up that I can one day break out for our crazies to hear. (bunette_bomber, 2015d)

Sean Ball made a fleeting appearance in one of the posts in which Amanda reminisced about Rex. In October 2014, Amanda reposted an old photograph of her and Rex clinking together two bottles of Mickey's Malt Liquor, relaxing after the children had gone to bed (Taylor, 2014a). Sean commented on the photograph as follows: 'I like this one quite a bit, I combines so many things I care about ... I miss that dude. So it's awesome seeing his pics, and I always love mickeys ... think I'll grab some of those on the way home'. The picture on the profile from which these comments originated is of Sean and Amanda together. So while she was important enough to him to place a picture of the two of them as his profile image, the same could not be said for Amanda. This was the only pre-murder post in which he appeared, and he was otherwise absent from her archive.

Turning to explore other family posts in her media archive, Amanda shows herself as a proud older sister, presenting her relationship with her sibling as a positive and fun-loving one. Her posts referred to two of them spending time together during her sister's breaks from university and highlighted how much Amanda missed her sister when she was away. Examples are a post referring to them making cupcakes together (brunette_bomber, 2014h) and an image of some chocolate-covered strawberries that her sister sent her as a gift (brunette_bomber, 2014i). A prominent theme within the posts about her sister is the structural context of the community in which they grew up. Amanda's pride at her sister having succeeded against the odds was very clear; she presented her as the exception to the rule. This is perhaps most obvious in the post Amanda made just after her sister won her place at university,

> I gotta say my little sister is the only person I've EVER been around that actually takes life serious. I see so many teenage girls who are just on a path of destruction … I thank God she avoided teenage pregnancy or never open that door to the world of drugs. She goes to school, always kept a job & will soon be on her way to … college. Ive got nothing but a load of respect & love for that little chica! If only this world had more people like her. I can only pray my daughter grows up to be just like her Auntie [heart emoji] (Taylor, 2013c).

Amanda, her sister and her mother all followed each other's accounts on Instagram and regularly commented on each other's posts, especially those in relation to family occasions like birthdays. There were no images of Amanda's mother anywhere in Amanda's archive, although she did include occasional references to other family members, such as an old picture of her grandmother as a young woman, who appeared to have been very glamorous (brunette_bomber, 2014j).

In summary, in the family category, Amanda showed herself in various family roles, including wife, mother and sister. She presented her children as important characters in her narrative and they were the subjects of most of the photographs she posted to Instagram and Facebook. However, there were also absences within this theme, particularly around motherhood. Amanda's text-based posts referred to her motherhood and she corresponded with her own mother through such posts, but there were no photographs of Amanda's mother in her archive and Amanda very rarely appeared with her children in the photographs she posted. In relation to how she showed others, Amanda never made disparaging or critical comments about her family members in her archive – they were always shown in a positive light.

She was complimentary towards them and expressed gratitude for their presence in her life. As such, family emerged as an important and significant social institution in Amanda's archive. The family she showed herself to have a presence in was portrayed as a warm, loving and 'perfect' one, despite the challenges that she identified within the local context in which the family was situated. However, in Amanda's Tumblr blog, there are no references to family at all. This part of her archive is dominated by another theme – violence – which is explored in the following section.

Violence: on and off screen

It is very clear from Amanda's archive that she was an avid fan of violent media. Posts categorised under this heading included those focusing on horror films, films featuring graphic violence, crime drama series about murder, a range of material relating to multiple murder (for example, serial killers and school shootings) and music in which violence and death were prominent themes. Over one quarter (n=166, 27.7%) of her Instagram posts and just over one fifth (n=137, 22.0%) of her Facebook posts were categorised under this heading. All of Amanda's 38 Tumblr posts featured violence and were much more graphic than her posts on Facebook and Instagram. As well as content similar to the violent media depicted in her Facebook and Instagram accounts, her Tumblr blog also included videos and images of people being – or about to be – subjected to violent assaults. It is also important to note that Amanda's archive included posts relating to media that may be considered more 'mainstream'. Indeed, around one fifth of posts in her Facebook archive (19.2%, n=119) fell into this category. These included posts about rhythm and blues music by artists like Lil Wayne, Chris Brown, Rihanna and Nicki Minaj, comedy films like Ted and the television show Workaholics. However, this theme became less prominent over time and indeed, only around one in 20 posts (5.5%, n=33) on her Instagram account – which she appeared to favour in later years – fell into this category. In addition, there were clear overlaps between Amanda's interest in violent media and everyday family life. For example, one video post showed her daughter playing with a Michael Myers doll[4] and putting the doll to bed (brunette_bomber, 2014k), and Amanda talked about her love for her son in the same post in which she celebrated Ted Bundy's birthday (Taylor, 2011c).

Despite violent media posts constituting a smaller proportion of her overall archive than those in the category of family, there were periods in which violent media was the dominant theme. In the four weeks prior to Charles' murder, Amanda focused most heavily on her Tumblr blog, where she created 39 posts, compared with 23 on Instagram and 11 on Facebook. Between June 2014 and February 2015, violent media featured prominently in her Instagram posts, ranging from 31.9% to 70% of monthly content during this period. Changes and shifts in Amanda's tolerance of media representations of violence are also evident when comparing earlier and later posts. For example, in December 2012, she stated that she could not finish watching the film VHS: 'I had my husband pause it in the middle I can't finish it. Itsnot scary just the murders in it feel so real now I'm stuck in this creeped out funk' (Taylor, 2012c). However, by March 2015, Amanda's Tumblr account not only featured a clip from this film, in which a man has his throat cut, but also included images of what appeared to be *real* acts of violence, suggesting that she came to be considerably less abhorred by this type of content.

Amanda included several photographs of her DVD collection on her Instagram feed. Among the titles are Cannibal Holocaust, All Hallows Eve, Three on a Meathook, Black Christmas, I Spit on Your Grave, Last House on the Left, American Psycho, Prom Night, Dexter, American Horror Story, Ed Gein, Bundy, Sensing Murder and The Ice Man (brunette_bomber, 2014l, 2015e). She was a fan of the television crime drama series Dexter, proudly commenting that she had all of the seasons of the show on DVD (brunette_bomber, 2014m). Her interest in the horror and violence genres was also evident from images taken around her home. Surrounding the television set were various pieces of horror paraphernalia, including plastic skulls and a fake spider's web. A photograph posted to Facebook showed Amanda's fireplace surrounded by posters and other memorabilia and was accompanied by the comment, 'I finally found my little posters [happy lil'mama!] My fireplace finally looks right. Cannibal Holocaust/ Army of darkness(Japanese print)/Last house on the left(original)/ Natural Born Killers/House of 1000corpses....*silly things like this make me happy* #horrorjunkie' (Taylor, 2013d). Amanda appeared to be aware of that her interest in horror and violent films was exceptional and unusual, using humour in her commentary. A photograph of the title screen for a film called Brutal Massacre is captioned 'My morning' (brunette_bomber, 2014n). Another post reads 'Starting my day with: #dawnofthedead' (brunette_bomber, 2014o).

Amanda had a penchant for two films in particular: Texas Chainsaw Massacre and Natural Born Killers. In relation to Texas Chainsaw Massacre, Amanda's interest went beyond simply posting about the film – it was *embodied*. She had two tattoos of Leatherface, the film's lead character, on her forearm. On her shoulder was a tattoo of another character from the film, Chop Top. The tattoos often appeared in her archive and received many compliments from her followers. In one post, she states that the Leatherface tattoo was 'Definitely most favorite thing on my body' (brunette_bomber, 2014p). She also had a tattoo of a quote from the film Dawn of the Dead on her feet. In relation to Natural Born Killers, Amanda appeared to idolise, romanticise and fantasise about the relationship between the film's main characters, Mickey and Mallory Knox. The film is about a road trip that starts with the murder of Mallory's abusive father. The couple then go on to kill multiple people at every stop they make on the road trip, each time leaving one person alive to tell their story to the media. The film presented the pair as cult heroes, made by the media. Amanda often quoted from the film and referred to herself and Rex as Mickey and Mallory Knox, using the hashtag #naturalbornkillers when posting images of the two of them together (see, for example, brunette_bomber, 2013a). Other posts included images from the film with comments about the lead characters, 'A couple that slays together stays together. #naturalbornkillers' (brunette_bomber, 2014q).

Amanda was also interested in real killers. Her interest included serial, spree and mass murderers, with a focus on school shooters emerging as particularly prominent in her Tumblr archive in March 2015. She posted an image of Seung-Hui Cho – the Virginia Tech shooter (Brunette Bomber, 2015a) – and reposted three videos of school-age boys with firearms that had been originally uploaded by others. Prior to this she had expressed an interest in school shootings, but it was largely reactive in nature, following unfolding news stories and responding to television documentaries on the topic. In relation to a school shooting in Nevada, she seemed keen to find out details of the killer as the story unfolded (Taylor, 2013e). She posted in relation to a documentary about TJ Lane, who killed three fellow students at a school in Chardon, Ohio in 2012. She liked the documentary and argued that 'killers aren't just born that way' (Taylor, 2014b). She also demonstrated a knowledge of several mass and spree killings, showing herself as something of an 'expert'. One example is her post noting that the month of April is a significant one for such events: 'April is such an insane month of terror. Waco massacre, Virginia Tech massacre, Columbine High School massacre, Boston Marathon bombing, Oklahoma City bombing. April blood showers bring May grave flowers' (Taylor, 2014c).

Amanda's showed herself as a serial killer enthusiast on her Instagram archive. This this went beyond simple fandom; she had not simply consumed and commented, but had directly corresponded with at least two serial killers – they had become part of her reality. She posted an image of a drawing Paul Runge had sent to her as a birthday gift on her Instagram feed (brunette_bomber, 2014r). The pencil drawing is a front cover of *Newsweek* featuring mugshots of Paul Runge and Amanda. Amanda commented: 'Today I received this awesome drawling as an early birthday present. I absolutely love it :) Paul Runge did him & I as Mickey & Mallory Knox #naturalbornkillers #serialkillers #paulrunge #prisonart #mickeymalloryknox #blood #lust #happybirthdaytome' (brunette_bomber, 2014r). The drawing alludes to a shared detailed knowledge of the film, as an issue of *Newsweek* featuring Mickey and Mallory flashes up momentarily during an early scene in the film. Amanda's archive also features images of correspondence from another serial killer, Roy Norris, who, with his accomplice Lawrence Bittaker, raped and murdered five young women in California in 1979. One such image shows an envelope containing a letter from him, on which he had written 'Greetings from California', commenting '& in today's mail…#roynorris #toolboxkiller #serialkiller #getinmyvan' (brunette_bomber, 2013b). She also posted an image of a Halloween card that she had spent two hours making to send to Charles Manson (brunette_bomber, 2013c). She referred to Ted Bundy as an 'amazing man' on the 22nd anniversary of his execution (Taylor, 2011d) and celebrated his birthday (Taylor, 2011c). She was also familiar with terminology relating to her interests, using the term 'murderabilia' frequently in hashtags.

Amanda also created her own murderabilia. She had a custom-made necklace that featured an image of school shooter TJ Lane on the pendant (brunette_bomber, 2013d). She also prepared a folder of newspaper clippings, love letters and notes relating to her and Rex's relationship, which she gave to Mariah three months before killing Charles, urging her to share the folder with authors and journalists who may one day want to write about her (Korth and Williams, 2015). In relation to this, Mariah commented: 'I think she just wanted the fame that they were so fascinated by' (Korth and Williams, 2015).

The way in which Amanda showed her interests in violence through social media demonstrated her association with and membership of a subculture around horror and violence. Members of this subculture actively produced and consumed their own content, creating spaces saturated with meanings and representations (Ferrell et al, 2001), their social media feeds an example of such fan spaces (Miller, 2011). Amanda engaged in conversations with Instagram followers and Facebook friends about particular films and television series she liked.

Her Instagram followers asked her to recommend horror films to watch and she discussed the television series Dexter with them (see, for example, brunette_bomber, 2014s). She shared her excitement about films soon to be released, such as The Purge Anarchy (Taylor, 2014d, 2014e, 2014f), Green Inferno (2014g) and VHS2 (Taylor, 2014h). She was an avid fan of Eli Roth's films and was very excited when one of her Instagram posts was 'liked' by a social media account appearing to belong to him (Taylor, 2014i). In relation to the film Evil Dead being made into a television show, she began her post, 'You guys …', as if addressing an audience of followers (brunette_bomber, 2014t). Amanda also recommended other Instagram accounts to follow, for example: 'If you like #murderabilia & #truecrime go follow her!' (brunette_bomber, 2015f).

In summary, violence was a prominent theme within Amanda's archive. Her interest in horror and violent films was longstanding, something that was a consistent feature over time and that became more prominent than the more mainstream interests in the earlier part of her archive. She permanently inscribed this interest on her own body through tattoos that paid homage to particular films and characters. Natural Born Killers was particularly meaningful to Amanda and came to form part of her identity as a wife and partner to Rex; fantasy and reality collided as she came to associate their relationship with that of the film's lead characters. Amanda demonstrated knowledge and awareness of searching and search-enabling practices. She used many hashtags, which not only demonstrated her ability to search for content but enabled others to *find* her posts. Amanda's identity as a member of a subculture around horror, homicide and violence was prominent throughout her social media archives. She portrayed a sense not just of being associated with this subculture but of being *immersed* within it, this immersion becoming particularly pronounced in the period preceding Charles' murder. Amanda's status within this subculture was enhanced by her correspondence with convicted serial killers. She was not simply consuming representations of these individuals; her reality and theirs had intersected on a personal level.

Self-portraits

The theme self-portraits was used to categorise posts that focused solely on Amanda. This included selfie photographs and text-based posts that expressed reflective feelings or sentiments about herself at particular points in time. Such posts made up just over one in 10 posts (12.1%, n=75) on her Facebook page and just under one in 10 posts (8.7%, n=52) on her Instagram feed. The early parts of her Facebook archive include some very direct statements about her thoughts and feelings and the issues she was coping with. Examples include the following:

> i am for real sad. bleh [frown emoji] (Taylor, 2011e)

> I can finally say after years and years of mad deep depression I am finally happy with life (Taylor, 2011f)

> Today i've been clean from alcohol , green, and opiates for two months … my body ='s hell but at least I've got full control of my mind and body back [smile emoji]:) I 'm proud of mah self (Taylor, 2011g)

However, these types of post do not appear in significant numbers beyond 2011. The only two posts in which Amanda directly addresses her own thoughts and feelings were made in the period following Rex's death in 2014. In one of these, she informed her followers about an art sale to raise money for Rex's funeral, and in the other she expressed thanks to people who had contributed. Extracts from the 2014 posts are as follows:

> … last Thursday I lost children's father , Rex. Its been really hard to accept & cope with what has happen but I'm so thankful for the love & support that's been sent my way for him & our family. It means the world. I wanted to put this out there, Lou Rusconi … is doing custom art and all proceeds will go towards helping Rex have the funeral he deserves … I don't want to accept the fact he's really gone. Thank you guys for all the emails, calls, donations on his funeral, just all this support. It helps so much & I promise to get back to all of you that's been there I just have to get my shit together first (brunette_bomber, 2014f)

> I suck at expressing myself towards..anything..i probably come off super ungratful , its really hard to be open with personal issues but nothing will compare to how much simple shit like this just seeing how much people care about rex means to me. Thank you all so ..so much [heart emoji] (brunette_bomber, 2014g)

Amanda's self-portraits after 2011 are largely image-based and take the form of selfie photographs. She posted her first selfie on Facebook in February 2012. From June 2014, her selfies became a regular feature of her archive, appearing up to seven times per month. Amanda's selfies are broadly similar – they are of her upper body, and she is smiling or has a neutral expression – and many appear to have been taken in a mirror, as she is holding her phone in many of the images. In some of the photographs, Amanda wears one of a variety of t-shirts that express her interest in serial killers, horror films and rock music. Amanda's selfies received a warm reception from her followers on Instagram, eliciting many 'likes' and compliments. Her selfies from June 2014 generated an average of 76 likes each and examples of comments include 'You really are very beautiful' (brunette_bomber, 2014u) and 'So gorgeous, always.' (brunette_bomber, 2015g). What accompanies the selfies is particularly interesting. Amanda often included lyrics from songs by a variety of artists and bands including Lana Del Rey, Marilyn Manson, GWAR and The Misfits. The quotes she used as captions for her selfies came from films like Texas Chainsaw Massacre, Natural Born Killers and The Devil's Rejects.

While Amanda's earlier selfies express her interest in horror films, serial killers and death, further 'showing' herself as a member of a subculture, the later ones, posted before Charles' killing, appear to be more sinister. The final selfie Amanda posted to Instagram carried the caption 'Freedom is a loaded shotgun' (brunette_bomber, 2015g). This is a lyric from the song Krank by German industrial rock band KMFDM. The lyrics to this song were also posted on a website by Eric Harris, one of the perpetrators of the 1999 Columbine High School massacre, before he carried out the shooting with accomplice Dylan Klebold. The band's music has since unfortunately become entwined in the loops and spirals around school shootings, as other school shooters have included it in their media practices – notably Pekka-Eric Auvinen, who carried out a shooting at a Finnish school in 2007 (Kiilakoski and Oksanen, 2011). The only selfie Amanda posted on her Tumblr blog included a quote. Accompanying a photograph in which she appears to have a wound on her throat is the caption 'Wrists are for girls. I'm slitting my throat' (Brunette Bomber, 2015b). This is a line from the 2000 Canadian film Ginger Snaps, which tells the story of two sisters who are fascinated with death, and who as children make a pact to die together.

Through her selfie photographs, Amanda 'showed' her physical self – an attractive woman in her twenties. However, these selfies are also interesting in terms of what they obscure – the vulnerabilities that were evident in her earlier text-based posts in which she shared feelings and emotions in a very direct manner. Instead, through her selfie photographs, Amanda presented herself as someone who was 'dark' and intriguing. She also enhanced her presence to select others through these selfies. Only those who shared her interests would have been likely to recognise the lyrics and quotes that accompanied her selfies, reinforcing her membership of a subculture. Indeed, journalists who explored her social media archives often did not appear to realise that the words Amanda was using were not her own.

The murder posts

Prior to killing Charles, Amanda posted twice on social media. The first post was uploaded to Facebook on the evening of Friday 3 April and was a music video of the song Sweet Jane by the Cowboy Junkies (Taylor, 201f5). The second was a similar post on Tumblr, uploaded in the early afternoon of Saturday 4 April – an image of Mickey and Mallory Knox with Sweet Jane playing in the background (Brunette Bomber, 2015c). Amanda captions the post 'All for you Rex', followed by a heart emoji. The focus on Natural Born Killers – and indeed the song Sweet Jane, which was part of the soundtrack to the film – is a continuous thread that links back to other posts in Amanda's media archive. As noted previously, Natural Born Killers appeared to be one of Amanda's favourite films and she had come to associate her relationship with Rex with the relationship between the film's two lead characters. Through posting this content, Amanda was not directly outlining what she was going to do the following day, but was alluding to it, using violent media as a symbol. This echoed the showing and presencing practices she had engaged in previously, cryptically using symbols and extracts from violent media that would only be understood by others with similar interests.

Following the murder, there were four posts. The first was the image of Amanda at the scene. This was described by a police officer at trial: 'Ms. Taylor with what appears to be the knife and Mr Taylor on the sofa in the background' (*Commonwealth of Virginia v Taylor*, 2015a, pp 198-9). The image was later uploaded to Amanda's Tumblr blog and sent to an online friend who ran a serial killers website. Both action and reflection narratives (Brookman, 2015) are evident here; Amanda was confirming that a crime has occurred *and* that she was responsible for it. She is keen to show her new identity as a killer and as such, the action narrative is arguably the strongest. There is simply an image, which tells the audience about the violence Amanda has enacted. The post was about evidencing the act, showing it to be visceral and real. She intended it to be seen by other individuals who gather around subcultures of violence. She was giving them exclusive access to this 'decisive moment' (Ferrell and Van de Voorde, 2010), where she had crossed the line from fan to celebrity, from consumer to creator of murderabilia. Charles is in the background of this photograph; the image is not about him. Just as he later became a minor character in playing the story of his own murder as it was told by the mainstream media, Amanda presented him as a small part in her own story of murder. Amanda was the subject, she was holding the knife, she had agency, she was in control; Charles was shown merely as an object. His personhood has been taken away, his corpse supporting the role in which Amanda cast herself—that of a killer. As someone familiar with the topic of murder and murderabilia, Amanda would have been aware of the attention that this post would generate. It could be argued that this was a ploy to create a fan following and generate media attention. If this was true, then life very much imitated art. Mickey and Mallory Knox always left one person alive at each place they killed to ensure that someone could tell the story to the media. In the 21st-century context of networked media, Amanda did not need a witness to tell her story; she could set the publicity machine in motion herself with a tap on a touchscreen.

The second post was on Facebook at around 5.30am the following day, after Amanda and Sean had spent the night in Tennessee: 'I proudly did this for Rex. I love my children but charlie killed my husband' (Taylor, 2015a). The third post – this time to Instagram – featured the news story about Amanda and Sean, accompanied by the following comment:

> Everything I did was for the right reasons. I stabbed my father in law to death because he destroyed my husband with drugs…depression. i wasn't the perfect wife but this was one last good thing i could do for rex i dont care what anyone thinks i loved rex more than the world. This was for you [heart emoji] seans dead, but I finally have closure with rex after charlie. If you keep looking for me more will die. Just let me get to the place rex and i always wanted and ill be free without having to kill more. Till we rot rex, till we fucking rot [heart emoji. (Cited in Murdock, 2015)

Amanda's desire to go on a killing spree had at this point diminished as a result of Sean's unwillingness to go along with this plan. Her media practices at this point represent a significant shift. She continued to show herself as a killer, describing what she did, but she also performed different identities. These was evident in her reflection narrative, which came to eclipse the action narrative at this point. She drew on her feminine social roles as widow and mother, including references to Rex and her children in the posts. She also changed the manner in which she showed Charles. Rather than showing him as a depersonified object, simply a corpse included in an image that 'proved' she was a killer, she constructed and presented him as an active agent. She engaged in victim blaming, accusing him of having brought about the death of her husband. This technique of neutralisation (Sykes and Matza, 1957) was an attempt to deny him the status of a victim and cast *him* in the role of the aggressor, pulling the victim role towards herself. However, she did not abandon her killer identity easily, stating: 'If you keep looking for me more will die' (Cited in Murdock, 2015). This would appear to be an attempt to continue the fantasy narrative straight from the script of Natural Born Killers, with Amanda presenting herself simultaneously as victim and aggressor, dual roles that assisted Mickey and Mallory Knox in acquiring cult hero status in the film. The inclusion of the news story about herself and Sean also supports this narrative and is eerily reflective of the drawing sent to her by Paul Runge (brunette_bomber, 2014r).

The final post came after Amanda had shot Sean and left him at the side of the road. She posted on her Instagram feed a photograph of a hand gun in what appeared to be her lap, accompanied by the comment: 'Alright ... it's about that time. Im going to go find my husband in Hell and finally be at peace. I love you mom and my beautiful crazies, i know youll give them the life i just couldnt after everything' (cited in Murdock, 2015). In this post, the action narrative of the homicide has gone; this post is saturated with reflection. Amanda cast the killer identity aside and omitted any mention of Charles. As such, she turned the spotlight firmly on herself and it could be argued that she was continuing to try to present herself as the victim. She highlighted her presence in a traditional social institution – the family – and identified her feminine social roles and identities as wife and mother. She presented herself as someone who cared about her children and expressed a wish as to who should look after them in her absence. Her words appeared to suggest that she was about to take her own life, but ultimately she did not do so. It could be argued that she was planning to commit suicide at another location. Whether or not her threat to harm herself was a real one, it had a very real effect – that of creating another scene in her fantasy and adding to the drama that she had created while 'on the run'.

Media behind bars

Amanda's media practices did not end with her arrest; rather, she continued (and at the time of writing continues) to show herself in various different ways. Police mugshots released to the mainstream media show her smiling broadly. This had the effect of differentiating her mugshots from the 'traditional' mugshot in which the suspect looks sullen and expressionless. Whether or not she intended to look different and stand out, this was certainly the effect. She gave an interview to Chris Hurst, a news anchor for the local WDBJ television news station. Frustrated at how the mainstream media were reporting Charles' murder, Amanda agreed to an interview with Hurst from jail and they had three telephone conversations (*Commonwealth of Virginia v Taylor*, 2015a). During these calls, Amanda compared murder to riding on a rollercoaster, saying: 'I was excited. I know it sounds bad, but I was really excited…. I know it's not right, but that was something I chose to do to feel better' (Austin, 2015). With regard to her method of killing, she stated that 'this was a personal kill … I wanted to watch him die' (Austin, 2015).

However, when the interview aired, Amanda was not happy with the coverage she received. She argued that the extracts shown on the television news did not accurately reflect the conversations: 'He cut it. He made it sound really bad' (*Commonwealth of Virginia v Taylor*, 2016, p 36). These comments suggest that Amanda was very concerned about how she was being shown by others. No longer able to show herself, she was dependent on others to produce and disseminate representations of her. She was desperately trying to regain control of the narrative. Incarcerated with no direct access to the internet, she no longer had the degree of control she had previously enjoyed through her posts on Tumblr, Instagram and Facebook. She wrote a threatening letter to Chris Hurst, threatening to harm him in the same way she had harmed Sean:

> Quit being such a scumbag. I told you my story wasn't over. You promised to stick around. You lied. Do you remember what happened to the last man to lie to me? I'm going to be the bullet that brings you to your knees. (*Commonwealth of Virginia v Taylor*, 2016, p 44)

Despite having confessed multiple times to Charles' murder, both on and offline, Amanda entered a plea of not guilty. As such, she secured a trial by jury – and the attention of the mainstream media that came with it. The courtroom provided another stage for Amanda, and indeed her behaviour during her trial and related hearings generated much media attention. She shouted out in court: 'Why do you have to stand there? Like can't you scoot over just a little?... I love you. Sorry I didn't see you, they had to stand in front of you. I'll see you next week' (*Commonwealth of Virginia v Taylor*, 2015b, p 17). This elicited the attention of a local journalist, who commented that Amanda 'was disruptive through much of the proceeding. She yelled out to someone in the crowd that she loved them. She also yelled at deputies to stop blocking her view' (Teague, 2015b).

Although she no longer had access to the internet, Amanda appeared keen to maintain a presence to others through social media and drew on the assistance of her friend Mariah. Mariah made several posts to Amanda's Facebook and Instagram accounts, confirming details of when her trial would take place and how people could write to her and send her messages and money. Amanda was successful in her attempt to show herself by proxy. As noted earlier in the chapter, Amanda attracted a considerable audience after killing Charles; the number of people following her on Instagram grew significantly and many of the comments posted on her account are very complimentary and supportive in nature. One comment on an image of the letter she forwarded to Mariah reads: 'Wow her hand writing is gorgeous' (brunette_bomber, 2015a). Other examples include: 'This case was shown on the peruvian TV (my country), and I feel bad for Amanda', and 'Tell her we said good luck dude' (brunette_bomber, 2015a). However, other comments heavily condemn her. Many posts express considerable disgust and a desire for vengeance, for example: 'Let her rot in prison, or get stabbed' (brunette_bomber, 2015b). Perhaps the most poignant comment, however, is one that poses a simple but important question: 'Why has everyone forgot about Charlie Taylor?' (brunette_bomber, 2015b).

Blurred lines: fantasies, realities and a crisis of being

The Ethnographic Media Practice Analysis for Criminology analysis of Amanda's social media archive has enabled a range of insights into her identities, values and interests. The exploration of her media practices of showing, presencing and archiving has facilitated both an examination of rich detail and an appreciation of context. Amanda performed a range of social identities via social media. Most of them focused on one institution – the family. Amanda was a mother, a sister, a daughter, a wife and then a widow. Her family-based social roles were not out of the ordinary in the local context; marriage and motherhood at a relatively early age were not particularly unusual. Indeed, she acknowledged her similarity to other young women of Christiansburg in the post congratulating her sister on getting into college. Amanda appeared immensely proud of her children, however, showing them to her Facebook friends and Instagram followers, with such content forming the largest category in her media archive. Despite this, she rarely showed herself alongside her children in the many photographs of them. In the context of our 'photographic culture', in which a photograph is not simply an image but part of our social being (Carney, 2010), this void in Amanda's archive is noteworthy. Her mother's comment that Amanda felt 'she wasn't good enough for her kids' (*Commonwealth of Virginia v Taylor*, 2015, p 263) is a powerful one when considering this absence. It could be argued that while she was proud of them, she was less proud of her performance in the role of their mother, a role that had constrained her and set the course for her life at an early age.

Alongside her identities within the family was Amanda's membership of subcultural groups, which she also performed on social media. She liked horror movies and films about violent crime, so much so that her body bore several tattoos paying homage to characters and lines from these films. Her association with these dark fan subcultures was not something she kept separate from her family identities. She and Rex shared these interests, she showed them in the same media spaces where she displayed her family roles, and images of her home and body demonstrate that these interests infused her everyday life and sense of *being* in the world. She romanticised Mickey and Mallory Knox from Natural Born Killers and projected this fantasy onto her relationship with her husband. Perhaps she admired what they represented – cult heroes who had gone from powerless to powerful and captured the attention of the world's media. Perhaps she empathised with the characters – both they and she were limited by their structural locations and the cultural norms, values and expectations that came along with this.

Amanda belonged to a subculture that celebrated and hero-worshipped *real-life* multiple killers in a similar way. She was familiar with the terminology of this subculture and was knowledgeable about the dates and circumstances of particular massacres and events. She further performed her belonging via a series of selfies accompanied by quotes and lyrics, the significance of which only fellow enthusiasts would understand. Her interest had extended as far as corresponding with convicted serial killers. She did not simply prosume mediated representations *of them*, she engaged in experiences *with them*. The boundary between the 'fan' and the 'iniquitous criminal celebrity' (Penfold-Mounce, 2009) had been broken, her life and theirs had connected. This was something Amanda was keen to show to others on Instagram. Amanda's Natural Born Killers fantasy and her access to real-life serial killers added a sense of the exotic and the exciting to her everyday, normal life as a young single mother in Montgomery County, Virginia. While she appeared uncomfortable showing herself as a mother, her self-portraits as a member of a dark subculture were confident and bold. She showed herself with lyrics and film quotes much more than she showed herself with her children. Her status within the subcultural groups that shared her interests in violence and murder was important to her. Amanda wanted to *be* somebody and through mainstream and social media, be *seen* to be somebody.

Amanda created murderabilia around the homicide long before she carried it out. She gave a folder of clippings, love letters and notes depicting hers and Rex's relationship to Mariah in early 2015. Amanda anticipated that journalists and authors would one day want to write about them. However, at this time, nothing that had happened in their lives would reach the thresholds of 'newsworthiness'; they were not interesting or unique (Jewkes, 2015). Amanda's actions in giving the folder to Mariah suggest that she was planning to do something that would make them newsworthy – becoming a multiple murderer would certainly achieve this end. This was an identity that both Amanda and Rex had admired and celebrated in others.

Amanda's Tumblr blog, created in March 2015, represented both an escalation and a separation. On Tumblr, Amanda did not show her family or maintain a presence to them. This was a dark repository; the content she uploaded and shared here was more violent and extreme than anything on Facebook or Instagram. This was a space in which she could create and maintain a darker, more violent presence to others. It was a place where these performances of self were not diluted or offset by her family identities. It was a space where she could *remediate* (Bolter and Grusin, 1999), crafting her own killing script from those of others, both real and fictional. The decision to commit murder in the month of April was most likely no coincidence – Amanda had acknowledged that this was a significant month for multiple murder and perhaps anticipated joining this macabre hall of fame. She left 'clues' on social media before she put her plan into action. Her Facebook friends, who included her mother, sister and extended family, may have interpreted the Sweet Jane music as simply a loving tribute to Rex, stemming from an unconventional but shared interest. However, when seen in the context of her Tumblr blog, the music took on another, more sinister meaning.

Charles' murder was more than the conflict resolution homicide she later presented it as. It was the culmination of Amanda's 'crisis of being' (Hayward and Young, 2004). In a society where self-fulfilment, celebrity and immediacy are valorised, the opportunities for Amanda to achieve these outcomes were limited. She broke these restraints and asserted her agency by killing. In so doing, she was treading the path of her heroes, both real and fictional. Her crisis of being was resolved through the convergence of fantasy and reality. The author argues that Charles' murder was a 'warm up'. Through killing an elderly, vulnerable man whom she knew, in circumstances over which she had a significant degree of control, she was able to 'test' whether she was capable of murder. Not able to carry out other killings due to the non-compliance of her temporary partner in crime, Amanda abandoned her plan. This is evident in the shift between action and reflection narratives, the former giving way to the latter as she realised that her goal of going on a murder spree reminiscent of that in Natural Born Killers was not going to materialise. She attempted to restore her family roles though social media, casting the killer aside and re-engaging with the wife and mother, roles she performed to her friends and family in the social media spaces where they were present. These audiences were not only people who would feel the impact of her actions most poignantly; more importantly, they would be useful to her in continuing to show herself from behind bars and in her attempts to maintain control over the narrative as the story unfolded in mainstream media. She also performed a victim narrative – a frame of reference in which criminology often understands women who kill.

While many would be tempted to focus on Amanda's consumption of violent media and 'blame' this for the crime she ultimately committed, the reality is considerably more complex and nuanced. Throughout most of her media archive, her consumption and production of representations of horror and violence were presented as socially acceptable, shown through Facebook and Instagram – spaces in which she also performed traditional, gendered roles and maintained family relationships. However, the line between fantasy and reality had always been blurred for Amanda; the characters and stories she admired and identified with offered the promise of something more than the life she had. They also provided the beginnings of a script that could achieve this end. It was not so much Amanda's *consumption* of violent media that matters in understanding this case. Rather, what matters is how she used networked media to perform a range of identities, some of which were violent and others that were not. In the same way that Amanda lived in and through media, so too she killed in and through media.

Amanda's media practices would appear to have more in common with Derek, the killer explored in the first case study in Chapter Five, than with Randy, the perpetrator considered in Chapter Six. While Amanda's portrayal of everyday life was less grandiose and fanciful than Derek's, her media practices came to embody fantasy more prominently in the period leading up to Charles' murder. Fantasy was important for Derek and Amanda in obscuring the mundane realities of their lives, their media practices used to portray selves that were more exciting and significant. Randy, on the other hand, did not claim the limelight for himself, instead using networked media to support his daughter's, and to a lesser degree his wife's, presentation of self – people on whom he depended for a sense of his own identity.

In the following chapter, the insights generated from the analysis of all three cases are considered in light of existing literature, identifying the broader structures and contexts in which people like Derek, Randy and Amanda confess to homicide on social media and considering the implications for future research and wider understandings of such phenomena.

Notes
[1] Throughout this chapter, grammatical errors and misspellings are left as they appear in the original source.
[2] 'ahs' is short for American Horror Story, a US horror television series.
[3] Most decongestants contain pseudoephedrine hydrochloride, which is used in the manufacture of methamphetamine.
[4] Michael Myers is one of the lead characters in the Halloween series of horror films.

EIGHT

Discussion: the complex contexts of social media homicide confessions

Throughout this book, the author has presented a range of themes, concepts, issues and cases at the intersection of media and homicide. The book aims to make better criminological sense of social media homicide confessions and develop more robust frameworks for the future study of such cases. The purpose of this final chapter is to outline the insights that have been generated from the three case studies and consider their implications for current theorising and future directions for research in this area. This chapter highlights the key findings in relation to the meanings and contexts of social media homicide confessions. It begins by outlining perpetrators' media practices *prior* to becoming involved in homicide before examining the confessions themselves, exploring continuities and changes. The chapter concludes with a consideration of future directions for research to develop better understandings of homicide in 21st-century networked society.

Writing the story: reality, fantasy and transgression in media

It was clear that social media was woven into the fabric of everyday life for each of the three perpetrators; they lived *in* media (Deuze, 2012). Their media practices – or what they were *doing* in relation to media (Couldry, 2012) – varied in nature and extent, and their experiences were unique and distinctive. However, several key themes emerged in relation to how they drew on social media to achieve a range of outcomes. They used social media to create representations of themselves and those around them. The stories of their lives that they told through social media were revealing in relation to their self-narratives, as characters occupying particular social roles and identities. Their practices also revealed their expectations of other people in the roles they occupied. Social media was a space in which their membership of social groups and institutions and the nature of their presence within them could be performed. An examination of roles, expectations and performances has enabled the author to situate the perpetrators within broader social and cultural contexts and consider the degree to which these structural frameworks constrained and enabled them.

The family emerged as a prominent social group in the perpetrators' archives. This is important to consider because in all three cases, victims were members of the perpetrator's immediate or extended families. Social media enabled them to perform social roles linked to the family and create a sense of presence within this social institution. What was common for all three perpetrators was that their performances of family via social media were highly idealistic and stylised. Derek presented himself as a successful patriarch. The family was a machismo prop to support his performance of other identities consistent with the American Dream – the sportsman and the self-help writer. The way in which he presented his family became more elaborate as his performance of other identities was embellished and exaggerated – most notably that of the writer. Amanda showed her happy, smiling children through photographs that dominated her archive and text-based posts in which she expressed her love for them and pride in them. Charles, her victim, was shown as a kindly grandfather taking his grandson and daughter-in-law to church. Family members were always portrayed in a positive light and as such, her family appeared idyllic and harmonious – a far cry from the picture of 'sheer desperation' in which scholars paint women who kill (Brookman, 2005). Randy supported the stories his family told about themselves on social media, complimenting his wife and expressing his pride in his daughter Emily – she was 'awesome' and 'beautiful', he was 'proud'. He 'liked' most of the things they posted on Facebook so was actively looking for opportunities to support them on social media.

However, while the idealistic presentations involved showing some elements of family, they also involved omitting, concealing or blurring others. Derek did not acknowledge Jennifer's personhood, portraying her only in her social role as his wife. He also hid from view the abusive and controlling nature of their relationship, the 'everyday terrorism' (Pain, 2014) that was entrenched in the household. A veneer of respectability is common among most abusers, who often present a different self in public to that behind closed doors (Richards et al, 2008). However, the more subtle indications of Derek's coercively controlling behaviour were not as well hidden as perhaps he may have thought – Jennifer's increasing presence within his videos suggested a correspondence in the intensity of Derek's monitoring and surveillance of her. Randy concealed Emily's illness, never referring directly to it on social media, a practice that stood in stark contrast to his wife Laurel's behaviour, as she regularly shared frustrations about Emily's migraines in these spaces. By focusing on showing Emily on social media, Randy concealed *himself*. What mattered was not *his* presence to others but Emily's; he appeared as an extension of her, living vicariously through her. These practices are characteristic of civil reputable familicide perpetrators, whose sense of self is nominal and whose emotional style is restrained and repressed (Websdale, 2010). Amanda omitted from her social media archive the break-up of her relationship with Rex, her felony conviction, her problems with mental health, Rex's addiction and the circumstances around his death. All of these issues and events would have severely fractured the idyllic picture of family life she painted, highlighting characteristics she shared with other female homicide perpetrators (Brookman, 2005; Schwartz, 2012).

The broader social and cultural contexts in which family lives and roles were embedded were also shown and concealed, present and absent in the perpetrators' archives. Derek alluded to a favourable structural position through his social media posts. The successful man dining out at the yacht club with his wife and daughter, the man playing golf at the country club and the 'pro', 'semi-pro', or 'retired pro' sportsman are suggestive of someone with considerably more economic resources than he had. While his many videos had a distinct feel of 'reality television' to them, inviting viewers into his private world, his narration of them was pure fantasy. Nowhere in his videos did he refer to his occupation or talk about his employment, even to complain about it, and in so doing, perhaps present a compelling narrative for his regular job moves. Derek did not show himself as a front-desk supervisor or allude to Jennifer's waitressing work in supporting the family. This would have compromised his patriarchal and machismo performance of self (Stevens, 1973). Context, structure and non-family social roles were largely absent from Randy's media archive; the self he presented only appeared to exist in relation to this institution. There was no mention of his work in his posts, or of the various sports teams he followed. His only link to broader structures in social media emerged *through* Emily when he celebrated her educational accomplishments and award of a place at university. As such, this further emphasised the sense of alienation and isolation associated with civil reputable familicide perpetrators (Websdale, 2010). Amanda rarely acknowledged her lack of economic resources, but when she did she presented it in a way that supported her positive depiction of family life. Her children were shown happily engaging in activities that were not expensive to facilitate – for example, a home-made ball pool and colouring books. Amanda did not narrate the challenges for young people in Montgomery County in fatalistic terms. She told tales of triumph over adversity rather than despair and frustration – for example, her sister defying the odds through graduating from high school and going to college.

As such, through social media, the perpetrators carefully crafted representations of themselves and others in family social roles and positioned them within broader cultural and structural contexts. This is not surprising given that the social media platforms on which family roles were displayed were those where the perpetrators were most likely to have links with friends and family. These were spaces in which they maintained their existing social relationships (Baym, 2010; Chambers, 2013) and presented themselves as friends and family knew them – as Derek Medina, Randy Janzen and Amanda Taylor. As such, the audiences for these performances were people from those intimate social circles, where people were connected to one another through family and friendship roles and occupied similar cultural and structural locations, suggesting that they were likely to judge each other with reference to these shared experiences.

In addition to family roles, social media was also an important stage for the performance of other identities for Derek and Amanda. Derek performed the identity of the sportsman and the writer, the latter emerging as dominant in the later parts of his media archive. His presentation of the sportsman – claiming to be professional or semi-professional – was saturated with fantasy and delusions of grandeur. It was not enough for him to present himself as someone who simply enjoyed the sports he engaged in; rather, he had to be someone of *superior* status, even if these claims were far removed from reality. In 2013, he came to take on the identity of the self-help writer. The books he wrote were largely nonsensical, short and littered with basic errors, with Derek seemingly unaware of his limitations in this area. As was true for his sportsman identity, Derek was not content to present himself as someone who was just getting started with writing; rather, he wanted to be seen as an established and prolific writer. He ensured that his self-published books were on sale via Amazon and Barnes and Noble, he set up his own 'brand' – 'emotional writer'. He was keen to share with his perceived audience of YouTube fans the fact that he written *six* books in *six* months, and he wore garments with 'writer' boldly emblazoned on them so no one was in any doubt as to his new identity. The mindful self-help writer was an identity wholly at odds with the real Derek Medina, who was an abuser. Derek's fantasising appeared to increase in scope and nature later in the archive. His narcissism was evident in these illusions of success, achievement, status and power (Raskin and Terry, 1998) and what others thought of him appeared to become more important over time. Derek used social media to perform identities he aspired to but did not fulfil – they were largely a fantasy. Derek built a fantasy life and fantasy identities on YouTube, where he also started to use his family to develop the narrative. In social media, fantasy and reality fused as Derek painted a picture of his life that he wanted people to see. Social media was an important locus of power for him too. It was a place where he could maintain control over Jennifer – who and what Jennifer was in social media was who and what she was *for* Derek (Stark, 2007). Rather than presenting himself and Jennifer as they were, he used social media to present how he thought they *should* have been. Derek's crisis of being (Hayward and Young, 2004) is clear to anyone looking at his YouTube channel and considering it in the context of what is known about him now. However, before he killed Jennifer, no one appeared to be looking at his YouTube channel. His audience of 'fans' did not exist. No one cared about what this strange man was doing in relation to media other than to make fun of his bizarre behaviour and 'crazy videos' (Benn, 2013). His sportsman and writer identities were not supported or endorsed by others. There is no evidence that anyone other than Derek himself attested to his membership of these communities and cultures. He simply went *unseen* as he evolved as an abuser and a narcissist.

Amanda's identity as a member of a horror and violence subculture was clear to see throughout her media archive. She was a fan of horror films, violent films and television series about violent crime. She idolised Mickey and Mallory Knox from the film Natural Born Killers and came to ascribe this to her relationship with her late husband. She admired multiple murderers, was knowledgeable about a range of cases, wrote to serial killers and appeared to have had established a regular correspondence with at least two such individuals. Her living room was decorated with various items of horror paraphernalia and murderabilia. Her body bore several tattoos inspired by her interests. She posted selfies captioned with lines from violent films and songs. Others endorsed these identities in regularly commenting on her posts, discussing films and television with her, admiring her tattoos and complimenting her on her selfies. Amanda posted this content alongside pictures of her children and family, her Instagram feed a stark juxtaposition of motherhood and violence, posting under the name 'brunette_bomber'. The transgression never appeared to elicit critical comment from any of her followers, even friends and family; it appeared to be simply 'just who she was'. In Amanda's reality, bizarre was the norm. Amanda's membership of a subculture and her *performance* of this membership through social media enabled her to do things that she was not able to do in any other area of her life – stand out from the crowd, be different. As a young mother in Montgomery County, Amanda was the rule rather than the exception. She may have stated, 'That's the only thing I was good at, was being a mom' (*Commonwealth of Virginia v Taylor*, 2016, p 38), but her motherhood made her just like everyone else. Her identity within horror and violence fan subcultures enabled her to be dangerous, edgy and exciting, going further than others, not simply consuming representations of violence but reaching out and making connections with serial killers. As such, social media offered Amanda both a space in which to perform traditional gendered roles and to demonstrate that she was *more* than a mother. She was admired, respected and endorsed by others in another role, a different identity. In presenting both identities in the same space, they offset and diluted one another. While her horror and violence interests were unusual, they came across as 'quirky' rather than deviant as the rest of her Instagram emphasised traditional, non-violent, caring and nurturing social roles. However, Amanda's creation of the Tumblr blog represented something altogether different. Again using the name 'Brunette Bomber', but pairing this with the handle 'letsbindtorturekill' in apparent homage to serial killer Dennis Rader, Amanda populated this space with images of graphic violence, the glorification of school shooters and what appeared to be a violent act of self-harm. There were no references to her children or family to balance or mitigate these extreme representations. In this space, Amanda was not a 'mother'; she left this identity behind at the login page. The creation of this dark repository was not just an escalation but was also a separation. Out of the view of friends and family, her media practices on Tumblr went unchecked, the only self she presented being one with an appetite for violence and violent media. While Facebook and Instagram embodied the 'social' in social media, Amanda's Tumblr account would be more accurately described as *antisocial* media.

It is clear that the media practices of these perpetrators prior to committing homicide were complex, unique and characterised by heterogeneity. However, what is also clear is that they served an important function in creating a presence to others through a range of social roles and identities. This presence to others was an *aspirational* one; the perpetrators were showing their lives on social media in the ways that they *wanted* to be seen. These roles and identities varied, some rooted in reality, others in fantasy, sometimes separate and sometimes overlapping. The audiences to which these selves were performed also varied. Sometimes they consisted of friends, family and those in close geographical proximity. At other times, these audiences encompassed subcultures, fans and followers – real or imagined. The showing of roles and identities in social media – both in relation to self and others – drew on broader social and cultural scripts and expectations. This included the identification of roles that carried status and how those occupying such roles should perform them. Having a presence in social media served a purpose for the perpetrators in performing aspirational representations of self. Visibility was a *weapon* they used to tackle the struggles and challenges of everyday life (Thompson, 2005) and present themselves as they wanted to be seen. However, what also emerged as key to the media practices of the perpetrators was *invisibility*. The things that they concealed, omitted and blurred were just as meaningful as the things they showed.

It is important to identify appropriate conceptual and theoretical frameworks within which to make sense of these practices of presencing, showing and concealing. While ideas like Goffman's *presentation of self* (1959) appear valuable, the author argues that they serve to abstract the perpetrator somewhat from the wider social context and do nothing to discourage the popular interpretations and mainstream media narratives of Derek, Randy and Amanda as aberrations, distinct and separate from the rest of us. Media practices take performances beyond the private realm. In showing themselves via networked media, the consumption and confirmation of their self-presentation was public. Networked technology was a powerful tool for establishing and maintaining their fantasies and their roles as characters within these fantasies. The context for the presentation of self has changed considerably since Goffman's seminal work. As such, there is a need for more robust conceptual and theoretical frameworks that are both appreciative of these shifts and attentive to the deeper structural currents that flow beneath the surface of a 21st-century networked society. The work of Hall and colleagues (Hall et al, 2008; Hall, 2012; Hall and Winlow, 2015) offers a promising framework. These authors draw on the work of Lacan (2006) and Žižek (2009) in drawing attention to infantile narcissism, enabled by the widespread acceptance of hedonism as an integral part of the reward structure in contemporary society. With the marketing industry of the mid-20th century acting as a primary catalyst, narcissism has become socially acceptable and indeed encouraged. In a technologically sophisticated, mass-mediated culture, we are able to justify and indulge our infantile narcissism under the guises of self-marketing, self-promotion or personal branding. Hall summarises the impact of these trends: 'the terror of insignificance, of remaining unrecognised by others, might now reign supreme as the most potent and extractable source of human energy' (2012, p 172). These endeavours serve to distract us from larger, more difficult questions about power, politics and citizenship. Media practices enabled all three perpetrators to forget or deny the devalued or negative aspects of their identities and amplify the valued roles and behaviours that accorded them status within their social context. Žižek describes this process as fetishist disavowal:

> This forgetting entails a gesture of what is called *fetishist disavowal*. 'I know but I don't want to know that I know, so I don't know'. I know it, but I refuse to fully assume the consequences of this knowledge, so that I can continue acting as if I don't know it. (Žižek, 2009, pp 45-6, emphasis added)

Fetishist disavowal was clear in the pre-homicide media practices of all three perpetrators considered in this book, and involved evoking what Cohen (2001) has referred to as literal denial. This stems from a deliberate avoidance of particular struggles or issues. Derek denied his identity as a coercively controlling abuser. Randy denied Emily's illness. Amanda denied the breakdown of her relationship, her felonies and mental health problems. Such denials and disavowals effectively protected Derek, Randy and Amanda from the consequences of acceptance and enabled the maintenance of fantasy, idealistic identities. It could be argued that they trapped themselves in 'the realm of the Imaginary' (Hall, 2012, p 208). They would continue to engage in fetishist disavowal via networked media when their real transgressions expanded to encompass homicide. This is explored in the following section.

Continuing the story: writing the homicide chapter

Just as the perpetrators' pre-homicide social media archives were varied, unique and heterogeneous, so too were the media practices they engaged in around the homicides they committed. While all three admitted responsibility for taking the lives of others, they did so in very different ways. The narratives were clearly rooted in perpetrators' social realities and structural locations. The confessions were tailored to particular audiences to achieve specific outcomes and as such, their nature and content was distinct. They represented both change and continuity in relation to their broader social media archives. This section considers these points in relation to each case and explores the implications for criminological understandings of social media homicide confessions.

Derek's macabre Facebook confession appeared to be aimed at two audiences: Jennifer's family and friends, and Derek's perceived community of 'fans'. Derek had been attempting to isolate Jennifer from her loved ones for several years. He had tried to get her to quit her job at Denny's, a place where she had many friends and loyal customers. He was likely instrumental in excluding any family members from their weddings. In showing her dead body to their family and friends via a strong action narrative (Brookman, 2015) in which he displayed the scene of the crime, he communicated his 'victory' to them. He had 'won', just as he had done so several times in his fantasy identity as a sportsman. Through changing the project to one of destruction (Dobash and Dobash, 2015), he had achieved his aim of complete control, isolating Jennifer from her loved ones and permanently taking her away from them. This represented a continuation of the way in which Derek exercised control through social media, deciding exactly how and to whom he showed himself and others. In addressing his following of 'fans' and saying 'You'll see me in the news', Derek continued to believe that others were interested in him and indeed, anticipated that more people would become interested in him given what he had just done. He needed to provide an explanation to his perceived followers, who – had they existed – may not have been sympathetic to this transgression in his performance from self-help author to abuser. He engaged in identity management here and donned a new identity – that of victim. When addressing this audience, the reflection narrative (Brookman, 2015) is the dominant one – the post is all about him, his story and his identity in terms of who *he* is and what will happen to *him*. In his story to his 'fans', Jennifer is simply a passing reference, a plot device that gets the next chapter to his story started but soon disappears from the narrative. Other continuities were evident in his post, most notably the choice to share a photograph of Jennifer's body. It was not enough to tell people he was a writer; rather, he had to *show* his books and *label* himself through his clothing. Similarly, it was not enough to tell people he was a killer; he had to *show* proof of this. However, one thing that Derek did not have control over was the capacity of the photograph to communicate the *real* dynamics of power and transgression (Ferrell and Van der Voorde, 2010). The photograph highlighted Jennifer's true identity as the victim and Derek's true identity as the aggressor. So powerful was this image that it spoke louder than the words Derek tried to use to justify his actions.

In showing this image, Derek's legitimacy as a self-determined 'victim' was quashed by a compelling counter-narrative of his own creation.

The audience for Randy's confession was considerably smaller than that for Derek. Given the importance he attached to his family and his dependence on them for a sense of his own identity, Randy's concern in writing his confession appeared to be solely to manage others' impressions of them. Connected to both Emily and Laurel through Facebook, he had commented on their posts and 'liked' their content on a regular basis. As such, he was aware of the importance of this social media space for Emily in managing her presence to others. Most important to him was ensuring that she continued to be seen in a positive light by the people who mattered to her and the people he anticipated may judge her after her death. This audience included her friends from school, members of the local performing arts community and people she had become connected to in the wider arts and cultural sphere in Canada and beyond. The visceral emotions expressed within the lengthy post and the direct acknowledgement of Emily's illness were at odds with Randy's previous media practices. Randy ascribed a crisis of being (Hayward and Young, 2004) to her, claiming that she had talent but would never be able to realise it. This stood in stark contrast to the hope that characterised earlier posts. So while the nature of homicide confession was distinct from the media practices that preceded it, the intention remained the same – to support Emily's management of identity. Even the reflection narrative (Brookman, 2015) within the post suggested this; Emily always central in the way Randy narrated aspects of himself, his life and his identity. Randy killed his family because through his increasing alienation and isolation (Websdale, 2010) he had convinced himself it was the only way to 'save' them. The homicide confession was the last time he would manage their presence to others and try to write his already nominal self out of the story, committing *existential* suicide prior to taking his own life.

Amanda confessed across a range of social media – Facebook, Instagram and Tumblr – and tailored her confessions to these different audiences. The intended audience for the graphic Tumblr photograph of Amanda with Charles' body were 'killer groupies'. These people were fellow members of the subculture she belonged to, who admired and glamorised murderers. The post was consistent with the rest of her Tumblr blog of violent imagery and glorification of homicide. In also sending the photograph to her online friend who ran a serial killers website, Amanda intended to present herself to these audiences in her new identity as a killer, enabling them to witness her transgression and the making of a spree killer – a strong 'action narrative'

(Brookman, 2015). She embraced the identity of killer and gloried in the visceral violence she had enacted. The Tumblr post is suggestive of a performance homicide, enacted for the camera, the will-to-representation evident (Yar, 2012; Surette, 2015a). Her Instagram posts continued the action narrative. She posted updates while 'on the run', inviting people on her journey as a killer. This content supplemented the murderabilia archive she had left with her friend Mariah. All of these artefacts would assist Amanda in her autobiographical account of the 'rise' of this wannabe iniquitous criminal celebrity (Penfold-Mounce, 2009). These posts were strongly reminiscent of reality television and rolling news, mimicking scenes from Natural Born Killers and turning Amanda's fantasies around the film into reality. Her Facebook posts were crafted for a different audience of friends and family. Reflection narratives became more dominant as she realised that her fantasy of a murder spree would not materialise and she resurrected her more well-worn identities of wife, widow, mother and victim. Taking on the identity as the victim involved the creation of an aggressor – a role in which Amanda cast Charles. No longer was he a kindly grandfather, but a toxic force whose actions had damaged her idyllic family. As such, these posts present her as the *defender* of her family, a mother and widow engaging in justifiable revenge in response to a threat.

All three confessions were performances. While the nature of the performance and the audience to whom it was addressed varied, they were all performances nonetheless, in which the perpetrators attempted to take control of the narrative around the homicides they committed. These performances were displayed in spaces where the intended audiences would see them; they were made to be seen by others and as such, they represent practices of search enabling (Couldry, 2012). Perhaps most importantly, these confessions were performances of self in a mediatised consumer culture (Hall et al, 2008), attempts to manage identity around the most serious of transgressions. Crises of being (Hayward and Young, 2004) were evident in the cases of all three perpetrators. As such, their management of the 'killer' identity was crucial, whether they fully embraced it, as was the case for Randy, or alternated between trying it on and casting it aside, as Derek and Amanda did. As such, visibility was a key weapon in their arsenal (Thompson, 2005). Poster's claims more than 20 years ago that the internet was facilitating an 'explosion of narrativity' (1995, p 91) and a burning desire to tell our stories holds true for these cases. Homicide confessions are no exception to this compulsion, reflective of the perpetrators' desire to tell their story and present themselves as particular types of character within it – including but not limited to that of killer and victim – and engaging in fetishist disavowal in so doing (Žižek, 2009).

The use of photographs was a particularly significant storytelling device for Amanda and Derek. As visual criminologists have noted, photographs are not merely images, but powerful parts of our lives that communicate our sense of being in the world (Carney, 2010). For Derek and Amanda, the photographs of their deceased victims represented 'decisive moments', where the significance of an event becomes such that it has to be captured by an image and the image itself becomes part of the event (Ferrell and Van de Voorde, 2010). For Derek, the photograph marked his 'win' – his success in destroying Jennifer and as such, gaining complete control over her. For Amanda, the photograph marked the birth of her new identity as a killer, one she had admired in others for many years and whose ranks she was now joining. In sharing these photographs on social media, Derek and Amanda were communicating to others that their sense of being in the world had shifted; they were now something *more* than they had been before. However, as noted previously, these photographs were much more powerful than Derek or Amanda's words or other posts in revealing the dynamics of the events. While Derek and Amanda may have tried to blame their victims and present themselves as justified in the homicides they committed, the photographs and the sharing of them simply reinforced their agency, choice, responsibility and culpability for their crimes. Randy's choice not to share any photographs of his family – either dead or alive – spoke to his embodiment of the civil reputable familicide perpetrator as someone who carefully shields their family from the threats they perceive in the outside world (Websdale, 2010).

The identity management practised by the perpetrators considered in this book took place within a wound culture, a pathological public sphere in which most of what people know about homicide is learned from what they see in the mainstream media (Seltzer, 1998, 2007, 2008; Surette, 2015b). People were drawn to these cases. People convened around the mediated scenes of violence, compelled to look at the broken bodies of the victims and the broken psyches of the perpetrators (Seltzer, 1998). As such, it is important to acknowledge the loops and spirals evident in the perpetrators' media practices (Ferrell et al, 2008, 2015). All three perpetrators will have watched crime news, crime drama, true crime documentaries and films about homicide. They will have encountered a variety of media products. These products may well have included shows like Crime Scene Investigation with its forensic realist depiction of violence, post-forensic crime dramas like The Wire, infused with complex narratives and personal stories, and reality crime television like America's Most Wanted or Crimewatch, depicting 'big bad' criminals (Jermyn, 2007, 2013). As such, they have some level of awareness of the meanings and representations associated with homicide. In the same way that mainstream media depictions of murder are stylised representations, sieved through a filter of newsworthiness and appealing to trends and appetites for particular types of product, so too are perpetrator-produced social media confessions. They are *representations*, perpetrator-constructed stories of homicide. The killers did not write these stories within a vacuum; they wrote them within wound culture, and as such, drew on the values, norms, identities and meanings inherent within it. Just as the 'cultural scripts' of school shooters are contextually and structurally situated (Newman et al, 2004; Kellner, 2008), so too were the media practices of the three perpetrators examined in this book. The world in which people confess to homicide on social media is one in which 'the street scripts the screen and the screen scripts the street ... the line between the real and the virtual is profoundly and irrevocably blurred' (Hayward and Young, 2004, p 259). This is particularly evident in Amanda's case. Her confessions and the dramatic way in which they were enacted drew on scripts from violent media and were particularly newsworthy, as were her attempts to elicit attention following her incarceration. Derek's confession also drew on mediated representations of homicide in assigning himself the status of the 'victim', aware of the power of this narrative even if unaware of how ludicrous it appeared in relation to his own case. Randy was quick to show remorse and take responsibility in his confession. He constructed Emily as an image of perfection, someone who had 'done everything' to try to address her migraines – an effective counter-narrative to the victim blaming and character assassination that sometimes features in sense making around homicides, particularly those involving female victims (Dowler et al, 2006; Monckton-Smith, 2012). Just as our general understandings of homicide are informed by mainstream media representations, so too are homicide confessions. They are infused with and surrounded by the loops and spirals that shape and reshape our understandings of homicide in contemporary society (Ferrell et al, 2008, 2015).

Several gatekeepers stood between the killers of the past and those who consumed their stories. In a pre-networked media age, killers wanting to attain celebrity status killed in a newsworthy way, targeting high-profile victims and/or making contact with mainstream media outlets to generate publicity around their crimes (Gekoski, 1998; Penfold-Mounce, 2009). These killers depended on news editors to determine whether or not their stories reached thresholds of newsworthiness. The perpetrators of murder-suicides often left behind letters explaining their actions to family and friends. They too could never be certain that these letters would reach their intended audience. They may have been concealed or destroyed by the people who discovered them. If not, once in an investigator's file, they may never have seen the light of day again. Essentially, whether perpetrator-produced stories of homicide in a pre-networked media era would be seen depended on the judgements and decisions of other people. If these stories did emerge, they did so second-hand, mediated and edited, the perpetrator's control of the narrative diminishing with every filter the story passed through. However, the tables have now turned; today's killers can share their stories of homicide in their own words at the tap of a touchscreen. This has enabled them a degree of control over the narrative that they would not previously have experienced. Social media appealed to the killers explored in this book because it enabled them to tell their stories and perform the identities of themselves and their victims in ways *they* wanted to be seen. Perpetrators both created and represented the homicides they committed. They went from consumers to producers, their content particularly marketable in 'wound culture' where the compulsion to gather around the torn mind of the killer and the torn body of their victim is considerable (Seltzer, 1998, 2007, 2008). Once the killers are arrested and imprisoned, their control over the narrative diminishes. They no longer have access to social media as a tool for the direct performance of self so they revert back to more 'traditional' means of attempting to be seen and heard. However, giving interviews to the mainstream media appeared to do Amanda's performance more harm than good. Media reports about Derek featured many interviews with former friends, who told stories of several of his previous alleged transgressions, both moral and legal, damaging his performance as the victim.

While mainstream media often took control of the homicide narrative away from the perpetrators, so too did another group of people – the friends and family of the victim, or the 'secondary victims' (Condry, 2010). Often creating content in the same spaces in which perpetrators had confessed to killing their relative or friend, secondary victims developed and shared counter-narratives. Within these narratives, they challenged the way in which the perpetrator had showed the victim and presented alternative and complementary narratives. Jennifer Alfonso's friends and family set up a memorial page for her on Facebook and one friend created a moving video montage of photographs. The performing arts community in Chilliwack established a memorial bursary for arts students in Emily Janzen's name on a crowdfunding platform and shared it via social media. People commenting on Amanda's Facebook posts reminded others that Charles was the victim and urged them not to forget him. So while the victims in the cases examined may have been silenced by the perpetrator, through images, videos and text, secondary victims were able to tell their stories through social media and re-humanise them, presenting them not simply as victims of a violent crime but as mothers, fathers, sisters, colleagues and friends. While there has always been scope for this, prior to the proliferation of networked media, secondary victims were reliant on mainstream media to cover their loved ones' story. Decisions to run these stories were not always based on sympathy or compassion but more often on newsworthiness and popular appeal (Rock, 1998). Therefore, when it comes to social media in homicide, it is not just the perpetrators who use it to tell stories. Secondary victims also use social media to challenge representations and present alternative narratives of the victim and their life. These voices have legitimacy and an important a role to play in countering the dominant discourses around homicide and the hierarchies of victimisation that continue to proliferate in contemporary society.

The social media homicide confessions described in this book were all characterised by continuity rather than change when seen in context of the perpetrators' broader media archives and other sources of knowledge about their lives. The threads evident in the murder posts could for the most part be followed back deep into their media archives. All three perpetrators continued to engage in fetishist disavowal (Žižek, 2009), but drew on additional states of denial in so doing in relation to the killings – interpretive and implicatory (Cohen, 2001). The interpretations of the homicides within the confessions emphasised valued identities and denied uncomfortable truths. Derek interpreted Jennifer's murder as an act of self-defence by an abused husband, casting himself in the role of the victim. Randy interpreted the familicide-suicide as an act of love, presenting himself as his family's protector. Amanda interpreted Charles' murder as a justified revenge for the death of her beloved Rex. The implications of the acts were denied and minimised. Derek quickly turned the focus on himself and what would happen to him, not openly considering the implications of Jennifer's death for her family and friends let alone expressing remorse. Randy acknowledged that people would judge him, but denied the wider implications of the familicide by emphasising the outcome of his family being 'pain free and in heaven' (Pynn, 2015). Amanda also quickly moved on, retreating back into the realm of the imaginary (Hall, 2012) in which she was simultaneously Mallory Knox, a grieving widow and a devoted mother. Homicide confessions are scenes in broader performances of self, chapters in books. The confessions explored in this book were not bizarre, one-off aberrations but parts of patterns of entrenched behaviour. Just as individuals do not suddenly change or snap when they kill, neither does what they do with media.

Future directions for research

Having outlined the key findings in relation to the three cases explored in this book and contextualised them in light of our understandings of homicide and media, it is important to consider how criminologists should proceed in continuing to make sense of homicide in a mediatised society where both understandings and actions swirl among a complex tangle of loops and spirals.

It is clear that examining the media practices of homicide perpetrators is valuable because it enables broader understandings of experiences of the internet or how it functions in particular ways for particular purposes (Ferrell et al, 2015). Media practices are an important element of constructing, shaping and maintaining identities, identities made in media and infused with mediated representations. As such, criminologists should continue to examine these practices. However, we should be careful to do so in context. As noted in the previous section, every killer who posts a confession on social media is writing a chapter within their own unique book and it is important to look at as much of the book as we can, not just the 'homicide' part of it. We also must acknowledge that we all engage in fetishist disavowal (Žižek, 2009) through our media practices. People like Derek, Randy and Amanda who confess to homicide on social media occupy the extreme end of a shared spectrum along which we all know, show, deny and conceal, performing identities tailored to contemporary ways of mediatised being (Hall et al, 2008). We should also encompass the stories of others, particularly victims, as told through their own social media archives and those of secondary victims, who position themselves as storytellers by proxy, speaking on behalf of their deceased friend or relative.

There is no reason why unorthodox sources – which are so often consigned to the 'intellectual dustbin' by orthodox criminologists (Ferrell et al, 2008) – cannot be explored alongside more traditional sources such as court transcripts and other documentary evidence to open as many windows and explore as many performative identities as possible. It is only though holistic and all-encompassing approaches like this that we can begin to better understand social media confessions and homicide in a networked culture. It is debatable whether social media has changed the world in any fundamental sense, but it has certainly changed our sense of *being* in the world, through enabling us to craft and reshape or self-narrative in ways we have never done so before (Couldry and Hepp, 2017). All of this occurs in a context in which infantile narcissism and hedonism is enabled and encouraged, where individuals engage in fetishist disavowal to deny their poverty, disenfranchisement, ignominy, marginalisation and other facets of their devalued identities (Hall et al, 2008; Žižek, 2009). By implication, shifts have occurred in the landscapes – or mediascapes – in which homicide occurs. Criminologists studying homicide need to adapt to the blurred lines and ever-changing territories of this world, in which networked media is embedded, embodied and everyday (Hine, 2015). This calls for methods that are mindful of this complexity and uncertainty, methods that are 'ragged around the edges' and 'not fully conceptualized or completed' (Ferrell et al, 2008). The Ethnographic Media Practice Analysis for Criminology approach applied to the cases in this book is one such method. Making sense of what people are doing with social media in relation to homicide should not be about quantification, seeking to develop arbitrary categories or 'types', or working out what the 'typical perpetrator' who confesses on social media 'looks like'. It should not be about trying to squash these realities into conceptual and theoretical frameworks developed for different experiences of the world and senses of being within it. It should be about highlighting and exploring the complex narratives and messy realities around which homicide in networked culture occurs.

A further concern for criminologists exploring homicide in contemporary contexts should be to continue to question and critique mainstream media representations of homicide. Despite the initial surge of interest in homicide cases involving social media (Yardley and Wilson, 2015), this appears to be subsiding. As social media has become part and parcel of everyday life, its presence in a homicide case is no longer sufficient on its own to make the case newsworthy. The author found very little general and academic awareness of the Charles Taylor case, unlike Jennifer Alfonso's murder or the Janzen familicide. As such, many cases of strategic importance risk going unseen and fading into the background as has been true for all technologies that were once 'new' (Marvin, 1997; Haddon, 2011; Deuze, 2012, 2014). Mainstream media continues to make judgements around which homicides we should care about and those we should be less concerned by. Therefore it could be argued that criminologists who have used mainstream media as a source for *identifying* cases of interest for study should now cast their net more widely. This is particularly important given tendencies to explain away perpetrators like Derek, Randy and Amanda as aberrations, denying their victims a place in meaningful debate encompassing the uncomfortable questions of power, status and authority that lurk in the shadows of contemporary homicide. Scholars should therefore explore other, newer spaces of cultural criminology (Hayward, 2012) where representations of homicide are created. Important among these are the spaces in which amateur 'armchair detectives' (Soothill, 1998) and 'websleuths' (Yardley et al, 2016) gather to discuss and debate a wide range of homicides, including the relatively unknown as well as the highly newsworthy. These communities often include victim advocates using these spaces to raise awareness of homicides that have been cast aside by mainstream media.

Linked to this, future research should take into account the changes that networked technologies have brought to bear on 'wound culture' (Seltzer, 1998, 2007, 2008). We continue to be drawn to the suffering and trauma of others, but networked media enables us to access representations of homicide like never before. The feeling that we can get 'closer' to homicide now is a widespread one among people interested in this topic, armchair detectives and criminologists alike. We feel that we have more direct access to these torn bodies and torn psyches than has been true in the past. We are now doing more than 'just looking' (Young, 2010b) as our worlds come to intersect with those of individuals affected by homicide (Yardley et al, 2015). In these immersive experiences, we are becoming part of these stories. We may not be *physically* present in the same way we would be in a traditional ethnography, but we are present nonetheless. As criminologists, this is something that we should be reflectively aware of – but not afraid of. Social media is crucially important for homicide scholars, not only in its function as a tool for perpetrators' performances of self but as a space of contemporary meaning making around homicide (Yardley et al, 2015, 2016). Social media is a key space of cultural criminology (Hayward, 2012). Criminologists should be present these spaces. However, as social media is rapidly becoming part of the furniture of everyday life, now is an important time to ensure that criminology is equipped to consider its meaning and significance in everyday homicide.

References

Note: Grammatical errors and misspellings in social media posts are left as they appear in the original source.

Adams, D. (2007) *Why do they kill? Men who murder their intimate partners,* Nashville, TN: Vanderbilt University Press.

Agnew, R. (1992) 'Foundation for a general strain theory of crime and delinquency', *Criminology,* 30(1): 47-87.

Albom, M. (2003) *The five people you meet in heaven,* New York, NY: Hyperion.

Alfonso, J. (2012) 'The mind of an Insane women', http://media.miamiherald.com/smedia/2013/09/17/17/42/8QDN5.So.56.pdf

Altheide, D. L. (1987) 'Reflections: Ethnographic content analysis', *Qualitative Sociology,* 10(1): 65-77.

Anon (2013) 'Facebook Update: Just killed my wife', *The Sun,* 10 August.

Anon (2015) 'Friend tried frantically to reach family after Facebook murder note', *Alberni Valley Times,* 11 May.

Appadurai, A. (1990) 'Disjuncture and difference in the global cultural economy', *Theory, Culture and Society,* 7(2): 295-310.

Aspden, K. and Hayward, K. J. (2015) 'Narrative criminology and cultural criminology: Shared biographies, different lives?', in L. Presser and S. Sandberg (eds) *Narrative criminology: Understanding stories of crime,* New York, NY: New York University Press, pp 235-59.

Atkinson, P. (1997) 'Narrative turn or blind alley?', *Qualitative Health Research,* 7(3): 325-44.

Atkinson, P. and Coffey, A. (2003) 'Revisiting the relationship between participant observation and interviewing', in: J. F. Gubriam and J. A. Holstein (eds) *Postmodern interviewing,* Thousand Oaks, CA: Sage, pp 109-22.

Atkinson, P. and Delamont, S. (2006) 'Rescuing narrative from qualitative research', *Narrative Inquiry,* 16(1): 164-72.

Austin, C. (2015) 'Amanda Taylor sentenced to life in prison for murder in Montgomery County', *Roanoke Times,* 12 November.

Bamberg, M. G. W. and Andrews, M. (eds) (2004) *Considering counter narratives: Narrating, resisting, making sense,* Amsterdam: Benjamins.

Bauwens, M. (2006) 'The political economy of peer production', *Post-autistic Economics Review,* 37(3): 33-44.

Baym, N. (1998) 'The emergence of online community', in S. G. Jones (ed), *Cybersociety 2.0,* Thousand Oaks, CA: Sage, pp 35-68.

Baym, N. K. (2010) *Personal connections in the digital age*, Cambridge: Polity.

Benn, E. S. (2013) 'Before the Facebook slaying: a lifetime of being ignored', *Miami Herald*, 18 August.

Berger, P. and Luckmann, T. (1966) *The social construction of knowledge: A treatise in the sociology of knowledge*, London: Penguin.

Biressi, A. and Bloom, C. (2001) *Crime, fear, and the law in true crime stories*, New York, NY: Palgrave.

Böckler, N. and Seeger, T. (2013) 'Revolution of the dispossessed: School shooters and their devotees on the web', in N. Böckler, T. Seeger, P. Sitzer and W. Heitmeyer (eds) *School shootings: International research, case studies and concepts for prevention*, New York, NY: Springer, pp 309-39.

Bolan, K. (2016) 'Homicide investigators busy in 2015', *Postmedia News*, 4 January.

Bolter, J.D. and Grusin, R. (1999) *Remediation: Understanding new media*, Cambridge, MA: MIT Press.

British Columbia Coroners Service (2016a) 'Coroner's Report into the Death of Emily Louise Janzen', Case no. 2015-0376-0086, Victoria, BC: Ministry of Justice.

British Columbia Coroners Service (2016b) 'Coroner's Report into the Death of Laurel Janzen', Case no. 2015-0376-0087, Victoria, BC: Ministry of Justice.

British Columbia Coroners Service (2016c) 'Coroner's Report into the Death of Shelly Diane Janzen', Case no. 2015-0376-0085, Victoria, BC: Ministry of Justice.

British Columbia Coroners Service (2016d) 'Coroner's Report into the Death of Randy Alan Janzen, Case no. 2015-0376-0088', Victoria, BC: Ministry of Justice.

Brooker, P., Barnet, J. and Cribban, T. (2016) 'Doing social media analytics', *Big Data and Society*, DOI: 10.1177/2053951716658060.

Brookman, F. (2005) *Understanding homicide*, London: Sage.

Brookman, F. (2015) 'The shifting narratives of violent offenders', in L. Presser and S. Sandberg (eds) *Narrative criminology: Understanding stories of crime*, New York, NY: New York University Press, pp 207-34.

Brookman, F. and Maguire, M. (2003) *Reducing homicide: A review of the possibilities*, London: Home Office.

Brown, S. (2006) 'The criminology of hybrids: Rethinking crime and law in technosocial networks', *Theoretical Criminology*, 10(2): 223-44.

Brown, S. (2011) 'Media/crime/millennium: Where are we now?', *Sociology Compass*, 5(6): 413-25.

Browne, A. and Williams, K. R. (1989) 'Exploring the effect of resource availability and the likelihood of female-perpetrated homicide', *Law & Society Review*, 23(1): 75–94.

Bruner, J. (2004) 'Life as narrative', *Social Research: An International Quarterly*, 71(3): 691–710.

Brunette Bomber (2015a) 'You have vandalized my heart', Tumblr, 19 March.

Brunette Bomber (2015b) 'Wrists are for girls, I'm slitting my throat', Tumblr, 4 March.

Brunette Bomber (2015c) 'All for you Rex', Tumblr, 4 April.

brunette_bomber (2013a) '#naturalbornkillers', Instagram, 7 October.

brunette_bomber (2013b) '& in today's mail...', Instagram, 17 March.

brunette_bomber (2013c) 'Ah all finished', Instagram, 10 October.

brunette_bomber. (2013d) 'Oh hey guess who received their t.j lane necklace!', Instagram, 19 June.

brunette_bomber (2014a) 'When I tell people I was raised in Florida', Instagram, 30 October.

brunette_bomber (2014b) 'Ah I don't even know..We tried', Instagram, 7 October.

brunette_bomber (2014c) 'My son colored me a beautiful boomer', Instagram, 24 July.

brunette_bomber (2014d) 'Already flipping his new wheels', Instagram, 26 December.

brunette_bomber (2014e) 'Spelling test practice! He's so smart, it amazes me', Instagram, 25 February.

brunette_bomber (2014f) 'I haven't been able to get this up any sooner', Instagram, 1 September.

brunette_bomber (2014g) 'I finally got around to seeing this on Facebook', Instagram, 5 October.

brunette_bomber (2014h) 'So my sister...loves her some sunflowers, we made these cute cupcakes today!', Instagram, 23 March.

brunette_bomber (2014i) 'We had a yummy knock at the door..thanks to my sister hundreds miles away', Instagram, 9 May.

brunette_bomber (2014j) 'We got a strong line of beauty running through my family ;)', Instagram, 29 March

brunette_bomber (2014k) 'Its time for Michael to take a nap', Instagram, 16 October.

brunette_bomber (2014l) 'I'm soooo friggin happy!', Instagram, 19 January.

brunette_bomber (2014m) 'So I gave in and bought asylum to add to the collection', Instagram, 28 February.

brunette_bomber (2014n) 'My morning', Instagram, 3 October.

brunette_bomber (2014o) 'Starting my day with: #dawnofthedead', Instagram, 16 December.

brunette_bomber (2014p) 'Definitely most favorite thing on my body', Instagram, 25 February.

brunette_bomber (2014q) 'A couple that slays together stays together. #naturalbornkillers', Instagram, 1 June.

brunette_bomber. (2014r) 'Today I received this awesome drawling as an early birthday present', Instagram, 9 March.

brunette_bomber. (2014s) 'Final season on sale at best buy, our collection is finally complete', Instagram, 19 January.

brunette_bomber (2014t) 'You guys I just read on fearnet that Sam Raimi is writing an Evil Dead TV show', Facebook, 25 July.

brunette_bomber (2014u) 'If I cut off your arms and cut off your legs', Instagram, 19 November.

brunette_bomber (2015a) 'Amanda's two-day trial for first degree murder will be November 12 & 13th at Montgomery County Courthouse', Instagram, 12 October.

brunette_bomber (2015b) 'Amanda wanted to clear a few things up', Instagram, 23 April.

brunette_bomber (2015c) 'Spent the day in Ellett Valley', Instagram, 22 March.

brunette_bomber (2015d) 'I came across this & HAVE to #throwbackthursdayit', Instagram, 6 March.

brunette_bomber (2015e) 'Crashing to one of my favorite filthy love stories', Instagram, 15 February.

brunette_bomber (2015f) 'Reposting this~The Death Merchant is finally on instagram!', Instagram, 5 March.

brunette_bomber (2015g) 'Freedom is a loaded shotgun', Instagram, 21 March.

brunette_bomber (2016) 'Amanda's article in #MasterDetective magazine released in the UK', Instagram, 13 April.

Bruns, A. (2008) *Blogs, Wikipedia, Second Life and beyond: From production to produsage*, New York, NY: Peter Lang.

Bucholtz, F. (2015a) 'Tragic Aldergrove murder shakes the community', *Langley Times*, 12 May.

Bucholtz, F. (2015b) 'Memorial service set for Janzen family', *Langley Times*, 26th May.

Buffardi, L. E. and Campbell, W. K. (2008) 'Narcissism and social networking web sites', *Personality and Social Psychology Bulletin*, 34(10): 1303-14.

Bullock, C. F. (2007) 'Framing domestic violence fatalities: Coverage by Utah newspapers', *Women's Studies in Communication*, 30(1): 34-63.

Burrell, G. and Morgan, G. (1979) *Sociological paradigms and organisational analysis*, Farnham: Ashgate.

Campbell, J. C., Glass, N., Sharps, P. W., Laughon, K. and Bloom, T. (2007) 'Intimate partner homicide review and implications of research and policy', *Trauma, Violence, & Abuse*, 8(3): 246-69.

Capote, T. (1965) *In cold blood: A true account of a multiple murder and its consequences*, London: Penguin Books.

Carney, P. (2010) 'Crime, punishment and the force of the photographic spectacle', in K. J. Hayward and M. Presdee (eds) *Framing crime: Cultural criminology and the image*, Abingdon: Routledge, pp 17-35.

Carney, P. (2015) 'Foucault's punitive society: Visual tactics of marking as a history of the present', *British Journal of Criminology*, 55(2): 231-47.

Carpenter, C. J. (2012) 'Narcissism on Facebook: Self-promotional and anti-social behavior', *Personality and Individual Differences*, 52(4): 482-6.

Carrabine, E. (2008) *Crime, culture and the media*, Cambridge: Polity.

Carter, H. (2010) 'Facebook killer sentenced to life for teenager's murder', *The Guardian*, 8 March.

Cashmore, E. (2014) *Celebirty culture* (2nd edn), Abingdon: Routledge.

Castells, M. (1996) *The network society*, Oxford: Blackwell.

CCV (Court Chatter View) (2015a) 'Derek Medina "Facebook Murder" Trial Day 7 Part 2 11/19/15', *YouTube*, 19th November.

CCV (2015b) 'Derek Medina "Facebook Murder" Trial Day 2 Part 2 11/12/15', YouTube, 12 November.

CCV (2015c) 'Derek Medina "Facebook Murder" Trial Day 1 Part 1 11/10/15', YouTube, 10 November.

CCV (2015d) 'Derek Medina "Facebook Murder" Trial DAUGHTER INTERVIEW Day 8 Part 4 11/20/15', YouTube, 20 November.

CCV (2015e) 'Derek Medina "Facebook Murder" Trial Day 8 Part 2 11/20/15', YouTube, 20 November.

CCV (2015f) 'Derek Medina "Facebook Murder" Trial Day 5 Part 5 11/17/15', YouTube, 17 November.

Chambers, D. (2013) *Social media and personal relationships: Online intimacies and networked friendship*, Basingstoke: Palgrave Macmillan.

Chan, S., Khader, M., Ang, J., Tan, E., Khoo, K. and Chin, J. (2012) 'Understanding "happy slapping"', *International Journal of Police Science & Management*, 14(1): 42-57.

Chibnall, S. (1977) *Law and order news: An analysis of crime reporting in the British press*, London: Tavistock.

Christie, N. (1986) 'The ideal victim', in E. A. Fattah (ed) *From crime policy to victim policy: Reorienting the justice system*, Basingstoke: Macmillan, pp 17-30.

cloudsinmycoffee59 (2013a) 'Talking about our problems is our greatest addiction. Break the habit. Talk about your joys – Rita Schiano', Instagram, 30 December.

cloudsinmycoffee59 (2013b) 'Get better Emily', Instagram, 17 November.

cloudsinmycoffee59 (2014a) 'Seek respect, not attention, it lasts longer', Instagram, 9 July.

cloudsinmycoffee59 (2014b) 'All great changes are preceded by chaos', Instagram, 30 May.

cloudsinmycoffee59 (2014c) '#tbt #1992 #mediterrean #barcelona #ladyinred #the love boat', Instagram, 24 July.

cloudsinmycoffee59 (2014d) '#flashbackfriday #mothersday #1996 #whatadoll #letsdobrunch #sweetheart', Instagram, 9 May.

cloudsinmycoffee59 (2014e) '#tbt #2002 #buildingcastlesinthesand #cultuslake', Instagram, 17 July.

cloudsinmycoffee59 (2014f) 'Some people create their own storms, then get upset when it rains', Instagram, 27 January.

cloudsinmycoffee59 (2014g) 'I don't hate you, I'm just disappointed you turned into everything you said you'd never be', Instagram, 2 April.

cloudsinmycoffee59 (2014h) 'Never push a loyal person to the point where they no longer give a damn', Instagram, 12 June.

cloudsinmycoffee59 (2014i) '#preachingit', Instagram, 6 May.

cloudsinmycoffee59 (2014j) '#mygirl #staystrong #gonnagetbetter #hangin', Instagram, 6 May.

cloudsinmycoffee59 (2014k) Untitled, Instagram, 27 June.

cloudsinmycoffee59 (2015a) 'Tell the negative committee that meets inside your head to sit down and shut up – Ann Bradford', Instagram, 5 January.

cloudsinmycoffee59 (2015b) '#sophie #goldenretriever #dogsofinstagram #puppy #pinkpolkadot #ribbons #rhodo #salonday', Instagram, 20 April.

cloudsinmycoffee59 (2015c) 'My girls #Vancouver #Canucks #hockey #playoffs #goldenretriever #sophie', Instagram, 17 April.

cloudsinmycoffee59 (2015d) 'cloudsinmycoffee59Thank you my sweet @emilyjanzen_1 for all the lovely #birthday #gifts', Instagram, 10 April.

cloudsinmycoffee59 (2015e) 'I can't keep calm it's my daughter's birthday', Instagram, 17 February.

cloudsinmycoffee59 (2015f) 'Women should empower each other instead of being so hateful and envious of one another', Instagram, 2 April.

cloudsinmycoffee59 (2015g) '#goldenretriever #sophie #dogsofinstagram #plaiddad #plaidonplaid #konggenius #powerchewer', Instagram, 7 March.

Cohen, S. (2001) *States of denial: Knowing about atrocities and suffering*, Cambridge: Polity.

Commonwealth of Virginia v Taylor (2010a) 'Case Details', Montgomery Christiansburg General District Court, GC10010754-00.

Commonwealth of Virginia v Taylor (2010b) 'Case Details', Montgomery Christiansburg General District Court, GC10010755-00.

Commonwealth of Virginia v Taylor (2011) 'Case Details', Montgomery Christiansburg General District Court, GC11008514-00.

Commonwealth of Virginia v Taylor (2012) 'Case Details', Montgomery County Circuit Criminal Division, CR12000635-00.

Commonwealth of Virginia v Taylor (2015a) 'Trial', Montgomery County Circuit Criminal Division, CR15000716-00.

Commonwealth of Virginia v Taylor (2015b) 'Motions', Montgomery County Circuit Criminal Division, CR15000716-00.

Commonwealth of Virginia v Taylor (2016) 'Sentencing and Probation Violation Hearing', Montgomery County Circuit Criminal Division, CR15000716-00.

Condry, R. (2010) 'Secondary victims and secondary victimization', in S.G. Shoham, P. Knepper, and M. Kett (eds) *International handbook of victimology*, Boca Raton, FL: CRC Press, pp 219-49.

Connell, R.W. and Messerschmidt, J.W. (2005) 'Hegemonic masculinity: Rethinking the concept', *Gender & Society*, 19(6): 829-59.

Cooper, M. and Eaves, D. (1996) 'Suicide following homicide in the family', *Violence and Victims*, 11(2): 99-112.

Couldry, N. (2004) 'Theorizing media as practice', *Social Semiotics*, 14(2): 115-32.

Couldry, N. (2012) *Media, society, world: Social theory and digital practice*, Cambridge: Polity.

Couldry, N. and Hepp, A. (2013) 'Conceptualizing mediatization: Contexts, traditions, arguments', *Communication Theory*, 23(3): 191-202.

Couldry, N. and Hepp, A. (2017) *The mediated social construction of reality*, Cambridge: Polity.

Crawford, T. (2015) 'With depression, you see the world through a dark cloud', *Postmedia News*, 9 May.

Cullen, D. (2009) *Columbine*, New York, NY: Twelve.

D'Cruze, S., Walklate, S. and Pegg, S. (2006) *Murder*, London: Routledge.

D'Orban, P. T. (1990) 'Female homicide', *Irish Journal of Psychological Medicine*, 7(1): 64–70

Debord, G. (1994) *The society of the spectacle* (trans), New York, NY: Zone Books.

Demmitt, J. (2016) 'Ball accepts plea deal, gets 41-year sentence for Montgomery County murder', *Roanoke Times*, 15 March.

Deuze, M. (2012) *Media life*, Cambridge: Polity.

Deuze, M. (2014) 'Media life and the mediatization of the lifeworld', in A. Hepp and F. Krotz (eds), *Mediatized worlds: Culture and society in a media age*, Basingstoke: Palgrave Macmillan, pp 207–20.

Dietz, P.E. (1986) 'Mass, serial and sensational homicides', *Bulletin of the New York Academy of Medicine*, 62(5): 477–91.

Dobash, R.E. and Dobash, R.P. (2009) 'Out of the blue: Men who murder an intimate partner', *Feminist Criminology*, 4(3): 194–225.

Dobash, R.E. and Dobash, R.P. (2015) *When men murder women*, Oxford: Oxford University Press.

Dowler, K., Fleming, T. and Muzzatti, S.L. (2006) 'Constructing crime: Media, crime, and popular culture', *Canadian Journal of Criminology and Criminal Justice*, 48(6): 837–50.

Durham, A.M., Elrod, H.P. and Kinkade, P.T. (1995) 'Images of crime and justice: Murder and the "true crime" genre', *Journal of Criminal Justice*, 23(2): 143–52.

Duwe, G. (2000) 'Body-count journalism', *Homicide Studies*, 4(4): 364–99.

Eagland, N. and Saltman, J. (2015) 'The heartbreaking Facebook confession that came before Thursday's fatal house explosion near Chilliwack', *Postmedia News*, 8 May.

Elks, S. (2013) 'Florida man "documents" murder of wife in Facebook photo', *The Times*, 9 August.

EmilyJanzen_1 (2013a) 'My dad knows how to cheer me up #hospital #sucks #flowers #daddysgirl', Instagram, 19 November.

EmilyJanzen_1 (2014a) 'My mom in the real breakfast club circa '74', Instagram, 27 April.

EmilyJanzen_1 (2014b) 'Sun hats and smelling daisies', Instagram, 28 May.

EmilyJanzen_1 (2014c) 'Macaroon pill case for a very sick emmy #earlychristmaspresent #mybestfriendrules #adorable', Instagram, 5 December.

EmilyJanzen_1 (2014d) 'Throwback with my two sopranos #tbt #idaho #2011 #lovethem', Instagram, 6 November.

EmilyJanzen_1 (2014e) 'Stop drop and selfie, thanks…caught me on my cheat day eating macaroons with the father', Instagram, 29 November.

EmilyJanzen_1 (2015a) 'Throwback Thursday w/ Sour Kangaroo & Gertrude McFuzz', Instagram, 23 April.

EmilyJanzen_1 (2015b) 'Happy Earth Day from me and my identical twin', Instagram, 22 April.

EmilyJanzen_1 (2015c) 'Transformation Tuesday #transformationtuesday #sickunibrow', Instagram, 21 April.

EmilyJanzen_1 (2015d) 'Cheat day is the best day – Chocolate covered strawberry inspired Nicecream!', Instagram, 20 April.

emmers_janzen (2013a) 'Being sick is just so blaaaahhh', Twitter, 27 September.

emmers_janzen (2013b) 'My dad is my bestfriend [sic] and I'm so proud of that', Twitter, 18 November.

emmers_janzen (2014a) 'I. Hate. The. Hospital. I. Am. Fed. Up. Meh.', Twitter, 17 April.

emmers_janzen (2014b) 'I'd love to be healthy annnnnnytime now', Twitter, 25 May.

emmers_janzen (2014c) 'WHY AM I ALWAYS SICK HOLY MOLY', Twitter, 4 July.

emmers_janzen (2014d) 'My dad just said ass tea at taco bell god dad', Twitter, 19 September.

emmers_janzen (2014e) 'My dad: I discovered youtube like 3 weeks ago. His buddy: What the hell is youtube?', Twitter, 26 September.

emmers_janzen (2014f) 'Don't know what I'd do without my dad', Twitter, 21 October.

emmers_janzen (2014g) 'My dad watches vines with me #bestdadever', Twitter, 27 November.

emmers_janzen (2015a) 'RT @KardashianReact "the text that starts 99% of family fights"', Twitter, 26 April.

emmers_janzen (2015b) 'YAS go nucks go', Twitter, 25 April.

emmers_janzen (2015c) 'I want to bite my docs bum and that's bad', Twitter, 25 April.

emmers_janzen (2015d) 'Doctors shouldn't be allowed to be so damn SEXY', Twitter, 25 April.

emmers_janzen (2015e) 'Being sick and having no one is the best life to live I highly recommend', Twitter, 24 March.

emmers_janzen (2015f) 'I need this life to be over', Twitter, 24 March.

emmers_janzen (2015g) 'I'm so tired of people making me feel guilty for being too sick to hangout', Twitter, 19 April.

emmers_janzen (2015h) 'Whenever I start to feel sorry for myself, I just thank God I'm still alive', Twitter, 24 April.

emmers_janzen (2015i) '"I care about you" *has a different girlfriend week later* #ihateboys', Twitter, 24 March.

emmers_janzen (2015j) 'Picking a career is hard af #whatdoidowithmylife', Twitter, 16 April.

emmers_janzen (2015k) 'Maybe I should start singing again', Twitter, 5 March.

Encheva, K., Driessens, O. and Verstraeten, H. (2013) 'The mediatization of deviant subcultures: An analysis of the media–related practices of graffiti writers and skaters', *MedieKultur: Journal of Medial and Communication Research*, 29(54): 8-25.

Evans, N. (2013) 'Facebook killer: He murders his wife then puts pic of her body on internet', Daily Mirror, 10 August.

Faberov, S. (2015) '"I proudly did this for Rex": Chilling confession of widowed mother of two obsessed with serial killers', *MailOnline*, 14 April.

Fabianic, D. (1997) 'Television dramas and homicide causation', *Homicide Studies*, 25(3): 195-203.

Fayerman, P. (2016a) 'Coroner silent on whether migraines contributed to Chilliwack/Aldergrove triple murder-suicide', *Langley Advance*, 7 March.

Fayerman, P. (2016b) 'Coroner silent on whether migraines contributed to Chilliwack triple homicide', *Chilliwack Times*, 8 March.

Ferguson, C. J. (2008) 'The school shooting/violent video game link: Causal relationship or moral panic?', *Journal of Investigative Psychology and Offender Profiling*, 5(1-2): 25-37.

Ferrell, J. (2005) 'Crime and culture', in C. Hale, K. Hayward, A. Wahidin and E. Wincup (eds) *Criminology*, Oxford: Oxford University Press, pp 139-55.

Ferrell, J. and Van de Voorde, C. (2010) 'The decisive moment: Documentary photography and cultural criminology', in K. J. Hayward and M. Presdee (eds) *Framing crime: Cultural criminology and the image*, Abingdon: Routledge, pp 36-52.

Ferrell, J., Hayward, K., and Young, J. (2008) *Cultural criminology*, London: Sage.

Ferrell, J., Hayward, K., and Young, J. (2015) *Cultural criminology* (2nd edn), London: Sage.

Ferrell, J., Milovanovic, D. and Lyng, S. (2001) 'Edgework, media practices, and the elongation of meaning: A theoretical ethnography of the Bridge Day event', *Theoretical Criminology*, 5(2): 177-202.

Fishman, M. and Cavender, G. (eds) (1998) *Entertaining crime: Television reality programs*, New York, NY: Aldine De Gruyter.

Flanders, J. (2013) *The invention of murder: How the Victorians revelled in death and detection and created modern crime*, London: Harper Press.

Flyvbjerg, B. (2006) 'Five misunderstandings about case-study research', *Qualitative Inquiry*, 12(2): 219-45.

Fortunati, L. (2002) 'The mobile phone: Towards new categories and social relations 1', *Information, Communication & Society*, 5(4): 513-28.

Fortunati, L. (2005) 'Is body-to-body communication still the prototype?', *The Information Society*, 21(1): 53-61.

Fox, J.A. and Levin, J. (2015) *Extreme killing: Understanding serial and mass murder* (3rd edn), Thousand Oaks, CA: Sage.

Fox, J. and Rooney, M.C. (2015) 'The Dark Triad and trait self-objectification as predictors of men's use and self-presentation behaviors on social networking sites', *Personality and Individual Differences*, 76: 161-5.

Frazier, S.H. (1975) 'Violence and social impact', in J.C. Schoolar and C.M. Gaitz (eds) *Research and the psychiatric patient*, New York,, NY: Brunner & Mazel, pp 191-200.

Fuchs, C. (2008) *Social media: A critical introduction*, London: Sage.

Fumano, D. (2015) '19 year old victim of apparent murder suicide near Chilliwack to be honoured with memorial and bursary fund', *Postmedia News*, 10 May.

Galtung, J. and Ruge, M. (1965) 'Structuring and selecting news', in S. Cohen and J. Young (eds) (1981) *The manufacture of news: Deviance, social problems and the mass media*, London: Constable, pp 62-72.

Geertz, C. (1973) *The interpretation of cultures: Selected essays*, New York, NY: Basic Books.

Gekoski, A. (1998) *Murder by numbers*, London: Andreas Deutsch.

Gergen, K. (2002) 'The challenge of absent presence', in J. Katz and M. Aakhus (eds) *Perpetual contact: Mobile communication, private talk, public performance*, Cambridge: Cambridge University Press, pp 227-41.

Goffman, E. (1959) *The presentation of self in everyday life*, New York, NY: Anchor Books.

Gruenewald, J., Chermak, S.M. and Pizarro, J.M. (2013) 'Covering victims in the news: What makes minority homicides newsworthy?', *Justice Quarterly*, 30(5): 755-83.

Gruenewald, J., Pizarro, J.M. and Chermak, S. M. (2009) 'Race, gender, and the newsworthiness of homicide incident', *Journal of Criminal Justice*, 37(3): 262-72.

Haddon, L. (2011) 'Domestication analysis, objects of study, and the centrality of technologies in everyday life', *Canadian Journal of Communication*, 36(2): 311-23.

Hall, S. (2012) *Theorizing crime and deviance*, London: Sage.

Hall, S. and Winlow, S. (2015) *Revitalizing criminological theory: Towards a new ultra realism*, Abingdon: Routledge.

Hall, S., Winlow, S. and s, C. (2008) *Criminal identities and consumer culture: Crime, exclusion and the new culture of narcissism*, Cullompton: Willan.

Harper, D. W. and Voigt, L. (2007) 'Homicide followed by suicide an integrated theoretical perspective', *Homicide Studies*, 11(4): 295-318.

Harvey, D. (1989) *The condition of postmodernity*, Oxford: Blackwell.

Hayles, K. (1999) *How we became posthumans*, Chicago, IL: University of Chicago.

Hayward, K. J. (2012) 'Five spaces of cultural criminology', *British Journal of Criminology*, 52(3): 441-62.

Hayward, K. J. and Young, J. (2004) 'Cultural criminology: Some notes on the script', *Theoretical Criminology*, 8(3): 259-73.

Henderson, P. (2015) 'BC Coroner will investigate tragic Chilliwack murder and suicide', *Chilliwack Times*, 13 May.

Henry, A. and Short, J. (1954) *Suicide and homicide*, Glencoe: The Free Press.

Hepp, A. and Krotz, F. (2014) 'Mediatized worlds: Understanding everyday mediatization', in A. Hepp and F. Krotz (eds) *Mediatized worlds: Culture and society in a media age*, Basingstoke: Palgrave Macmillan, pp 1-15.

Hepp, A., Hjarvard, S. and Lundby, K. (2015) 'Mediatization: Theorizing the interplay between media, culture and society', *Media, Culture & Society*, online ahead of print, DOI: 10.1177/0163443715573835.

Hickey, E. W. (2010) *Serial murderers and their victims* (5th edn), Belmont, CA: Wadsworth.

Hine, C. (2015) *Ethnography for the internet: Embedded, embodied and everyday*, London: Bloomsbury Academic.

Hjarvard, S. (2008) 'The mediatization of society: A theory of the media agents of social and cultural change', *Nordicom Review*, 29(2): 105-34.

Hjorth, L., Burgess, J. and Richardson, I. (2012) *Studying mobile media: Cultural technologies, mobile communication and the iPhone*, London and New York, NY: Routledge.

Honigsbaum, M. (2005) 'Concern over rise of "happy slapping" craze: Fad of filming violent attacks on mobile phones spreads', *The Guardian*, 26 April.

Hough, R.M. and McCorkle, K.D. (2017) *American homicide*, Thousand Oaks, CA: Sage.

Howie, L. (2012) *Witnesses to terror*, Basingstoke: Palgrave Macmillan.

Hughes, M. (2010) 'Teenager jailed for Facebook murder', *The Independent*, 23 June.

Hughes, O. (2009) 'Partner guilty of Facebook murder', *Daily Post*, 11 September.

Indiegogo (2016) 'Emily Janzen Memorial Bursary Fund', www.indiegogo.com/projects/emily-janzen-memorial-bursary-fund#.

Janzen, Emily (2014a) 'Accepted to UBC for Opera Performance', Facebook, 11 April.

Janzen, Emily (2014b) Untitled photograph, Facebook, 28 October.

Janzen, Emily (2014c) 'The kindest soul I've ever known', Facebook, 19 August.

Janzen, Emily (2015a) Untitled photograph, Facebook, 17 April.

Janzen, Emily (2015b) 'This is so important. As someone who has been suffering with chronic pain for over two years, it's 100% relatable', Facebook, 7 April.

Janzen, Emily (2015c) 'Hot cross buns, hot cross buns', Facebook, 5 April.

Janzen, Randy (2012) Untitled photograph, Facebook, 10 July.

Janzen, Randy (2014a) Untitled photograph, Facebook, 19 August.

Janzen, Randy (2014b) Untitled photograph, Facebook, 21 August.

Jeffries, D. (2015) 'Family of Rex and Charles Taylor speak out on Amanda Taylor', *WSLS 10*, 24 April.

Jenkins, H. (2006) *Convergence culture: Where old and new media collide*, New York, NY: New York University Press.

Jensen, V. J. (2001) *Why women kill: Homicide and gender equality*, Boulder, CO: Reinner.

Jermyn, D. (2007) *Crime watching: Investigating real crime TV*, London: IB Taurus.

Jermyn, D. (2013) 'Labs and slabs: Television crime drama and the quest for forensic realism', *Studies in History and Philosophy of Science, Part C: Studies in History and Philosophy of Biological and Biomedical Sciences*, 44(1): 103-9.

Jewkes, Y. (2015) *Media and crime* (3rd edn), London: Sage.

Jewkes, Y. and Yar, M. (eds) (2010) *Handbook of internet crime*, London: Routledge.

Johnstone, J. W. C., Hawkins, D. F. and Michener, A. (1994) 'Homicide reporting in Chicago dailies', *Journalism & Mass Communication Quarterly*, 71(4): 860-72.

Kane, L. (2015) 'Friend tried frantically to reach BC family after Facebook murder note', *Canadian Press*, 9 May.

Kellner, D. (2008) *Guys and guns amok: Domestic terrorism and school shootings from the Oklahoma City bombing to the Virginia Tech massacre*, Boulder, Co: Paradigm.

Kennedy, H. (2006) 'Beyond anonymity, or future directions for internet identity research', *New Media and Society*, 8(6): 859-76.

Kiilakoski, T., and Oksanen, A. (2011). 'Soundtrack of the school shootings: Cultural script, music and male rage', *Young*, 19(3): 247-69.

Klevens, J. (2007) 'An overview of intimate partner violence among Latinos', *Violence Against Women*, 13(2): 111-22.

Klevens, J., Shelley, G., Clavel-Arcas, C., Barney, D.D., Tobar, C., Duran, E.S., ... and Esparza, J. (2007) 'Latinos' perspectives and experiences with intimate partner violence', *Violence Against Women*, 13(2): 141-58.

Knight, S. (2010) *Crime fiction since 1800: Detection, death, diversity*, Basingstoke: Palgrave Macmillan.

Korth, R. (2015) 'FBI now involved in death inquiry', *Roanoke Times*, 8 April.

Korth, R. and Williams, T. (2015) 'Friend: Amanda Taylor was released from mental facility before father-in-law's death', *Roanoke Times*, 9 April.

Kozinets, R. V. (2015) *Netnography: Redefined* (2nd edn), London: Sage.

Lacan, J. (2006) *Ecrits*, London: Norton.

Lane, J. (2016) 'The digital street: An ethnographic study of networked street life in Harlem', *American Behavioral Scientist*, 60(1): 43-58.

Larkin, R.W. (2007) *Comprehending Columbine*, Philadelphia, PA: Temple University Press.

Larkin, R.W. (2009) 'The columbine legacy: Rampage shootings as political acts', *American Behavioral Scientist*, 52(9): 1309–26.

Larkin, R.W. (2013) 'Legitimated adolescent violence: Lessons from Columbine', in N. Böckler, T. Seeger, P. Sitzer and W. Heitmeyer (eds) *School shootings: International research, case studies and concepts for prevention*, New York, NY: Springer, pp 159-76.

Laurel-E-Janzen (2016a) 'Janzen/Cusiter: Information about Laurel Elizabeth Cusiter', genealogy.com, www.genealogy.com/ftm/j/a/n/Laurel-E-Janzen/WEBSITE-0001/UHP-0001.html.

Laurel-E-Janzen (2016b) 'Janzen/Cusiter: Information about William Cusiter', genealogy.com, www.genealogy.com/ftm/j/a/n/Laurel-E-Janzen/WEBSITE-0001/UHP-0002.html.

Laurel-E-Janzen (2016c) 'Janzen/Cusiter: Information about Evelyn Annabelle Myers', genealogy.com, www.genealogy.com/ftm/j/a/n/Laurel-E-Janzen/WEBSITE-0001/UHP-0003.html.

Laurel-E-Janzen (2016d) 'Janzen/Cusiter: Information about Randy Alan Janzen', genealogy.com, www.genealogy.com/ftm/j/a/n/Laurel-E-Janzen/WEBSITE-0001/UHP-0202.html.

Laurel-E-Janzen (2016e) Janzen/Cusiter: Information about Henry Janzen, genealogy.com, www.genealogy.com/ftm/j/a/n/Laurel-E-Janzen/WEBSITE-0001/UHP-0348.html.

laureljanz (2012a) 'Dinner at Deluxe in White Rock with dear hubby', Twitter, 8 April.

laureljanz (2012b) 'Happy Birthday to my timid little husband Randy Janzen', Twitter, 12 June.

laureljanz (2013a) 'Back in the ER. Day 13 of a migraine from hell', Twitter, 16 October.

laureljanz (2013b) 'Really missing @emmersjanzen #sad #ChristmasAgony #ER #packed no doctors #lovemyfamily #bestrongemily', Twitter, 25 December.

laureljanz (2014a) 'My daughter has had a #migraine for 11 months. Don't know what else to do #sadtweets #chronicmigraines #stop', Twitter, 17 July.

laureljanz (2015a) 'Just because Titus is pretty doesn't mean he won't mess you up, especially your hair', Twitter, 25 April.

laureljanz (2015b) 'RT @MigraineChecked "You are strong!"', Twitter, 24 April.

laureljanz (2015c) 'RT @CMigraineProbs "Never wait more than 3 months for another round of botox"', Twitter, 24 April.

laureljanz (2015d) 'So lost. My daughter has suffered #daily #migraine #headaches for 515 days #broken', Twitter, 26 January.

laureljanz (2015e) 'Watching someone I love in unbearable pain everyday for 18 months and I feel helpless #migraine #weneedhelp @FraserHealth', Twitter, 9 March.

Lees, S. (1997) Ruling passions: Sexual violence, reputation and the law, Buckingham: Open University Press.

Licoppe, C. (2004) 'Connected presence: The emergence of a new repertoire for managing social relationships in a changing communication technoscape', Environment and Planning D, 22(1): 135-56.

Liem, M. (2010) 'Homicide followed by suicide: A review', Aggression and Violent Behavior, 15(3), 153-61.

Liem, M. and Koenraadt, F. (2008) 'Familicide: A comparison with spousal and child homicide by mentally disordered perpetrators', Criminal Behaviour and Mental Health, 18(5): 306-18.

Liem, M. and Reichelmann, A. (2014) 'Patterns of multiple family homicide', Homicide Studies, 18(1): 44-58.

Liem, M., Hengeveld, M. and Koenraadt, F. (2009a) 'Domestic homicide followed by parasuicide: A comparison with homicide and parasuicide', *International Journal of Offender Therapy and Comparative Criminology*, 53(5): 497–516.

Liem, M., Levin, J., Holland, C. and Fox, J. A. (2013) 'The nature and prevalence of familicide in the United States 2000–2009', *Journal of Family Violence*, 28(4): 351–8.

Liem, M., Postulart, M., and Nieuwbeerta, P. (2009b) 'Homicide-suicide in the Netherlands', *Homicide Studies*, 13(2): 99–123.

Lister, M., Dovey, J., Giddings, S., Grant, I. and Kelly, K. (2009) *New media: A critical introduction* (2nd end), London: Routledge.

Lundby, K. (2009) 'Media logic: Looking for social interaction', in K. Lundby (ed) *Mediatization: Concept, changes, consequences*, New York, NY: Peter Lang, pp 101–19.

Lundman, R.L. (2003) 'The newsworthiness and selection bias in news about murder', *Sociological Forum*, 18(3): 357–86.

Madianou, M. and Miller, D. (2013) 'Polymedia: Towards a new theory of digital media in interpersonal communication', *International Journal of Cultural Studies*, 16(2): 169–87.

Maguire, M. (2002) 'Crime statistics', in M. Maguire, R. Morgan, and R. Reiner (eds) *The Oxford handbook of criminology* (2nd edn), Oxford: Oxford University Press, pp 322–75.

Mann, B.L. (2009) 'Social networking websites: A concatenation of impersonation, denigration, sexual aggressive solicitation, cyber-bullying or happy slapping videos', *International Journal of Law and Information Technology*, 17(3): 252–67.

Mann, C.R. (1996) *When women kill*, Albany, NY: State University of New York Press.

Manning, J. (2015) 'The social structure of homicide-suicide', *Homicide Studies*, 19(4): 350–69.

Manovich, L. (2001) *The language of new media*, Cambridge, MA: MIT Press.

Marvin, C. (1997) *When old technologies were new*, Oxford: Oxford University Press.

Marzuk, P.M., Tardiff, K. and Hirsch, C. S. (1992) 'The epidemiology of murder-suicide', *Journal of the American Medical Association*, 267(23): 3179–83.

Mathieson, T. (1997) 'The viewer society: Michael Foucault's "Panopticon" revisited', *Theoretical Criminology*, 1(2): 215–34.

McAdams, D. P. (2006) *The redemptive self: Stories Americans live by*, New York, NY: Oxford University Press.

McLuhan, M. (1964) *Understanding media: The extensions of man*, Cambridge, MA: MIT Press.

McLuhan, M. (1968) *Understanding media*, London: Sphere.

McQuail, D. (2010) *McQuail's mass communication theory*, London: Sage.

Medina, Derek (2011a) 'CORAL GABLES 10 YEAR REUNION AT THE HARD ROCK CASINO', YouTube, 14 August.

Medina, Derek (2011b) 'DEREK MEDINA GOING IN THE MOSH PIT OF HELL SUICIDE SILENCE MAYHEM FESTIVAL 2011', YouTube, 15 August.

Medina, Derek (2011c) 'CIRCLE OF DEATH AND INJURIES SUICIDE SILENCE MAYHEM', YouTube, 15 August.

Medina, Derek (2011d) 'our first time october31,2011 celebrating it at south beach 50k people on 10-31-11', YouTube, 1 November.

Medina, Derek (2011e) 'DEREK MEDINA WINNING THE GOLD', YouTube, 2 May.

Medina, Derek (2011f) 'FORMER PRO BASKETBALL P', YouTube, 29 October.

Medina, Derek (2011g) 'HOUSE OF TERROR 2011', YouTube, 29 October.

Medina, Derek (2011h) 'HARDEST GAME TO WIN', YouTube, 29 October.

Medina, Derek (2012a) 'DEREK MEDINA 10/10 THAT'S 100 PERECENT SHOOTING FROM THE FIELD', YouTube, 6 January.

Medina, Derek (2012b) 'derek medina training with the temp boxing trainer BEFORE PRO EXHBITION FIGHT', YouTube, 3 April.

Medina, Derek (2012c) 'APA POOL PLAYER CLEANING UP EVERYTHING ON THE POOL TABLE', YouTube, 18 March.

Medina, Derek (2012d) 'PRO EXIBITION ROUND 2', YouTube, 26 March.

Medina, Derek (2012e) 'Pro exibition fight derek vs kode / use vs australia on royal / KODE PHILP', YouTube, 26 March.

Medina, Derek (2012f) 'JULY8,2012 TRYING TO GET BACK IN SEMI PRO BASKETBALL SHAPE AT 30YEARS OLDD', YouTube, 8 July.

Medina, Derek (2012g) 'MARLINSVSCARDINALS JUNE25,2012 GETTING PLAYERS FROM BULL PEN TO WAVE TO CAMERATO', YouTube, 25 June.

Medina, Derek (2012h) 'Call of duty mw3 action multitournament action NYC', YouTube, 27 December.

Medina, Derek (2012i) 'Call of duty mw3', YouTube, 28 December.

Medina, Derek (2013a) 'Rip Jennifer Alfonso', Facebook, 8 August.

Medina, Derek (2013b) 'Im going to prison or death sentence for killing my wife', Facebook, 8 August.

Medina, Derek (2013c) 'USA vs Puerto Rico marlins park march12,2013', YouTube, 12 March.

Medina, Derek (2013d) 'USA Sloan Stevens beating up on Russia', YouTube, 19 March.

Medina, Derek (2013e) 'Retired semi pro player Derek medina vs Josh Rodriguez', YouTube, 13 June.

Medina, Derek (2013f) 'Work hard play hard part one', YouTube, 6 August.

Medina, Derek (2013g) 'Work hard play hard part2', YouTube, 6 August.

Medina, Derek (2013h) 'Um NCAA ranked2in the country feb19,2013make acc history13-', YouTube, 19 February.

Medina, Derek (2013i) *How I saved someone's life and marriage and family problems thru communication*, Montgomery, AL: E-Book Time.

Medina, Derek (2013j) *World just ask yourself why we are living a life full of lies and how I an emotional writer made all of my professional dreams come true blocking society's teachings*, Montgomery, AL: E-Book Time.

Medina, Derek (2013k) Emotional Writer, www.emotionalwriter.com.

Medina, Derek (2013l) 'March21,2013 new book release', YouTube, 21 March.

Medina, Derek (2013m) 'Attention world save your self', YouTube, 22 April.

Medina, Derek (2013n) 'The world needs to read this book', YouTube, 2 February.

Medina, Derek (2013o) '6books created in 6 months by author Derek medina', YouTube, 1 August.

Medina, Derek (2013p) 'Miami Dade vs ROLLINS COLLEGE Debate tournament march30,2013 MICHAEL DUNLAP', YouTube, 30 March.

Medina, Derek (2013q) 'Curry heaven at the marina', Facebook, 7 August.

Medina, Derek (2013r) 'Our view', Facebook, 7 August.

Medina, Derek (2013s) 'Summer fun', Facebook, 7 August.

Medina, Derek (2013t) 'Summer 2013 sailing camp at our yacht club', YouTube, 24 July.

Medina, Derek (2013u) 'My 89year old grandma is my number one fan of my 6books', YouTube, 11 July.

Mehdizadeh, S. (2010) 'Self-presentation 2.0: Narcissism and self-esteem on Facebook', *Cyberpsychology, Behavior, and Social Networking*, 13(4): 357-64.

Miami Dade Police Department (2013) 'Sworn Statement of Derek V. Medina', 8 August, Case Number PD130808291623.

Milivojevic, S. and McGovern, A. (2014) 'The death of Jill Meagher: Crime and punishment on social media', *International Journal for Crime, Justice and Social Democracy*, 3(3): 22-39.

Miller, J. (2014) 'The fourth screen: Mediatization and the smartphone', *Mobile Media & Communication*, 2(2): 209-26.

Miller, V. (2011) *Understanding digital culture*, London: Sage.

Monckton-Smith, J. (2012) *Murder, gender and the media: Narratives of dangerous love*, Basingstoke: Palgrave Macmillan.

Monckton-Smith, J., Williams, A. and Mullane, F. (2014) *Domestic abuse, homicide and gender: Strategies for policy and practice*, Basingstoke: Palgrave Macmillan.

Morash, M., Bui, H.N. and Santiago, A.M. (2000) 'Cultural-specific gender ideology and wife abuse in Mexican-descent families', *International Journal of Victimology*, 7(1-3): 67-91.

Murdock, S. (2015) 'Woman allegedly kills father-in-law in retaliation: Explains why she fled on social media', *Huffington Post*, 9 April.

Muschert, G.W. (2007) 'Research in school shootings', *Sociology Compass*, 1(1): 60-80.

Muschert, G.W. (2013) 'School shootings as mediatized violence', in N. Böckler, T. Seeger, P. Sitzer and W. Heitmeyer (eds) *School shootings: International research, case studies and concepts for prevention*, New York, NY: Springer, pp 265-81.

Newman, K. S., Fox, C., Harding, D. J., Mehta, J. and Roth, W. (2004) *Rampage: The social roots of school shootings*, New York, NY: Basic Books.

O'Hagan, A. (2015) 'Who's the alpha male now, bitches?', *London Review of Books*, 37(2): 3-6.

Oksanen, A., Hawdon, J. and Räsänen, P. (2014) 'Glamorizing rampage online: School shooting fan communities on YouTube', *Technology in Society*, 39(5): 55-67.

ONS (Office for National Statistics) (2016a) 'Compendium: Focus on Violent Crime and Sexual Offences: Year ending March 2015', www.ons.gov.uk/peoplepopulationandcommunity/crimeandjustice/compendium/focusonviolentcrimeandsexualoffences/yearendingmarch2015.

ONS (2016b) 'Statistical bulletin: Crime in England and Wales: Year ending March 2015', www.ons.gov.uk/peoplepopulationandcommunity/crimeandjustice/bulletins/crimeinenglandandwales/2015-07-16.

Ortega, G. and Dixon, L. (2013) 'Tears and frustration at Hialeh wake for mom in Facebook killing', *Miami Herald*, 12 August.

Ortega, G., Ovalle, D. and Brown, J. K. (2013) 'Police release video of Derek Medina, confessed Facebook killer', *Miami Herald*, 9 August.

Ovalle, D. (2013a) 'South Miami man who kills wife and posts photo on Facebook makes first court appearance', *Miami Herald*, 9 August.

Ovalle, D. (2013b) 'South Miami man who posted picture of dead wife on Facebook pleads not guilty', *Miami Herald*, 29 August.

Ovalle, D. (2013c) 'Accused Facebook killer Derek Medina denied bail after all-day hearing', *Miami Herald*, 15 October.

Ovalle, D. (2015a) 'Prosecution: Pride, rage fuelled South Miami Facebook killer', *Miami Herald*, 10 November.

Ovalle, D. (2015b) 'Defense for Miami Facebook killer: Wife abused him', *Miami Herald*, 18 November.

Ovalle, D. (2015c) 'Miami jury adjourns for the night in trial of accused "Facebook" killer', *Miami Herald*, 24 November.

Ovalle, D. (2015d) 'Accused killer wants trial by judge, not jury', *Miami Herald*, 22 January.

Ovalle, D. (2016) 'Life in prison for South Miami's Facebook killer', *Miami Herald*, 5 February.

Pain, R. (2014) 'Everyday terrorism: Connecting domestic violence and everyday terrorism', *Progress in Human Geography*, 38(4): 531–50.

Palasinski, M. (2013) 'Turning assault into a "harmless prank" – teenage perspectives on happy slapping', *Journal of Interpersonal Violence*, 28(9): 1909–23.

Papacharissi, Z. (ed) (2011) *A networked self: Identity, community and culture on social network sites*, New York, NY and London: Routledge.

Paton, N. and Figeac, J. (2015) 'Expressive violence: The performative effects of subversive participatory media uses', *Journal for Communication Studies*, 8(1): 231–56.

Paulsen, D.J. (2003) 'Murder in black and white: The newspaper coverage of homicide in Houston', *Homicide Studies*, 7(3): 289–317.

Peelo, M., Francis, B., Soothill, K., Pearson, J. and Ackerley, E. (2004) 'Newspaper reporting and the public construction of homicide', *British Journal of Criminology*, 44(2): 256–75.

Penfold-Mounce, R. (2009) *Celebrity culture and crime: The joy of transgression*, Basingstoke: Palgrave Macmillan.

Perilla, J.L., Bakeman, R. and Norris, F.H. (1994) 'Culture and domestic violence: The ecology of abused Latinas', *Violence and Victims*, 9(4): 325–39.

Peters, J. (2015) 'Coroner to investigate Janzen deaths', *Chilliwack Progress*, 12 May.

Polk, K. (1994) *When men kill: Scenarios of masculine violence*, New York, NY: Cambridge University Press.

Polk, K. (1999) 'Males and honour contest violence', *Homicide Studies*, 3(1): 6-29.

Poster, M. (1995) 'Postmodern virtualities', in M. Featherstone and R. Burrows (eds) *Cyberspace/Cyberbodies/Cyberpunk,* Thousand Oaks, CA: Sage, pp 79-95.

Poster, M. (1999) 'Underdetermination', *New Media & Society*, 1(1): 12-17.

Pritchard, D. and Hughes, K.D. (1997) 'Patterns of deviance in crime news', *Journal of Communication*, 47(3): 49-67.

Pynn, L. (2015) 'Social media grows as confessional tool; With more people sharing their crimes online, police hit the Internet to collect the evidence', *Vancouver Sun*, 9 May.

Rabin, C. (2014) 'Accused Facebook killer defense team wants victim tested for bath salts', *Miami Herald*, 29 January.

Rader, N.E., Rhineberger-Dunn, G.M. and Vasquez, L. (2016) 'Victim blame in fictional crime dramas: An examination of demographic, incident-related, and behavioral factors', *Women & Criminal Justice*, 26(1): 55-75.

Raskin, R. and Terry, H. (1988) 'A principal-components analysis of the Narcissistic Personality Inventory and further evidence of its construct validity', *Journal of Personality and Social Psychology*, 54(5): 890-902.

Rettie, R. (2009) 'Mobile phone communication: Extending Goffman to mediated interaction', *Sociology*, 43(3): 421-38.

Rice, R. E. (1999), 'Artifacts and paradoxes in new media', *New Media & Society*, 1(1): 24-32.

Richards, L., Letchford, S. and Stratton, S. (2008) *Policing domestic violence*, Oxford: Oxford University Press.

Riessman, C. K. (2001) 'Analysis of personal narratives', in J. F. Gubriam and J. A. Holstein (eds) *Handbook of interview research: Context and method*, Thousand Oaks, CA: Sage, pp 695-710.

Riessman, C. K. (2008) *Narrative methods for the human sciences*, Thousand Oaks, CA: Sage.

Ritzer, G. and Jurgenson, N. (2010) 'Production, consumption, prosumption: The nature of capitalism in the age of the digital "Prosumer"', *Journal of Consumer Culture*, 10(1): 13-36.

Robertz, F.J. (2004) *School shootings*, Frankfurt: Polizeiwissenschaft.

Rock, P. (1998) *After homicide*, Oxford: Clarendon Press.

Ryan, T. and Xenos, S. (2011) 'Who uses Facebook? An investigation into the relationship between the big five', *Computers in Human Behavior*, 27(5): 1658-64.

Sandberg, S., Oksanen, A., Berntzen, L. E. and Kiilakoski, T. (2014) 'Stories in action: The cultural influences of school shootings on the terrorist attacks in Norway', *Critical Studies on Terrorism*, 7(2): 277-96.

Sassoon, L. (2015) 'Dad murders family over migraine hell', *Sunday Mirror*, 10 May.

Schildkraut, J. and Donley, A.M. (2012) 'Murder in black: A media distortion analysis of homicides in Baltimore in 2010', *Homicide Studies*, 16(2): 175-96.

Schildkraut, J. and Elass, H.J. (2016) *Mass shootings: Media, myths and realities*, Santa Barbara, CA: Praeger.

Schulz, W. (2004) 'Reconstructing mediatization as an analytical concept', *European Journal of Communication*, 19(1): 87-101.

Schwartz, J. (2006a) 'Effects of diverse forms of family structure on female and male homicide', *Journal of Marriage and Family*, 68(5): 1291-312.

Schwartz, J. (2006b) 'Family structure as a source of female and male homicide in the United States', *Homicide Studies*, 10(4): 253-78.

Schwartz, J. (2012) 'Comparing men and women who kill', in M. DeLisi and P.J. Conis (eds) *Violent offenders: Theory, research, policy, and practice*, Burlington, MA: Jones and Bartlett, pp 185-205.

Seltzer, M. (1998) *Serial killers: Death and life in America's wound culture*, New York, NY: Routledge.

Seltzer, M. (2007) *True crime: Observations on violence and modernity*, New York, NY: Routledge.

Seltzer, M. (2008) 'Murder/media/modernity', *Canadian Review of American Studies*, 38(1): 11-41.

Senft, T. (2008) *Camgirls: Celebrity and community in the age of social networks*, New York, NY: Peter Lang.

Senft, T. (2013) 'Microcelebrity and the branded self', in J. Harvey, J. Burgess and A. Bruns (eds) *A companion to new media dynamics*, Maiden, MA: Wiley-Blackwell, pp 346-54.

Senft, T. and Baym, N. K. (2015) 'What does the selfie say? Investigating a global phenomenon', *International Journal of Communication*, 9: 1588-606.

Sentencing Council (2016) 'New guidelines proposed for the sentencing of young offenders', www.sentencingcouncil.org.uk/news/item/new-guidelines-proposed-for-the-sentencing-of-young-offenders.

Shortland, G. (2016) 'Widow stabbed her ex father-in-law to death and then posted a selfie with his body on social media', *The People*, 31 January.

Silverstone, R. (1999) 'What's new about new media?', *New Media & Society*, 1(1): 10-12.

Silverstone, R. (2007) *Media and morality: On the rise of the mediapolis*, Cambridge: Polity.

Simons, H. (2009) *Case study research in practice*, London: Sage.

Sinclair Janzen, Laurel (2014a) Untitled photograph, Facebook, 30 July.

Sinclair Janzen, Laurel (2014b) Untitled photograph, Facebook, 24 July.

Sinoski, K., Crawford, T., Carman, T. and Robinson, M. (2015) 'Shocking triple murder in BC as Randy Janzen apparently confesses on Facebook to killing daughter, wife, sister', *Postmedia News*, 9 May.

Sitzer, P. (2013) 'The role of media content in the genesis of school shootings: The contemporary discussion', in N. Böckler, T. Seeger, P. Sitzer and W. Heitmeyer (eds) *School shootings: International research, case studies and concepts for prevention*, New York, NY: Springer, pp 283-308.

Smith, E. L. and Cooper, E. (2013) *Homicide in the US known to law enforcement 2011*, Washington, DC: US Department of Justice.

Smith, K., Taylor, P. and Elkin, M. (2013) *Crimes detected in England and Wales 2012/13*, London: Home Office.

SoFlaRocks (2013) 'JENNIFER ALFONSO RIP MEMORIAL PICTURE VIDEO TRIBUTE', YouTube, 12 August.

Solis, G. (2013) 'Pastor describes confessed Facebook killer Derek Medina as a "complex, multidimensional person"', *Miami Herald*, 10 August.

Soothill, K. (1998) 'Armchair detectives and armchair thieves', *The Police Journal*, April: 155-9.

Soothill, K., Peelo, M., Francis, B., Pearson, J. and Ackerley, E. (2002) 'Homicide and the media: Identifying the top cases in *The Times*', *The Howard Journal of Crime and Justice*, 41(5): 1-14.

Sorenson, S.B., Manz, J.G.P. and Berk, R.A. (1998), 'News media coverage and the epidemiology of homicide', *American Journal of Public Health*, 88(10): 1510-14.

Soulliere, D. (2003) 'Prime time murder: Presentations of murder on popular television justice programs', *Journal of Criminal Justice and Popular Culture*, 10(1): 12-38.

Stack, S. (1997) 'Homicide followed by suicide: An analysis of Chicago data', *Criminology*, 35(3): 435-54.

Stark, E. (2007) *Coercive control: How men entrap women in personal life*, Oxford: Oxford University Press.

Steffensmeier, D.J. and Allan, E. (1996) 'Gender and crime: Toward a gendered theory of female offending', *American Review of Sociology*, 22(1): 459-87.

Steffensmeier, D.J. and Haynie, D. (2000a) 'Gender, structural disadvantage, and urban crime: Do macrosocial variables also explain female offending rates?', *Criminology*, 38(2): 403-38.

Steffensmeier, D.J. and Haynie, D. (2000b) 'The structural sources of urban female violence in the United States: A macrosocial gender-disaggregated analysis of adult and juvenile homicide offending rates', *Homicide Studies*, 4(2): 107-34.

Stevens. E. (1973) 'Marianismo: The other face of machismo', in A. M. Pescatello (ed) *Female and male in Latin America*, Pittsburgh, PA: University of Pittsburgh Press, pp 90-101.

Stone, A. R. (1995) *The war of desire and technology at the close of the mechanical age*, Cambridge, MA: MIT Press.

Strum, B. (2015) 'Facebook family massacre', *New York Post*, 9 May.

Suler, J. (2004) 'The online disinhibition effect', *CyberPsychology & Behavior*, 7(3): 321-6.

Sumiala, J., and Tikka, M. (2011) 'Reality on circulation: School shootings, ritualised communication, and the dark side of the sacred', *Journal for Communication Studies*, 4(2): 145-59.

Summerscale, K. (2016) *The wicked boy: The mystery of a Victorian child murderer*, London: Bloomsbury.

SuperLola59 (2011) 'Shaw TV', YouTube, 9 January.

Surette, R. (2015a) 'Performance crime and justice', *Current Issues in Criminal Justice*, 27(2): 195-216.

Surette, R. (2015b) *Media, crime and criminal justice: Images and realities* (5th edn), Belmont, CA: Wadsworth.

Sutfin, H. (2015) 'Social media confessions', Sword and Scale, 17 June, http://swordandscale.com/social-media-confessions.

Sykes, G. M. and Matza, D. (1957) 'Techniques of neutralization: A theory of delinquency', *American Sociological Review*, 22(6): 664-70.

Tamminga, M. (2015) 'There is not anger, just sadness around this tragedy', *Langley Times*, 11 May.

Tanenbaum, L. (2000) *Slut!: Growing up female with a bad reputation*, New York, NY: Harper Collins.

Taylor, Amanda (2011a) 'Damiens first day of school', Facebook, 30 August.

Taylor, Amanda. (2011b) 'filling people's bellys 11-5', Facebook, 30 July.

Taylor, Amanda (2011c) 'I'm so thankful to have such a happy healthy handsome hyper little monster', Facebook, 24 November.

Taylor, Amanda (2011d) '22 years ago an amazinggg man was executed', Facebook, 24 January.

Taylor, Amanda (2011e) 'i am for real sad. bleh [frown emoji]', Facebook, 17 August.

Taylor, Amanda (2011f) 'I can finally say after years and years of mad deep depression I am finally happy with life', Facebook, 14 April.

Taylor, Amanda (2011g) 'Today I've been clean from alcohol , green, and opiates for two months..', Facebook, 21 November.

Taylor, Amanda (2012a) 'I love being out & seeing people melt over how adorable my children are', Facebook, 19 December.

Taylor, Amanda (2012b) 'Aw my sweet angel is a month today!', Facebook, 16 December.

Taylor, Amanda (2012c) 'So this movie 'VHS' has put me in the weirdest mood', Facebook, 16 December.

Taylor, Amanda (2013a) 'Go buy cookies & lemonade from my monster at his friends mamas yardsale', Facebook, 28 September.

Taylor, Amanda (2013b) 'I earned massive mummy points with this one. I got this ADORABLE seashell pool at wal-mart for $2 today', Facebook, 30 October.

Taylor, Amanda (2013c) 'I gotta say my little sister is the only person I've EVER been around that actually takes life serious', Facebook, 7 March.

Taylor, Amanda (2013d) 'I finally found my little posters [happy lil'mama!]', Facebook, 21 February.

Taylor, Amanda (2013e) 'Ugh I'm out & can't watch the news and my phone won' pull it up', Facebook, 21 October.

Taylor, Amanda (2014a) Untitled photograph, Facebook, 15 October.

Taylor, Amanda (2014b) 'ran across this video..I'm not a big fan of b.o.t.d.f but after this I gained so much respect', Facebook, 3 March.

Taylor, Amanda (2014c) 'April is such an insane month of terror', Facebook, 16 April.

Taylor, Amanda (2014d) 'Omfg. Yes', Facebook, 12 February.

Taylor, Amanda (2014e) 'United We Purge', Facebook, 17 July.

Taylor, Amanda (2014f) 'I can't waiiiiiiiiit. LET US PURGE!', Facebook, 14 July.

Taylor, Amanda (2014g) '40 more days you guyssss. September cant come soon enough', Facebook, 27 July.

Taylor, Amanda (2014h) 'Now that I got my 'The Purge Anarchy' fix, I'm anxiously waiting for October', Facebook, 20 July.

Taylor, Amanda (2014i) 'Little things in life that make me ridiculously happy', Facebook, 15 July.

Taylor, Amanda (2015a) 'I proudly did this for Rex', Facebook, 5 April.

Taylor, Amanda (2015b) 'Amanda wanted to let everyone know ~ you can create an account on jpay.com', Facebook, 30 April.

Taylor, Amanda (2015c) 'Amanda wanted to let you guys know she's been transferred to a prison near Richmond, VA', Facebook, 13 April.

Taylor, Amanda (2015d) 'Spent the day down in Ellett Valley', Facebook, 22 March.

Taylor, Amanda (2015e) Untitled image, Facebook, 30 August.

Taylor, Amanda (2015f) Untitled post (Sweet Jane music video), Facebook, 3 April 2015.

Taylor, Amanda (2016) 'Reposting for those asking for Amanda's address', Facebook, 18 August.

Teague, B. (2015) 'Amanda Taylor disruptive in court, defense awaits mental health records', *WSLS 10*, 4 November.

Thomas, K.A., Dichter, M.E. and Matejkowski, J. (2011) 'Intimate versus nonintimate partner murder: A comparison of offender and situational characteristics', *Homicide Studies*, 15(3): 291-311.

Thompson, J.B. (2005) 'The new visibility', *Theory, Culture and Society*, 22(6): 31-51.

Toch, H. (1969) *Violent men: An inquiry into the psychology of violence*, Chicago, IL: Aldine.

Turkle, S. (1995) *Life on the screen*, London: Weidenfold and Nicolson.

Turnbull, S. (2010) 'Crime as entertainment: The case of the TV crime drama', *Continuum: Journal of Media & Cultural Studies*, 24(6): 819-27.

Turnbull, S. (2014) *The TV crime srama*, Edinburgh: Edinburgh University Press.

United States Census Bureau (2016) 'Montgomery County, Virginia', www.census.gov/quickfacts/map/INC910214/51121.

Virginia Courts Case Information (2016) 'Montgomery County Circuit – Criminal Division', http://ewsocis1.courts.state.va.us/CJISWeb/circuit.jsp.

Walklate, S. and Petrie, S. (2013) 'Witnessing the pain of suffering: Exploring the relationship between media representations, public understandings and policy responses to filicide-suicide', *Crime Media Culture*, 9(3): 265-79.

Wall, D. (2007) *Cybercrime: The transformation of crime in the information age*, Cambridge: Polity.

Ward, C. (2011) 'With suspect serving life, DuPage prosecutors opt to drop murder charges', *Chicago Tribune*, 25 August.

Websdale, N. (2010) *Familicidal hearts: The emotional styles of 211 killers*, Oxford: Oxford University Press.

Weiss, A. and Chermak, S.M. (1998) 'The news value of African American victims: An examination of the media's presentation of homicide', *Journal of Crime and Justice*, 21(2): 71-88.

Whelan, D. (2016) 'What does our obsession with true crime podcasts say about us?', Vice, 16 December, www.vice.com/read/what-does-our-obsession-with-true-crime-podcasts-say-about-us-814.

Williams, R. (2013) 'Florida man arrested after admitting he killed his wife and posting picture of dead body on Facebook', *The Independent*, 9 August.

Wilson, M. and Daly, M. (1998) 'Lethal and non-lethal violence agaist wives and the evolutionary psychology of male sexual proprietariness', in R.E. Dobash and R.P. Dobash (eds) *Rethinking violence against women*, Thousand Oaks, CA: Sage, pp 199-230.

Wilson, M., Daly, M. and Daniele, A. (1995) 'Familicide: The killing of spouse and children', *Aggressive Behavior*, 21(4): 275-91.

Wiltenburg. J. (2004) 'True crime: The origins of modern sensationalism', *The American Historical Review*, 109(5): 1377-404.

Woo, A. and Kane, L. (2015) 'Community grieves "amazing" young woman, family', *The Globe and Mail*, 9 May.

Wykes, M. (2010) 'Harm, suicide and homicide in cyberspace: Assessing causality and control', in Y. Jewkes and M. Yar (eds) *Handbook of internet crime*, London: Routledge, pp 369-94.

Yar, M. (2012) 'Crime, media and the will-to-representation: Reconsidering relationships in the new media age', *Crime, Media, Culture*, 8(3): 245-60.

Yar, M. (2013) *Cybercrime and society* (2nd edn), London: Sage.

Yardley, E. and Wilson, D. (2015) 'Making sense of "Facebook murder"? Social networking sites and contemporary homicide, *The Howard Journal of Criminal Justice*, 54(2): 109-34.

Yardley, E., Wilson, D. and Kennedy, M. (2015) '"TO ME ITS [SIC] REAL LIFE": Secondary victims of homicide in newer media', *Victims and Offenders,* online ahead of print, DOI: 10.1080/15564886.2015.1105896.

Yardley, E., Wilson, D. and Lynes, A. (2014) 'A taxonomy of male British family annihilators, 1980-2012', *The Howard Journal of Criminal Justice*, 53(2): 117-40.

Yardley, E., Wilson, D., Lynes, A. G. T. and Kelly, E. (2016) 'What's the deal with "websleuthing"? News media representations of amateur detectives in networked spaces', *Crime, Media, Culture,* online ahead of print, DOI: 10.1177/1741659016674045.

Yin, R.K. (1994) *Case study research: Design and methods*, Thousand Oaks, CA: Sage.

Young, A. (2005) *Judging the image: Art, value, law*, London: Routledge.

Young, A. (2010a) *The scene of violence: Cinema, crime, affect*, Abingdon: Routledge.

Young, A. (2010b) 'The scene of the crime: Is there such a thing as "just looking"?', in K.J. Hayward and M. Presdee (eds) *Framing crime: Cultural criminology and the image*, Abingdon: Routledge, pp. 83–97.

Young, A. (2014) 'From object to encounter: Aesthetic politics and visual criminology', *Theoretical Criminology*, 18(2): 159–75.

Young, J. (2011) *The criminological imagination*, Cambridge: Polity.

Žižek, S. (2009) *Violence*, London: Profile Books.

Legislation

Corporate Manslaughter and Corporate Homicide Act 2007 (c. 19), London: The Stationery Office.

Infanticide Act 1938 (c.1), London: The Stationery Office.

Road Traffic Act 1988 (c. 1), London: The Stationery Office.

Index

Page numbers in *italics* refer to figures and tables.